The Dynamics of Coercion

Successful coercion should be relatively simple for the United States. Since the demise of the Soviet Union, the United States is without rivals in military might, political influence, or economic strength. Yet despite the lopsided U.S. edge in raw power, regional foes persist in defying the threats and ultimatums brought by the United States and its allies. This book examines why some attempts to strong-arm an adversary work while others do not. It explores how coercion today differs from coercion during the Cold War. It describes the constraints on the United States emanating from the need to work within coalitions and the restrictions imposed by domestic politics, and it assesses the special challenges likely to arise when an adversary is a non-state actor or when the use of weapons of mass destruction is possible. In particular, this book attempts to understand how features of American-style coercion create opportunities for, and give adversaries incentives to employ, certain counter-coercive strategies.

Daniel Byman is a policy analyst with the RAND Corporation and the Research Director of RAND's Center for Middle East Public Policy. Before coming to RAND, he worked as a political analyst for the U.S. government. He received his Ph.D. in political science from MIT and has held several prestigious fellowships. Dr. Byman is the author of several books and numerous monographs and articles in the field of international relations.

Matthew Waxman is an attorney and policy consultant in Washington, D.C. He has worked as a consultant on issues of American foreign and defense policy and international law at the RAND Corporation, and he served as law clerk to Supreme Court Justice David H. Souter and U.S. Court of Appeals Judge Joel M. Flaum. Mr. Waxman received his J.D. from Yale Law School.

Dr. Byman and Mr. Waxman have collaborated on numerous published studies for the U.S. Department of Defense and U.S. Air Force, including *Confronting Iraq: U.S. Policy and the Use of Force Since Desert Storm* (RAND, 2000) and *Air Power as a Coercive Instrument* (RAND, 1999). Their work has also appeared in leading American and British journals, including *International Security* and *Survival.*

The Dynamics of Coercion

RAND Studies in Policy Analysis

Editor: Charles Wolf, Jr., Senior Economic Advisor and Corporate Fellow in International Economics, RAND

Policy analysis is the application of scientific methods to develop and test alternative ways of addressing social, economic, legal, international, national security, and other problems. The RAND Studies in Policy Analysis series aims to include several significant, timely, and innovative works each year in this broad field. Selection is guided by an editorial board consisting of Charles Wolf, Jr. (editor), and David S. C. Chu, Paul K. Davis, and Lynn Karoly (associate editors).

Also in the series:

David C. Gompert and F. Stephen Larrabee (eds.), *America and Europe: A Partnership for a New Era*

John W. Peabody, M. Omar Rahman, Paul J. Gertler, Joyce Mann, Donna O. Farley, Jeff Luck, David Robalino, and Grace M. Carter, *Policy and Health: Implications for Development in Asia*

Samantha F. Ravich, *Marketization and Democracy: East Asian Experiences*

Gregory F. Treverton, *Reshaping National Intelligence for an Age of Information*

Robert J. MacCoun and Peter Reuter, *Drug War Heresies: Learning from Other Vices, Times, and Places*

Further Praise for *The Dynamics of Coercion*

"Questioning why strong nations such as the United States fail to intimidate much weaker foes, Byman and Waxman offer a fresh analysis of the concept and the strategy of coercion within the context of the post cold-war security environment. This well-organized and rigorous analysis offers a fine synthesis between classical thinking about coercion and its new dimensions, such as domestic and coalition politics, casualty sensitivity, humanitarian coercion, and coercion against weaker rivals armed with weapons of mass destruction. Anyone concerned with the new challenges to American hegemony will find this book indispensable reading."
—Uri Bar-Joseph, *University of Haifa*

"Byman and Waxman tackle some of the most important issues underlying American foreign policy: When do coercive strategies succeed? Why do they fail so often? Their book substantially improves the state of theory about coercion while offering straightforward, clear-headed advice to analysts and policy makers."
—Daryl Press, *Dartmouth College*

The Dynamics of Coercion

American Foreign Policy and the Limits of Military Might

Daniel Byman
RAND

Matthew Waxman
RAND

PUBLISHED BY THE PRESS SYNDICATE OF THE UNIVERSITY OF CAMBRIDGE
The Pitt Building, Trumpington Street, Cambridge, United Kingdom

CAMBRIDGE UNIVERSITY PRESS
The Edinburgh Building, Cambridge CB2 2RU, UK
40 West 20th Street, New York, NY 10011-4211, USA
10 Stamford Road, Oakleigh, VIC 3166, Australia
Ruiz de Alarcón 13, 28014 Madrid, Spain
Dock House, The Waterfront, Cape Town 8001, South Africa

http://www.cambridge.org

First published 2002

Printed in the United States of America

Typeface Sabon 10/13 pt. *System* MS Word [AU]

A catalog record for this book is available from the British Library.

Library of Congress Cataloging in Publication data available

ISBN 0 521 80991 6 hardback
ISBN 0 521 00780 1 paperback

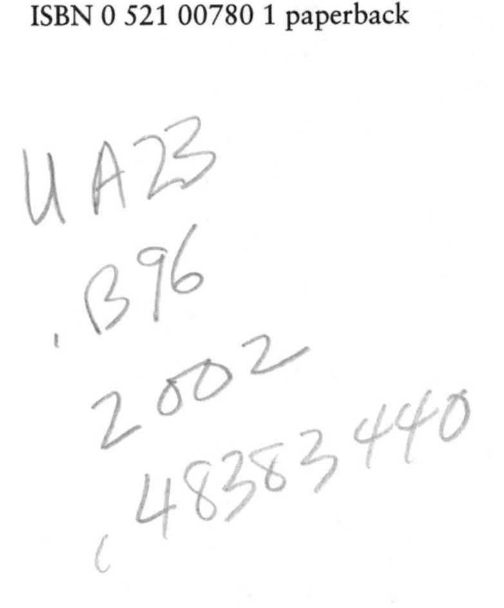

To Josh and Benjamin, my joy

D.L.B.

To Merle and Steve, for everything

M.C.W.

Contents

Foreword *page xi*
Preface *xiii*
Acknowledgments *xv*

1 Introduction 1
Defining coercion 3
The role of inducements 9
Models of coercion 10
Coercion today: old wine in new bottles? 14
Challenges to coercion today 18
Structure 21

PART ONE: COERCIVE STRATEGY MAKING 25

2 The theory of coercion 30
Measuring coercion 31
Coercion as a dynamic contest: key analytic concepts 37
The path ahead 46

3 Coercive mechanisms 48
Commonly used mechanisms 50
Second-order coercion 82
Conclusion 85

4 Coercive instruments 87
Air strikes 88
Invasions and land grabs 99
The threat of nuclear attack 102
Sanctions and international isolation 105
Support for an insurgency 117

Combinations 120
Conclusion 123

PART TWO: THE CONTEXT OF COERCION TODAY 125

5 Domestic politics and coercion 130
Justifying force 132
U.S. casualty sensitivity 134
Sensitivity to adversary civilian suffering 137
U.S. political constraints and adversary counter-coercion 142
The asymmetry of constraints 148
Conclusion 150

6 Coercion and coalitions 152
Why coalitions? 154
Limits imposed by coalitions 158
Coalitions and adversary counter-coercion 171
Conclusion 172

7 Humanitarian coercion and nonstate actors 175
Humanitarian intervention and coercion 176
The decision to intervene 177
Common tasks during a humanitarian intervention 181
Constraints on humanitarian coercion 183
The challenge of nonstate adversaries 190
Nonstate actors and counter-coercion 194
Conclusion 199

8 Weapons of mass destruction and U.S. coercion 201
Understanding the danger 203
WMD and escalation dominance 212
Beyond the brink: how WMD use affects coercion 216
Implications for coercive contests 218
Conclusion 224

PART THREE: THE FUTURE OF U.S. COERCION 227
Challenges to strategy making 229
Why policy makers and analysts disagree 234
Coercion dynamics and credibility traps 236
Final words 239

Bibliography 241
Index 265

Foreword

The September 11, 2001, terrorist attacks on the World Trade Center and the Pentagon reinforced what pundits and policy makers have said for years: in the post-Cold War era, the rules of international relations have changed. Despite repeating this truism, analysts and scholars have made little progress in comprehending the challenges and opportunities of the current era, particularly those regarding the uses of military force. The September 11 attacks should shake us out of this analytic inertia, pushing us to address new threats such as terrorism while ensuring a strong defense against traditional challenges.

The Dynamics of Coercive Force is an important contribution to analysis in the field. Although the book was written before the fateful September attacks, it illuminates the daunting problems inherent in countering terrorism. Indeed, it explores the fundamental paradox of America's technological superiority: How can a small band of men, armed with obsolete weapons, operating in a country devastated by war, pose a direct threat to U.S. security? Why is it so difficult for the United States, given its overwhelming military and technological edge, to counter this threat?

In answering these questions, Daniel Byman and Matthew Waxman provide a sophisticated analysis of the use of force, explaining the constraints stemming from our political system and the challenge of coordinating diplomatic and military efforts. Perhaps most important, they examine the use of coercion on both sides of a confrontation as viewed by each side, and they describe how terrorist groups, rogue states, and other adversaries exploit U.S. vulnerabilities to advance their cause.

These are but a few of the issues addressed in this thoughtful and timely book. Other challenges range from intervening in humanitarian crises to countering foes armed with chemical, biological, or nuclear weapons. The authors' analysis avoids breathless proclamations that today's challenges are completely new. Instead, they draw on a range of historical experiences even as they focus on truly novel features of the current international system.

If knowledge is one foundation of power, assimilating the lessons of this book will assist the United States and its allies in meeting the challenges they confront today.

Charles Wolf, Jr.
Series Editor
September 30, 2001

Preface

This book is intended to revive a once-active discussion about limited war. The stark danger of a nuclear conflict during the Cold War generated a burst of creative thinking on conflict in general and limited war in particular that engaged some of the best minds of a generation. That intellectual ferment was not surprising: the fearsome specter of nuclear war lingered behind every diplomatic confrontation and peripheral conflict during that period.

However, the end of the Cold War ushered in an era in which limits to conflict arise from the low stakes at issue (for the United States), rather than from the potential cataclysm that could result from escalation or miscalculation. Many of the lessons learned during the Cold War are still valid, but many are not or need refinement. Analysis has not kept pace with the changing circumstances.

The research for this book began with a RAND study on how air power might become a more effective coercive instrument. The analysis was expanded in a series of articles addressing coercive strategies against Iraq and Serbia and assessing how adversaries respond to perceived U.S. weaknesses. It was soon clear, however, that a focus on one instrument, one country, or one aspect of coercion unnecessarily limited the applicability of the findings and at times misled readers in their thinking about the problem more broadly.

This book offers new thinking on coercive force, informed by both the lessons of the past and the new dynamics that have emerged since the fall of the Berlin Wall. As such, it examines the lessons of Cold War crises to gain insights into problems associated with the threat and use of force in general, but it pays particular attention to identifying constraints that have emerged or evolved in the post–Cold War era. These include constraints related to casualty sensitivity, coalition cohesion, humanitarian intervention, and weapons of mass destruction.

The book is not intended to be a comprehensive analysis of coercion in the post–Cold War era—it does not review every instance of coercion, give every type of force equal treatment, or detail the full range of adversary responses to coercive threats. Although it reaches broad judgments on the use of force in general, it focuses on the experience of the United States and the unique freedoms of and constraints on U.S. strategy making, in the hope of advancing the thinking in a once-vibrant field of inquiry and offering insights relevant to policy making.

In writing this book, the authors drew on several of their previously published articles and RAND reports (selections of which have been reprinted here with permission): Daniel Byman, "After the Storm: U.S. Policy Toward Iraq Since 1991," *Political Science Quarterly*, Winter 2000; Daniel Byman and Matthew Waxman, "Defeating U.S. Coercion," *Survival*, Summer 1999; Daniel Byman and Matthew Waxman, "Kosovo and the Great Air Power Debate," *International Security*, Spring 2000; Daniel Byman, Kenneth Pollack, and Matthew Waxman, "Coercing Iraq: Lessons from the Past," *Survival*, Fall 1998; Daniel Byman and Matthew Waxman, *Confronting Iraq: U.S. Policy Since Desert Storm*, RAND, 2000; Daniel Byman, Matthew Waxman, and Eric Larson, *Air Power as a Coercive Instrument*, RAND, 1999; Daniel Byman, Ian Lesser, Bruce Pirnie, Cheryl Benard, and Matthew Waxman, *Strengthening the Partnership: Military Cooperation with Relief Agencies*, RAND, 2000. Some of the arguments in Chapters 2 and 4 were presented in "Kosovo and the Great Air Power Debate"; parts of Chapters 5 and 6 (on the roles of domestic politics and coalition dynamics in coercion) draw on *Air Power as a Coercive Instrument*; and Chapter 7 draws on *Strengthening the Partnership*.

Acknowledgments

We owe a debt to a number of friends and colleagues for their many insights and thoughtful criticisms. Jeremy Shapiro deserves our greatest thanks. He influenced our research and thinking at almost every stage and proved a tough but fair (and, at times, somewhat bemused) critic. Brent Sterling also read large portions of this manuscript and offered a range of valuable comments. Nora Bensahel, David Earnest, F. Gregory Gause III, Thomas McNaugher, Forrest Morgan, Karl Mueller, Kenneth Pollack, Daryl Press, and Dan Prieto all read portions of this work or previous versions—our thanks to them all. Kenneth Pollack also influenced our thoughts on efforts to coerce Iraq. Alan Vick deserves credit and our appreciation for initiating this project at RAND and helping it through its most difficult formative stages. Steve Hosmer, Zalmay Khalilzad, Ben Lambeth, Eric Larson, and Abram Shulsky also contributed to our initial thinking. In addition, Eric Larson wrote the chapter on domestic politics in the RAND study on coercive air power. We drew on that chapter in this book, though we wish to stress that he may disagree with a number of our conclusions.

We received administrative assistance and support from The RAND Corporation and a number of individuals. Charles Wolf helped transform a disparate collection of articles and monographs on coercion into a final product. Scott Parris was our guide at Cambridge University Press. Rachel Fischer Alberts, a kind neighbor as well as superb editor, tightened our prose. Judy Lewis smoothed a bumpy publication process and helped us overcome many administrative hurdles before they became overwhelming. Jeri O'Donnell conducted a thorough final edit, improving the book's flow and correcting many errors.

Acknowledgments

1

Introduction

Coercion—the use of threatened force, and at times the limited use of actual force to back up the threat, to induce an adversary to change its behavior—should be easy for the United States. Since the demise of the Soviet Union, the United States is without rivals in military might, political influence, and economic strength. U.S. conventional and nuclear forces dwarf those of any adversaries, and the U.S. economy remains the largest and most robust in the world. Because of these overwhelming advantages, the United States can threaten any conceivable adversary with little danger of a major defeat or even significant retaliation. Yet coercion remains difficult. Despite the United States' lopsided edge in raw strength, regional foes persist in defying the threats and ultimatums brought by the United States and its allies. In confrontations with Somali militants, Serb nationalists, and an Iraqi dictator, the U.S. and allied record of coercion has at best been mixed over recent years. Consider perhaps the starkest example, coming at the close of the century: 78 days of intensive NATO bombing were required to convince Serbian President Slobodan Milosevic to back down and withdraw his forces from Kosovo. Even then, NATO failed to stop the Milosevic regime's campaign of ethnic terror.

Despite its mixed record of success, however, coercion will remain a critical element of U.S. foreign policy. The end of the Cold War created a world in which the United States faces no peer competitor. Instead, it faces extreme uncertainty. Although the Cold War world was hardly as stable or as predictable as many people now recall, the U.S. military did have a well-defined mission: deter a conflict with the Soviet Union and, if deterrence fails, defeat Soviet forces. Such a pressing mission thankfully is missing today. Yet because the identity of threats is less clear, deterrence becomes harder while coercion becomes more necessary. The United States faces too many low-level threats to forecast each one and deter it with a credible warning.

While the post–Cold War era has witnessed vast changes, military force remains a vital foreign policy instrument. Sanctions, political pressure, and other tools for influencing states are important, but they have proven neither reliable nor efficient in stopping aggression or changing the behavior of committed adversaries. Force may be the last instrument policy makers want to use—and it too has obviously proven far from reliable or efficient—but the absence of effective alternatives elevates its importance.

Coercive force is a particularly critical element of U.S foreign policy. The United States has not waged an all-out war to defeat a foe since World War II. Even in the long, bloody, and bitter Korean and Vietnam wars, Washington limited its involvement and strove to convince adversary governments and their major-power sponsors not to accept unconditional surrender but to make concessions. In recent years, this trend toward limited war for limited means has accelerated. In the Balkans, the Persian Gulf, Haiti, Somalia, and elsewhere, the United States has sought to coerce regional foes and rivals rather than defeat them.

This book is primarily concerned with U.S. coercive strategy making. There are, however, other major and regional powers that have faced similar perplexities concerning the use of military force and threats. Since the end of the Cold War, Russia has supported insurgents and used economic pressure to intimidate former Soviet states such as Georgia, Moldova, and Tajikistan. China has engaged in a bitter war of words, and at times used demonstrative missile attacks to back up its rhetoric, in a largely unsuccessful attempt to influence Taiwanese elections and policy with respect to independence. Israel has supported an army of sympathizers in southern Lebanon and conducted repeated air raids on Hezbollah guerrilla targets in an unsuccessful attempt to end Hezbollah raids. The might of these coercers should have been enough to overwhelm their adversaries, but, as with the United States, it has not always translated into leverage.

What are the elements of successful coercion? How does today's coercion differ from that of the Cold War? Why do some attempts to strong-arm an adversary work while others do not? Might coercive threats make matters worse by steeling the resolve of adversaries? What barriers commonly impede coercive strategies? Do some coercive threats diminish the effectiveness of other foreign policy tools? To answer these questions, this book draws on the long and varied history of the use of force, by both the United States and other states, to inform its general arguments about conditions under which coercive strategies are likely to succeed and the key challenges facing U.S. policy makers. It explores how emerging trends and contemporary political pressures affect U.S. coercion today and how they will affect U.S. coercion in the future.

DEFINING COERCION

Coercion is not destruction. Coercive strategies are most successful when threats need not even be carried out. Although some destruction is often part of coercion, coercion succeeds when the adversary gives in while it still has the power to resist.

Coercion is best understood in opposition to what Thomas Schelling termed "brute force": "Brute force succeeds when it is used, whereas the power to hurt is most successful when held in reserve. It is the threat of damage, or of more damage to come, that can make someone yield or comply."[1] Coercion may be thought of, then, as getting the adversary to act a certain way via anything short of brute force; the adversary must still have the capacity for organized violence but *choose* not to exercise it.[2]

We define coercion as we do to emphasize that it relies on the threat of future military force to influence an adversary's decision making but may also include limited uses of actual force. The limited use of actual force may form a key component of a coercion strategy if its purpose is to enhance credibility or demonstrate the type of price that continued defiance will bring. Limited uses of force sway an adversary not only because of their direct and immediate destructive impact but because of their effects on the adversary's perceptions of future force and the adversary's vulnerability to it. For example, military strikes against some of an enemy's fielded forces might help induce the enemy to withdraw the rest of its forces by making defense of a particular territory harder

1 Thomas C. Schelling, *Arms and Influence* (New Haven, CT: Yale University Press, 1966), p. 3.

2 Robert A. Pape, *Bombing to Win* (Ithaca, NY: Cornell University Press, 1996), p. 13.

and riskier, by reducing the enemy's ability to repel subsequent strikes, and by demonstrating one's willingness to resort to military means. Coercion is about how those military strikes affect an adversary's subsequent decision making and policy moves.

The line between coercion and brute force is not always easy to discern. Once an armed conflict begins, an adversary's behavior will always be dictated by a combination of brute force and threatened (coercive) force. Nonetheless, pure or near-pure cases of coercion and brute force do exist. In 1994, the United States effectively coerced the military regime in Haiti to step down by threatening an imminent military invasion. No force was actually applied before the junta conceded, although the United States did send forces to help manage the transition. The regime capitulated due to the credible threat of future U.S. action. An example of brute force is Nazi Germany's 1941 invasion of Russia to conquer territory and seize resources (Operation Barbarossa). German forces conquered areas of western Russia without attempting to elicit surrender.[3] The Israeli demolition of Iraq's nuclear reactor at Osiraq in 1981 is another example of brute force.[4] Although destruction of the reactor set back Iraq's nuclear program, it was not expected to change Iraqi policy—nor did it—and may even have increased Baghdad's desire to acquire nuclear weapons.

Those who reject the distinction between brute force and coercion might respond that all state behavior, especially surrender, is always volitional to some extent. In no instance, the argument might go, has a state been so decimated in battle that it had a complete absence of choice. But there are degrees of choice that must be considered. Generally, as an adversary absorbs more and more destruction, the proportion of its decisions that are motivated by the threat of future destruction declines. This is because the destruction of more and more of the adversary's assets narrows the adversary's range of options and, in some

3 We do not know what concessions Stalin might have been willing to make, but given the military balance at the time and the German advances up to that point, it seems reasonable to believe that the two sides might have agreed on a settlement similar to the 1917 Brest-Litovsk treaty. If Germany had accepted such terms from Stalin, Germany would have "won" the war. Only Hitler could have considered such a victory inadequate. (See Richard J. Overy, *Why the Allies Won* [New York: W.W. Norton, 1996], pp. 14 and 19.)

4 See Karl Mueller, "Denial, Punishment, and the Future of Air Power," *Security Studies,* Vol. 7, no. 3 (Spring 1998), pp. 182–228.

cases, leaves the adversary less and less to lose in the future. Brute force, by contrast, eliminates the adversary's options completely. Allied operations against Nazi Germany illustrate this point. Even in May 1945, Nazi Germany was physically capable of continuing the war despite Berlin's capture. But it certainly had fewer options than it had had earlier in the war, at the commencement of the Combined Bomber Offensive in 1943, when it had yet to suffer serious damage to its homeland. Understanding the relative contributions that brute force and coercion make to an adversary's actions is critical to informing policy about minimal uses of force and avoiding the need to escalate actual uses of force.

Most crises involving coercion fall along the continuum between pure brute force and coercion. The goal of the coercer is usually not total destruction but the use of enough force to make the threat of future force credible to the adversary. Counterinsurgency campaigns, for example, are typically designed to dislodge and eradicate pockets of resistance, but the government waging such a campaign usually will accept the voluntary disbanding and disarmament of rebels. Some conflicts may ultimately be resolved through brute force because one side's attempts at coercion may be met by refusals to negotiate. It is only in rare cases—such as campaigns of genocide—that one side will not settle for the other side's surrender.

Distinguishing brute force from coercion is similar to the debate over what constitutes pornography or art: coercion is often in the eye of the beholder. Some studies on coercion classify World War II and the Korean War as coercion, while others focus on cases solely involving the threat of force or token uses of force. Of course, such incredible variance in case selection has analytic consequences, leading to conclusions that might not be appropriate along the entire force spectrum.

This book does not completely escape this trap. We too draw on a range of cases to illustrate our conclusions. We focus most of our attention on cases in which all participants clearly understood that additional force could have been used and would have produced operational benefits. Thus, NATO operations in the Balkans, the use of force against Iraq following Desert Storm, and other instances of limited force are mined for their insights. At times we incorporate lessons from uses of force such as those of the United States and its allies in Vietnam and Korea, instances that fall nearer to the brute force end of the continuum. These cases often yield implications about the effectiveness of a particular coercive instrument (e.g., air power) that remain valid and useful regardless of the level of overall force used. However, we try to base our conclusions on cases that truly represent limited force, as these represent the most common types of challenges the United States will face in the coming decades.

Once distinguished from brute force, coercion is typically broken down into two subcategories: compellence and deterrence.[5] Compellence involves attempts to reverse an action that has already occurred or to otherwise overturn the status quo, such as evicting an aggressor from territory it has just conquered or convincing a proliferating state to abandon its nuclear weapons programs. Deterrence, in contrast, involves attempts to prevent an as yet unmaterialized action from occurring in the first place, such as dissuading an aggressor from trying to conquer a neighboring state or convincing a country that desires nuclear weapons not to seek them.

Patrick Morgan offers a further, valuable distinction between *general deterrence* and *immediate deterrence*. General deterrence involves preventing an action, whether it is planned or not; general deterrent threats are always present to some degree. Immediate deterrence focuses on a specific, planned event.[6] An example of general deterrence is the U.S.

5 Our definition draws on the work of several leading scholars. In his seminal work *Arms and Influence*, Thomas Schelling introduces the term *coercion* and notes that it includes efforts to discourage through fear (deterrence) and efforts to actively change an existing situation (compellence) (Schelling, *Arms and Influence*, pp. 72–73). Alexander George defines coercive diplomacy as "efforts to persuade an opponent to stop or reverse an action; . . . coercive diplomacy is a defensive strategy that is employed to deal with the efforts of an adversary to change a status quo situation in his own favor" (Alexander George and William E. Simons, eds., *The Limits of Coercive Diplomacy* [Boulder, CO: Westview Press, 1994], pp. 7–8). George and Simons, however, are explicitly referring to defensive uses of coercion, noting that the use of threats to persuade a victim to give up something of value is better designated as a blackmail strategy. This distinction has analytic value, but our focus explores how blackmail, deterrence, and other forms of coercion reinforce one another, leading us to adopt a broader definition. Robert Pape defines coercion as "efforts to change the behavior of a state by manipulating costs and benefits" (Pape, *Bombing to Win*, p. 4). He uses *coercion* similarly to how Schelling uses *compellence*.

6 See Patrick M. Morgan, *Deterrence: A Conceptual Analysis* (Beverly Hills, CA: Sage Library of Social Science, 1977) for more on these concepts.

treaty with Japan that is intended to secure Japan against any aggressor. An example of immediate deterrence is the 1970 Israeli warning to Syria not to escalate after its initial failure to invade Jordan: the warning prevented a particular, imminent invasion from materializing.[7]

In practice, however, compellence is difficult to distinguish from deterrence and to separate from the level of threat inherent to the overall security environment. As David Baldwin argues, "From a purely semantic standpoint, any deterrent threat can be stated in compellent terms, and any compellent threat can be stated in deterrent terms."[8] Reversing a completed action versus deterring a future, planned action (immediate deterrence) is rarely a clear-cut division. Both actions ultimately boil down to inducing the adversary to choose a different policy than it otherwise would.[9] Classifying cases as compellence as opposed to immediate deterrence is always speculative to some degree, given the inherent opacity of enemy intentions. Indeed, even general deterrence and compellence are codependent, as success or failure in coercion affects the coercing power's general reputation to some degree and thus its overall ability to deter. Moreover, the specific policies of compellence and deterrence are inextricably related because, as discussed later, the success or failure of coercive threats affects the coercer's general reputation and therefore its ability to coerce successfully in the future.[10]

7 T. N. Dupuy, *Elusive Victory: The Arab Israeli Wars, 1947–1974*, 3rd ed. (Dubuque, IA: Kendall/Hunt Publishing, 1992), p. 381. Dupuy argues that Syrian President Nur al-Din al-Attasi considered escalation but was dissuaded by the threat of Israeli intervention.

8 David A. Baldwin, "Power Analysis and World Politics: New Trends and Old Tendencies," *World Politics,* Vol. 31, no. 1 (January 1979), p. 188.

9 Although this distinction remains useful for delineating different types of deterrence behavior (and the challenges inherent to each), it is far crisper in the nuclear, as opposed to conventional, context. The use of nuclear weapons by either side would represent a massive escalation and break from the status quo. Conventional force, in contrast, can range from highly destructive to minimal in its impact.

10 For works on the reputation effects of deterrence and coercion, see Uri Bar-Joseph, "Variations on a Theme: The Conceptualization of Deterrence in Israeli Strategic Thinking," *Security Studies,* Vol. 7, no. 3 (Spring 1998), pp. 145–181; Ted Hopf, *Peripheral Visions: Deterrence Theory and American Foreign Policy in the Third World, 1965–1990* (Ann Arbor: University of Michigan Press, 1994); Paul K. Huth, "Reputations and Deterrence," *Security Studies,* Vol. 7, no. 1 (Fall 1997), pp. 72–99; Patrick M. Morgan, "Saving Face for the Sake of Deterrence," in

Figure 1.1 illustrates the difficulty of drawing clear lines between compellence and deterrence and between different types of deterrence. General demands to Iraq, such as "Don't invade Kuwait," appear to fall clearly in the deterrence camp, whereas calls to withdraw seem like compellence. The in-between areas are more ambiguous. "Don't go further" involves both stopping an existing action and avoiding a future one—both immediate deterrence and coercion. Moreover, a call to withdraw carries with it an implicit demand not to engage in the offense again and affects the credibility of the deterrence call to not in-

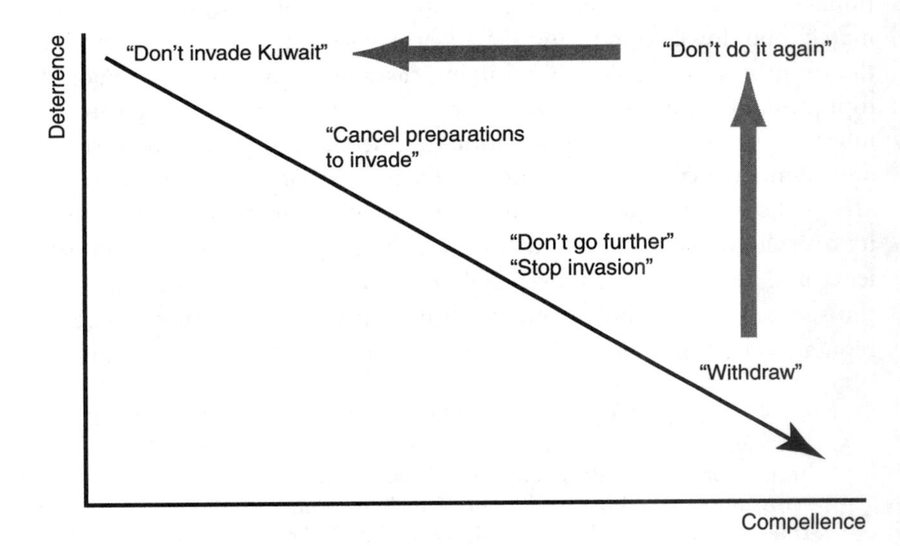

Figure 1.1. Deterrence and Compellence Blur in Practice

Psychology and Deterrence, Richard Ned Lebow, Robert Jervis, and Janice Gross Stein, eds. (Baltimore, MD: Johns Hopkins University Press, 1985), pp. 125–152; and Jonathan Shimshoni, *Israel and Conventional Deterrence: Border Warfare from 1953 to 1970* (Ithaca, NY: Ithaca University Press, 1988). Evidence for the reputation hypotheses is mixed (see Huth, "Reputations and Deterrence," pp. 92–93). In general, the reputation effect is stronger when it involves the same countries. For an overview, see Jonathan Mercer, *Reputation and International Politics* (Ithaca, NY: Cornell University Press, 1996).

vade Kuwait in the future. The arrows in Figure 1.1 suggest the linkage between the general deterrence statement of "Don't invade" and the compellent demand of "Withdraw." As the figure highlights, these analytic categories have value, but they overlap considerably.

The primary focus of this book is the compellence subset of coercion, but given that deterrence is a closely related phenomenon (both actions use the threat of force to manipulate an adversary's decision-making calculus), we incorporate insights and examples drawn from both. As such, the term *coercion* is used throughout this work to include both phenomena.

THE ROLE OF INDUCEMENTS

The flipside of threatening an adversary with economic or political sanctions is the offering of inducements for compliance. The United States gave billions of dollars to Egypt and Israel to sweeten the Camp David accords and provided aid to Belarus, Ukraine, and Kazakhstan in exchange for their giving up their nuclear programs. Germany gave 50 billion DM to the Soviet Union to encourage its withdrawal of troops from East Germany.[11] Inducements such as these are common. Even as coercive pressure is being applied, coercers often use inducements to encourage cooperation and to ease implementation problems by allowing an adversary to "save face" or otherwise play down the costs of concessions.

Traditionally, most coercive strategies focus either on raising the costs to an adversary of continued provocations or on denying the benefits of defiance. Inducements, however, reverse this focus. Instead of raising the costs of defiance, inducements increase the value of concessions. In addition, inducements can decrease the political costs of capitulation for an adversary, enabling leaders to claim victory even in defeat. When inducements are combined with more-traditional forms of coercion, resolution of a dispute is more likely.[12] Of course, a balance is necessary. Coercers may fear that concessions will be viewed as

11 Daniel W. Drezner, "The Trouble with Carrots: Transaction Costs, Conflict Expectations, and Economic Inducements," *Security Studies,* Vol. 9, no. 1–2 (Autumn 1999–Winter 2000), p. 188.

12 George and Simons, *The Limits of Coercive Diplomacy,* pp. 28–29; and David Baldwin, "The Power of Positive Sanctions," *World Politics,* Vol. 24, no. 1 (October 1971), pp. 19–38.

signs of weakness, and concessions alone may lead to blackmail, but offering a carrot with the coercive stick makes yielding more palatable to an adversary. The Cuban missile crisis represents perhaps the most commonly cited use of specific inducements as part of a coercive strategy. In addition to threatening an invasion of Cuba, the Kennedy administration offered to remove U.S. missiles from Turkey and to promise not to invade Cuba—concessions that both allowed the Soviets to save face and served the Kremlin's broader strategic ambitions.

This book does not explore the use of inducements in any depth. Instead we focus on the threat and use of limited force. This neglect, however, should not obscure the importance of inducements: carrots and sticks, when combined, are often more effective than sticks alone.[13]

MODELS OF COERCION

Most standard explorations of coercion rely on a cost-benefit model to explain whether coercion succeeds or fails.[14] These models predict outcomes by comparing the expected costs and benefits of a particular action. In his study of strategic bombing as an instrument of coercion, for example, Robert Pape uses such a model: "Success or failure is decided by the target state's decision calculus with regard to costs and benefits. . . . When the benefits that would be lost by concessions and the probability of attaining these benefits by continued resistance are exceeded by the costs of resistance and the probability of suffering these costs, the target concedes."[15] Coercion should work when the anticipated suffering associated with a threat exceeds the anticipated gains of defiance.

13 To be sure, inducements carry heavy costs to the coercer, in terms of immediate payments and the precedent of paying a potential future adversary today for uncertain compliance tomorrow. Also, some adversary regimes resist what the coercer views as generous concessions. (Drezner, "The Trouble with Carrots," pp. 189–191.)

14 In addition to Pape's and Schelling's works, the many other major works on coercion that employ a rationalist, cost-benefit approach include Bruce Bueno de Mesquita, *The War Trap* (New Haven, CT: Yale University Press, 1981); and Christopher H. Achen and Duncan Snidal, "Rational Deterrence Theory and Comparative Case Studies," *World Politics,* Vol. 41, no. 2 (January 1989), pp. 143–169.

15 Pape, *Bombing to Win*, pp. 15–16.

We too use a cost-benefit model as a starting point, because it focuses attention on four basic elements of coercive threats: benefits, costs, probabilities, and perceptions. Benefits are a simple concept—the value to the adversary of a particular action—though appreciating all the factors that go into a precise calculation of benefits is ultimately impossible. The benefits to Iraq of resisting U.S. demands to leave Kuwait included the possession of Kuwait, along with the political gains the Iraqi government saw in holding it. Saddam Husayn and other Iraqi decision makers may also have expected to reap domestic political benefits from the move, in addition to perhaps improving Iraq's future bargaining position among the Persian Gulf states.

Costs, the other side of the coercion coin, are the price an adversary expects to pay to pursue a particular action. Saddam must have anticipated at least the possibility that the United States and its allies would carry out their threats and attack his forces. On the other hand, once committed to holding Kuwait, Saddam probably saw a risk to his domestic political position if he gave in to Western threats. When considering a coercer's threat, an adversary looks at costs associated with continued resistance versus costs associated with complying with the coercer's demands.

Because coercion is about altering decision making, analyses of coercion focus not on some objectively "real" costs and benefits of various policy choices but on what the adversary perceives as costs and benefits. These perceived costs and benefits are products of the magnitude of the dangers and profits the adversary sees ahead for a given path and the probability of their occurrence. Saddam knew he might face a U.S. nuclear strike during the Gulf standoff, but the probability of such a contingency was low. He might also have perceived the likelihood of a coalition ground invasion as low too, perhaps underestimating the coalition's resolve and accordingly discounting the costs of that possibility when weighing his options. Another adversary might have understood the threats issued to Saddam very differently, perhaps thinking it more likely that the United States would intervene to roll back Iraqi aggression in 1990.

The cost-benefit model of state decision making has—appropriately—been critiqued from many angles. One set of critiques points to empirical studies showing that human beings often deviate from rational decision making and argues that states may also do so, and for similar reasons. Cultural differences, overconfidence about low-probability events, unreasonable assumptions about an adversary's knowledge of one's own thoughts and decision-making process, and improper generalizations from small events are only a few of the common problems that distort "rational" decision making and make it difficult to predict.[16] Drawing on "prospect theory," Jack Levy argues that leaders often take more risks to preserve their position than to enhance it and will engage in high-risk activity after losses in territory or other key political assets. Leaders also value "sunk costs"—the price they have already paid in blood, treasure, and political capital in pursuing the strategy—more than a strictly rational approach would suggest. Because leaders are usually highly averse to loss, outside pressure may cause them to follow policies that are failing, despite the contrary predictions of a simple cost-benefit analysis of the behavior.[17]

Policy makers may also be sensitive to how coercive threats are framed. For example, empirical studies suggest that people are more likely to accept a medical treatment if it is described as having a 90 percent survival rate rather than a 10 percent mortality rate, even though these two descriptions are identical in terms of the patient's probable survival. Because coercion tends to be framed as a threat, and thus in a negative manner, individuals may be more obstinate than rationality would suggest.[18]

Another limit of cost-benefit models is their failure to provide insight into what particular decision makers may value. In economics, the cost-benefit model is quite useful because the ultimate goals of decision making can be derived from profit motive. Politics, however, lacks such clarity. Some leaders value power, others security, and still others

16 For a review, see Colin Camerer, "Individual Decision-Making," in *The Handbook of Experimental Economics* (Princeton, NJ: Princeton University Press, 1995), pp. 587–703.

17 Jack Levy, "Prospect Theory, Rational Choice, and International Relations," *International Studies Quarterly,* no. 41 (1997), p. 93, and "Loss Aversion, Framing, and Bargaining: The Implications of Prospect Theory for International Conflict," *International Political Science Review,* Vol. 17, no. 2 (1996), p. 189. Levy's findings have significant implications for coercion. Loss aversion suggests that compellence, as traditionally defined, is harder than traditional deterrence. In addition, policy makers may take more risks to prevent losses than to achieve gains.

18 See Levy, "Prospect Theory, Rational Choice, and International Relations," and "Loss Aversion, Framing, and Bargaining," for a review.

glory. Even if leaders have identical goals, they may place different emphases on them. Without a detailed knowledge of a policy maker's goals and priorities, it is difficult to use the cost-benefit model with any hope of predictive accuracy.

Still another line of critique calls into question whether it is accurate or valuable to think about state decision making in terms of a unitary actor. Leaders do not always act in the interests of their country and people. At times, leaders may undertake risky foreign policy behavior to avoid or put off defeat at the polls or a loss of support from key elites.[19] Coercers must recognize that some states generally act in a unitary fashion, while the behavior of others depends largely on the goals and concerns of certain groups of elites or a few individuals.

The different agendas of important factions and bureaucracies may shape an adversary's collective decisions. In his famous explanation of this phenomenon, Graham Allison assessed the Cuban missile crisis using three different decision-making paradigms, two of which focus on how organizations and their leaders—not unitary states—make decisions. Allison proposes that it is the outputs of organizational processes and interorganizational bargaining rather than the decisions of a monolithic government that often explain important state behavior.[20] Other scholars have developed organizational explanations, applying them to such diverse phenomena as the development of military doctrine and nuclear safety.[21] Coercers thus should focus on the relative influence of important substate actors and the flexibility of organizations in order to enhance the effectiveness of their strategy. Certainly regimes are *not* individuals. It is necessary in applying any model of

19 For an excellent description of how this problem affects conflict, see George W. Downs and David M. Rocke, "Conflict, Agency, and Gambling for Resurrection: The Principle-Agent Problem Goes to War," *American Journal of Political Science,* Vol. 38, no. 2 (May 1994), pp. 362–380. For a broader overview, see Alexander Wendt, "The Agent-Structure Problem in International Relations Theory," *International Organization,* Vol. 41, no. 3 (Summer 1987), pp. 335–370.

20 Graham T. Allison, *Essence of Decision* (Glenview, IL: Scott, Foresman and Company, 1971), pp. 79–95 and 162–184.

21 See, for example, Barry Posen, *Sources of Military Doctrine: France, Britain, and Germany Between the World Wars* (Ithaca, NY: Cornell University Press, 1984); and Scott D. Sagan, *The Limits of Safety: Organizations, Accidents, and Nuclear Weapons* (Princeton, NJ: Princeton University Press, 1993).

state decision making to take into account a regime's unique attributes. As Schelling notes:

> Analogies with individuals are helpful; but they are counterproductive if they make us forget that a government does not reach a decision in the same way as an individual in a government. Collective decision depends on the internal politics and bureaucracy of government, on the chain of command and on the lines of communication, on party structures, on pressure groups, as well as on individual values and careers.[22]

Unfortunately, since Schelling's writing, analysts have made limited progress on learning how regime variations shape coercive diplomacy.

Each of these critiques is valid, to the extent that one wishes to use a generic cost-benefit model to predict specific behavior. But the cost-benefit approach still yields tremendous value in thinking about coercion and the effectiveness of coercive strategies. We use it as a heuristic device to elaborate the concepts presented in the next several chapters and the key factors affecting U.S. coercion presented in later chapters. But we also use the remainder of this book to explain the limits of a strict cost-benefit approach in the hope of yielding a more nuanced understanding of state decision making in the face of threats.

COERCION TODAY: OLD WINE IN NEW BOTTLES?

The study of coercion has long been associated with Cold War concerns, particularly the question of how to wield nuclear threats. This book focuses on the post–Cold War world, but many of the concepts and challenges that shape coercion today are not new. Basic factors identified by previous scholars—escalation, credibility, domestic support, and so on—remain pertinent to an analysis of coercion regardless of the era. Because of these continuities, we draw on the experience of the Cold War era and the findings of many scholars writing during that period to back our conclusions. The end of the Cold War, however, requires a corresponding shift in analytic emphasis. No longer does the prospect of a massive nuclear exchange dominate, and limit, U.S. actions. Because many of the particular dynamics that affect coercion have shifted since the fall of the Soviet Union, we carefully examine more-recent U.S. military crises as well as Cold War–era attempts by powers, such as Israel, that were not locked in a nuclear rivalry.

22 Schelling, *Arms and Influence*, p. 86.

Coercion, as an abstract notion and as a particular foreign policy strategy, received a great deal of scholarly attention during the 1960s and 1970s, when authors and policy makers considered how each superpower used threats of nuclear attacks to manipulate its rival. Works on nuclear coercion by Albert Wohlstetter, Herman Kahn, and others shaped the application—and nonapplication—of nuclear weapons to crises.[23] Scholars and policy makers also examined how to use limited amounts of force to pursue strategic interests in remote parts of the world without sparking wider conflagrations.

Among the best and most widely cited works on coercion from the 1960s and 1970s are those of Thomas Schelling, Alexander George, and William Simons. In *Arms and Influence*, Schelling develops the theoretical structure of coercion theory, applying his prior work on the strategy of conflict to argue that rational adversaries routinely use the threat of military force as an integral part of their diplomacy.[24] He concludes that by gradually raising the costs of resistance, a party could induce an adversary, eager to avoid future costs, to concede. In *The Limits of Coercive Diplomacy* and other works on the subject, George and Simons take an empirical approach, reviewing a series of case studies to draw lessons regarding the success and failure of coercive threats. Examining evidence from various international crises, they analyze contextual variables and their effects on parties' reactions to threats. The authors attempt to draw lessons of direct relevance to policy makers regarding the ingredients of successful strategies combining diplomatic efforts with minimal applications of force. Among the most important insights are their conclusions that the relative strengths of parties' motivations and the clarity and urgency of their objectives are critical determinants of successful coercive diplomacy.[25]

23 For the most famous, see Albert Wohlstetter, "The Delicate Balance of Terror," *Foreign Affairs,* Vol. 37, no. 2 (January 1959), pp. 213–236; Herman Kahn, *On Thermonuclear War* (Princeton, NJ: Princeton University Press, 1960); Henry Kissinger, *The Necessity for Choice* (New York: Harper & Row, 1961); and Morton Halperin, *Limited War in the Nuclear Age* (New York: John Wiley and Sons, 1963). For a review, see Lawrence Freedman, *The Evolution of Nuclear Strategy* (New York: St. Martin's Press, 1981).

24 Schelling, *Arms and Influence*; and Thomas C. Schelling, *The Strategy of Conflict* (Cambridge, MA: Harvard University Press, 1960).

25 In addition to George and Simon's *The Limits of Coercive Diplomacy*, see Alexander George, *Forceful Persuasion* (Washington, DC: United

A number of other scholars have added valuable insights to these pioneering works. William Simons's independent work on escalation offers broad insights from a range of cases on one of the most important aspects of successful coercion: the ability to inflict costs while denying an adversary the capability to do so. Robert Jervis, Richard Ned Lebow, Janice Gross Stein, and other scholars explore the rationality assumption inherent to Schelling's work and find it wanting. They argue that "abstract rationality fails to provide an adequate description of how states actually behave."[26] David Baldwin has also made valuable contributions, explaining the situational nature of power and the choices that often go into a particular strategy of coercion.[27]

The years immediately following the end of the Cold War—and the U.S.-led coalition's overwhelming military victory in the 1991 Gulf War—saw a change in the focus of scholarship on coercion, including a shift from nuclear threats to air power and economic sanctions as coercive tools. When the allied coalition's heavy reliance on precisely targeted air power against Iraqi assets renewed interest in the use of limited force—particularly strategic bombing—to achieve strategic objectives, Colonel John Warden was one of those who argued that air power could be used to incapacitate enemy leaders and paralyze enemy war making.[28] Pape, by contrast, conducted a review of various coercive uses of air power and found that denial—targeting a state's military strategy for controlling the objectives in dispute—has proven the only meaningfully effective use of coercive air power.[29] Interest in sanctions also grew in the post–Cold War era, in large part due to the

States Institute of Peace, 1991); and Alexander L. George and Richard Smoke, *Deterrence in American Foreign Policy: Theory and Practice* (New York: Columbia University Press, 1974).

26 Richard Ned Lebow, "Conclusions," in Robert Jervis, Richard Ned Lebow, and Janice Gross Stein, eds., *Psychology and Deterrence: Perspectives on Security* (Baltimore, MD: Johns Hopkins University Press, 1985), p. 204.

27 Baldwin, "Power Analysis and World Politics," pp. 161–194, and "The Power of Positive Sanctions." Also see David A. Baldwin, "The Sanctions Debate and the Logic of Choice," *International Security*, Vol. 24, no. 3 (Winter 1999–2000), pp. 90–136.

28 John A. Warden III, "Employing Air Power in the Twenty-First Century," in *The Future of Air Power in the Aftermath of the Gulf War*, Richard Shultz, Jr., and Robert L. Pfaltzgraff, Jr., eds. (Maxwell Air Force Base, AL: Air University Press, 1992), p. 57.

29 Pape, *Bombing to Win*, p. 11.

explosive increase in the imposition of sanctions by both the United States and the United Nations and the view that geostrategic realignments made possible more broadly based international cooperation in isolating "rogue" states. As with air power, the debate has focused both on whether sanctions are effective at all and, if so, when they should be used.[30]

This shift in focus from the nuclear to the conventional and even to the economic reflects a number of global transformations. At a geopolitical level, the position of the United States as the sole superpower, it is sometimes argued, gives it tremendous leverage when it chooses to flex its military muscle with authority. On the other hand, the lack of common, vital interests and the increases in global interdependence may negate many potential advantages of unipolarity, particularly those associated with the U.S. nuclear arsenal.

Technological change also shapes strategy making and influences the effectiveness of coercive strategies. Just as interwar air power theorists like Giulio Douhet prophesied that the advent of air power would negate long-held, basic principles about the way conflicts would be waged, many of today's scholars and commentators hint or state that conflicts in the Information Age will be fundamentally and radically different, requiring that strategic principles be accordingly rebuilt from scratch. Other observers respond that the vast technological transformations overhauling the way conflict is waged leave intact the basic foundations of military and national security strategy.

Beneath all these arguments about the conditions of the Cold War versus those of the post–Cold War and the waves of the future is a de-

30 The most cited, and most criticized, compendium on sanctions is Gary Clyde Hufbauer et al., *Economic Sanctions Reconsidered*, 2nd ed. (Washington, DC: Institute for International Economics, 1990). Useful articles on sanctions are Elizabeth S. Rogers, "Using Economic Sanctions to Control Regional Conflicts," *Security Studies,* Vol. 5, no. 4 (Summer 1996), pp. 43–72; Jonathan Kirshner, "The Microfoundations of Economic Sanctions," *Security Studies,* Vol. 6, no. 3 (Spring 1997), pp. 32–64; and Robert A. Pape, "Why Economic Sanctions Do Not Work," *International Security,* Vol. 22, no. 2 (Fall 1997), pp. 90–136. For excellent and subtle arguments about economic coercion in general, see Jonathan Kirshner, *Currency and Coercion: The Political Economy of International Monetary Power* (Princeton, NJ: Princeton University Press, 1995); and David A. Baldwin, *Economic Statecraft* (Princeton, NJ: Princeton University Press, 1985).

bate about the value of history. Is history a promising tool for understanding coercion in the future? Or is the world changing so rapidly that reliance on history could lead the United States down wrong paths?

This book derives from a cautious belief in the former. Coercion, by definition, is about using threats of force and limited actual force to manipulate adversary decision making. Such manipulation is timeless; all historical eras have seen the strong shape the world according to their will by coercing the weak (and attempts by the weak to manipulate the strong). Israelites tried to coerce Canaanites, Persians tried to coerce Athenians, and so on. Each era of history has its own dynamics, but many elements of these dynamics are eternal. Reliance on history, however, should be tempered by a recognition of its limits. Fighting the last war is a sure recipe for defeat in the next one. Analysts and policy makers must recognize how changes in the world today—social, economic, technological, and political—affect the application of many of the basic analytic concepts that are timeless.

CHALLENGES TO COERCION TODAY

The experience of the United States and other strong powers suggests that objective, qualitative measures of power seldom determine foreign policy success or failure. Many of the military assets that the United States and other strong powers can bring to the table often are of little or no utility against a particular adversary—a phenomenon that David Baldwin labels "the paradox of unrealized power."[31] The United States failed to coerce North Vietnam; Russia failed to coerce Chechen guerrillas to give up their struggle; Israel has pulled out of Lebanon. These instances and many others evince the importance of vital, if rather ineffable, factors. Will and credibility matter as much as, and often more than, the overall balance of forces. At times, a coercer may have preponderant power in a general sense but lack specific means to influence an adversary.

It is the dynamic nature of coercion that helps explain its failure. Just as the United States and other major powers try to exploit their adversaries' weaknesses, adversaries tailor their actions to exploit U.S. and major world power weaknesses. Adversaries generally avoid exposing themselves to the coercer's strengths. They employ weapons of the

31 Baldwin, "Power Analysis and World Politics," p. 163.

weak, such as guerrilla warfare, and try to exploit the humanitarian conscience or political sensitivities of the coercing powers in an effort to fracture public opinion. Though the coercing power may possess an apparent supremacy of strength, it often lacks the ability or will to apply that strength and inflict costs. Domestic constraints and the concerns of allies often hinder the coercer's ability to escalate, while the adversary may be able to counterescalate by holding hostages, killing soldiers, splitting coalitions, or otherwise inflicting costs on the coercer.

This book attempts to understand coercion from an adversary's point of view, in terms of the incentives that the key features of U.S.-style coercion give adversaries to employ certain counter-coercive strategies. Coercion is a dynamic contest that evolves during the course of crises. Whether a reactive, adaptive foe will yield in the face of threats depends on the levels of threat or motivation present at the time U.S. demands are issued, the adversary's options for undermining U.S. strategies, and the ways in which the United States reacts and adapts to those options.

Many problems facing the United States and other world powers arise from difficulties exploiting adversary vulnerabilities with the instruments at hand. At times, the United States uses its military forces and economic might poorly, leading to policy failure. In many instances, however, the true pressure points of an adversary are difficult to affect or, equally important, to identify in the first place. The United States finds itself able only to place indirect pressure on a foe, targeting the population at large or the national infrastructure rather than threatening the position of the few elites who make decisions. Many of the coercer's most powerful tools, such as air strikes or nuclear weapons, are of limited utility. These powerful destructive instruments are vital in an all-out war but have proven inappropriate or difficult to apply when the confrontation involves limited war for limited ends. "The theme of such explanations," Baldwin further elaborates, "is not 'he had the cards but played them poorly,' but rather 'he had a great bridge hand but happened to be playing poker.'"[32]

These broader points must be placed within the context of U.S. foreign policy today and in the near future. The assumptions and constraints that shaped U.S. foreign policy in the Cold War differ considerably from those shaping U.S. policy today. Four key sets of challenges will confront policy makers in the coming decades: constraints on the

32 Baldwin, "Power Analysis and World Politics," p. 164.

use of force emanating from domestic politics; constraints imposed by coalition partners; difficulties associated with humanitarian intervention; and dangers involved in confronting adversaries armed with weapons of mass destruction (WMD).

Both the level and the robustness of domestic support for coercive operations influence the conduct of those operations and their chances of success. Public support is critical to sustaining credible coercive strategies. Policy makers, however, regularly impose restrictions on U.S. military operations—such as limiting the size of forces, the type of missions, and the length of an operation—to gain or maintain public support. In addition, concerns about ensuring public support may lead to a choice of one coercive instrument over others. Air strikes in particular are increasingly seen by the U.S. public and many policy makers as a low-cost, low-commitment tool, even though from a purely military standpoint they are not always an ideal instrument. These preferences and restrictions then impede (or, more rarely, strengthen) coercive diplomacy, preventing escalation or otherwise hindering U.S. efforts. Adversaries tend to exploit U.S. domestic political concerns, particularly sensitivities regarding U.S. and enemy civilian casualties, to counter coercive threats.

Another challenge comes from U.S. allies or other international partners and actors. The United States regularly conducts coercive operations in partnership with other states, and intracoalition relations have tremendous effects on coercive diplomacy. Allies offer the United States access to bases overseas, and their participation enhances domestic U.S. support for operations. Differences among coalition partners, however, can restrict options for escalation. The objectives and responses of divergent members often reduce the credibility of coalition threats, permitting adversaries to widen intracoalition rifts and further obstruct coercive operations.

The end of the Cold War has also seen repeated efforts by the United States to intervene for humanitarian reasons, in which case little or no traditionally vital U.S. interest is immediately at stake and restrictions on the use of force are tight. In such crises, the United States often finds itself confronting nonstate actors, such as communal militias and international terrorist organizations. Though U.S. assets dwarf those of even the most capable nonstate foes, U.S. resolve in humanitarian interventions is often limited while that of the local actors is high. In addition to their higher level of commitment, nonstate actors pose special coercion challenges in that they often lack identifiable and targetable assets. Moreover, the nonstate organization's very structure impedes coercion because its leadership often exercises only limited control over its component parts. Thus, even if leadership decision making can be modified, changes to policy may not trickle down to those who carry it out.

Finally, it is increasingly likely that the United States will confront an adversary armed with nuclear, chemical, or biological weapons. Over 20 states possess chemical weapons, about ten probably have a biological weapons program, eight have a nuclear capacity, and several others are seeking all of the above.[33] Indeed, U.S. conventional superiority has increased the incentives for adversaries to acquire WMD. The most obvious implication for coercion is that a WMD-armed adversary—no matter how otherwise weak or how dangerous its foreign policies—can threaten its neighbors and offset U.S. regional influence or military might. Yet the specter of WMD can help as well as harm U.S. coercive diplomacy. Precisely because WMD-armed adversaries are potentially so threatening to U.S. interests, U.S. resolve and political support for intervention, and hence the credibility of U.S. threats, may reach their apex against such adversaries.

STRUCTURE

This book is divided into three parts. Part I, which comprises Chapters 2 through 4, examines the ingredients of coercive strategies, including the instruments of coercion and the mechanisms by which adversary behavior is influenced. Chapter 2 begins the examination with a theoretical discussion of coercion. Many disputes and false lessons about coercion have resulted from imprecise and faulty definitions of the problem. The concepts introduced in Chapter 2 are then used both to survey the historical record of coercion and to examine the context in which it will be practiced in the future. Chapter 3 focuses on the processes by which coercive pressure influences adversary decision making. It identifies a number of mechanisms for generating desired responses to coercive threats and discusses how they work in practice. Chapter 4 concludes the general discussion of coercive strategy making by describing

33 Monterey Institute, "Chemical and Biological Weapons Resource Page," http://cns.miis.edu/research/dbw/possess/htm (accessed on April 4, 2000).

various instruments of coercion and how they can be used to trigger the mechanisms discussed previously.

Part II consists of Chapters 5 through 8. It draws on the theoretical and conceptual overview of Part I to explore how today's security environment and various political pressures shape U.S. coercive strategy making and affect its prospects for success. Chapter 5 discusses how domestic constraints in the United States shape U.S. attempts to coerce. Chapter 6 assesses how participation in multinational coalitions limits the application of force. In both of these chapters, the focus is on how adversaries exploit these potential weaknesses in an effort to counter-coerce the United States. Chapters 7 and 8 then examine several of the emerging challenges in the post–Cold War world. Chapter 7 evaluates coercion in the context of humanitarian intervention, paying particular attention to efforts to threaten and use force against nonstate actors; Chapter 8 addresses the other end of the intervention spectrum, examining how a regional adversary's possession of WMD affects U.S. attempts to coerce.

Part III concludes the book by outlining some general principles of effective coercive strategy making. Within the context of ever-shifting technology, politics, and security issues, it attempts to highlight key challenges that will constrain the application of force.

Consistent with our basic argument about the value of history, this book draws from a wide range of past cases of coercion and coercive threats. Several criteria guided our selection of cases. First, we looked for high-profile and well-known cases, such as the Vietnam conflict and the U.S. attempt to coerce Serbia in 1999, to ensure that the most historically significant cases, which are often the ones best researched by scholars, were included and properly understood. Second, we looked for cases that show the limits and advantages of various coercive instruments and strategies—in other words, several cases were included specifically because they illustrate a rare, but important, point about coercion. Third, we looked for cases that involved factors most germane to the post–Cold War world so that we could identify the factors that matter most today. Clearly, however, the cases examined in this book represent neither a universal set of coercion cases nor even a representative sample thereof.[34]

34 We recognize the methodological tension in building conclusions on such a limited sample. The conclusions we present should be considered

Writing on coercion requires modesty. Not only are we building on the work of several giants in political science, but the topic itself defies easy description. The range of policies that fall under the term *coercion* is broad, encompassing most uses of force and many other forms of aggressive diplomacy. Any work of this kind therefore requires generalizations. There is no recipe for success, and a key theme of this book is the obvious but often ignored fact that history, theory, and other means of drawing general insights are often insufficient for providing guidance in a particular crisis. There will always be exceptions to the conclusions we draw. Our conclusions are not to be read as a blueprint for coercive strategies, but as a set of architectural rules of thumb for designing appropriate policies to fit the unique circumstances of crises.

hypotheses derived from the cases in question rather than theories tested on these cases.

Part One

Coercive Strategy Making

Coercive strategy making

The decision to confront an adversary is only the first of many decisions that policy makers make when deciding to coerce. Basic questions immediately arise: What are the objectives of the confrontation? In what ways is the adversary vulnerable? What means are at hand for targeting these vulnerabilities? The answers to these questions make up the coercer's strategy, which is the means-end chain expected to produce the desired results.[1] The coercive strategy specifies the coercer's objectives, how it plans to achieve those objectives, and which instruments it will use to do so.

Figure I.1 offers a simple conceptual framework for thinking about coercive strategies in terms of three key elements: the instrument

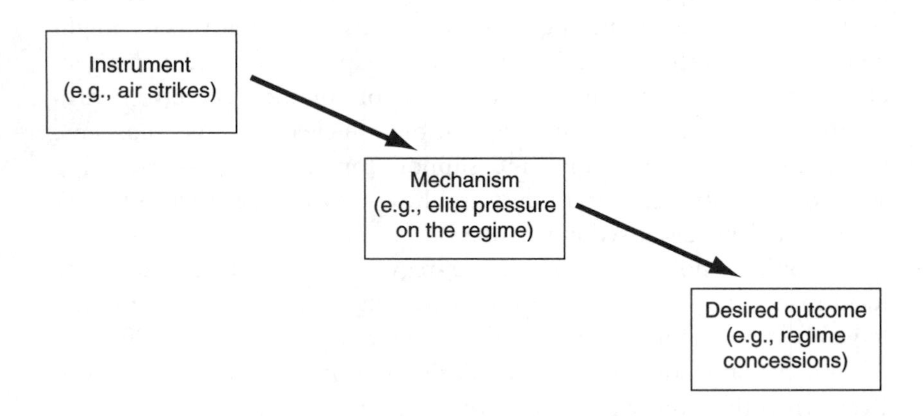

Figure I.1. Framework for Analyzing Coercive Strategy Making

1 This approach to coercive strategy making follows Barry Posen's use of the term *grand strategy*, applying it to the specifics of a confrontation involving coercion. (See Barry R. Posen and Andrew L. Ross, "Competing Visions for U.S. Grand Strategy," *International Security,* Vol. 21, no. 3 [Winter 1996–1997], pp. 5–53; and Posen, *Sources of Military Doctrine.*)

wielded, the mechanism used, and the desired outcome.[2] In short, the instrument is the means of threatening to inflict costs on an adversary, the mechanism is the process by which the threat of infliction of costs generates adversary responses, and the outcome is the overall goals the coercer seeks.

NATO operations against Serbia in 1999 help illustrate these concepts. During Operation Allied Force, NATO tried to force Serbian President Slobodan Milosevic to make concessions in part by attacking strategic targets in Serbia proper, such as the electric grid and the facilities of regime supporters. NATO planners believed that as the destruction mounted, key regime supporters and the population at large would become disgruntled with Milosevic's leadership, forcing him to cede autonomy to Kosovo or risk losing power. In other words, NATO sought to use air attacks (a coercive instrument) on strategic targets to generate popular and elite disaffection (the theorized mechanisms) that would favorably influence Milosevic's decision making and lead him to accept terms similar to the Rambouillet accords (desired concessions).

These three components are analyzed in Chapters 2, 3, and 4. Chapter 2 begins with a discussion of how coercion works, focusing on the basic concepts of the topic and the often nebulous nature of "success" in coercion. Chapter 3 follows with an exploration of the "black box" of decision making, exploring possible reasons why an adversary might concede in the face of coercive pressure. Chapter 4 concludes this general discussion by presenting an overview of common coercive instruments—air strikes, land-based operations, nuclear threats, economic sanctions, political pressure, and support for insurgency—describing some of their strengths and limits and how they can be used to trigger the mechanisms discussed in Chapter 3.

It should be noted that coercive strategy making often represents the ideal rather than the reality of policy making. At times policy makers have no strategy for coercion at all. A cynic would say that politicians often focus on increasing their popularity, not on overall policy success. Even when they know force will not work or is not an effective instru-

2 Pape briefly details a similar schematic, noting that a coercive air (and, logically, all coercive instrument) strategy might look like "force → targets → mechanism → political change" (see Pape, *Bombing to Win*, p. 56; and Mueller, "Denial, Punishment, and the Future of Air Power, p. 186). Alan Vick of RAND deserves our thanks for helping us construct our arguments in this manner.

ment against the target in question, they may use it anyway, simply because they believe it will be to their advantage politically. Even a less cynical perspective suggests that in some conflicts policy makers' time horizons are focused on the short term rather than on long-term success. Moreover, in many crises, leaders may see their country's interests as limited and thus not meriting a serious and integrated overall strategy. In such cases, the means-end chain used to coerce may not be internally consistent and thus will be unlikely to produce measurable success.

2

The theory of coercion

Coercion is a commonly used term, yet one that lacks an agreed-upon definition. As stated in Chapter 1, we define *coercion* as the use of threatened force, and at times the limited use of actual force to back up the threat, to induce an adversary to behave differently than it otherwise would. In short, coercion is about manipulating an adversary's policy choices and decision making. Critical to applying this definition in practice is the recognition that coercion does not operate only in one direction, with a coercer threatening a coercee. In virtually any military crisis, both parties (or more) will attempt to coerce each other.

Recognizing the dynamic nature of coercion yields two key, closely related insights. The first is that successful coercion requires discovering and threatening an adversary's *pressure points*. Pressure points are much more than those areas sensitive to the adversary—they are also areas the adversary cannot impenetrably guard. The second insight is that coercive threats are most likely to succeed when the coercer achieves *escalation dominance*, which is the ability to increase the threatened costs to an adversary while denying the adversary the opportunity to neutralize those costs or to counterescalate.

This chapter introduces these concepts and what they mean for the study of coercion. We also explore how to measure coercion and what factors contribute to its success. Related questions on why coercion works and how it is carried out are discussed in Chapters 3 and 4, respectively.

MEASURING COERCION

Coercion is difficult to measure. What does it mean to say that a coercive strategy was successful? If an adversary yields in the face of a threat but was likely to do so even before the threat was issued, is that coercion? Is it fair to say coercion worked if the adversary concedes to some but not all demands? Many past studies have tried to simplify these issues and have presented skewed conclusions as a result. Such measurement difficulties cannot be overcome completely, but it is critical that they be recognized if history is to be used to inform an understanding of coercion.

Combinations and synergies

Current debates about coercive instruments (air strikes, economic sanctions, and so on) tend to focus on one instrument in isolation rather than considering the effects of several instruments in combination. The result is a misassessment of the value of particular coercive instruments. Pape's critical appraisal of why the bombing of adversary populations does not lead to adversary capitulation is often wrongly used as evidence for the ineffectiveness of air power as a coercive instrument at all. This has contributed to an underestimation of air power's value. As Richard Overy pointed out about the bombing campaign against Germany and Japan: "There has always seemed something fundamentally implausible about the contention of bombing's critics that dropping almost 2.5 million tons of bombs on tautly-stretched industrial systems and war-weary urban populations would not seriously weaken them. . . . The air offensive was one of the decisive elements in Allied victory."[1] Overy's point is not that air power won the war single handedly, but that air power contributed significantly to Allied success, as did victories at sea and on land. Each instrument by itself was inadequate; together they packed a considerable punch. Coercive instruments must be understood in context, not in isolation.

The difficulties of dissecting adversary decision making to assess the impact of particular coercive pressures are considerable. Analysts typically are tempted to focus on an adversary state's observed behavioral response—Did the state *do* what the coercer wanted?—and correlate

1 Overy, *Why the Allies Won*, p. 133.

that response to particular events. This is a misleading substitute for the more fundamental issue of whether a specific threat, in the context of other pressures, significantly affected an opponent's decision making. A narrow focus on whether a coercive instrument either achieved objectives or failed outright leads to arbitrary and misleading coding of coercive strategies, because even limited, contributory effects, when combined with those of other coercive instruments, may be enough to force a policy change where an instrument in isolation might have failed.[2]

The effects of the instruments are not just additive; at times their combined impact is greater than the sum of the individual contributions. The 1999 Kosovo crisis illustrates how air attacks can interact synergistically with the threat of ground invasion. The threat of ground war at the outset of the Kosovo crisis carried immense potential costs for Serbia, but the likelihood of a ground war was small. As the intensity of NATO air attacks increased, however, the destruction of Serb forces and infrastructure enabled NATO potentially to launch a ground campaign at less cost to itself and at more cost to the Serbs—the softening up of Serbian defenses needed before a ground push had been accomplished by the air attacks. Milosevic's most obvious counter to NATO threats of physical invasion—inflicting heavy casualties on NATO forces—was in part offset by the air supremacy that NATO would have enjoyed and the devastation that air power would have inflicted in conjunction with ground forces. In analyzing Serbian decision making, variables such as "the threat of ground invasion" should be viewed not in terms of whether the threat existed—even in the face of ardent denials by Clinton administration officials, it remained a possibility—but in terms of whether a surge in its probability, made possible by air attacks and diplomatic maneuvers, contributed to the Serbian decision to capitulate.[3]

A proper assessment of the value of various coercive instruments also needs to recognize that coercive pressure does not exist only at particu-

2 As Barry Watts argues, mapping coercion to binary rankings is highly reductionist and wrongly assumes that complex campaigns can be reduced to zero or one (Barry M. Watts, "Theory and Evidence in Security Studies," *Security Studies*, Vol. 7, no. 2 [Winter 1997–1998], p. 136).

3 Daniel L. Byman and Matthew C. Waxman, "Kosovo and the Great Air Power Debate," *International Security*, Vol. 24, no. 4 (Spring 2000), pp. 25–28; and Barry R. Posen, "The War for Kosovo: Serbia's Political-Military Strategy," *International Security*, Vol. 24, no. 4 (Spring 2000), p. 62.

lar moments. Military capabilities and other forms of pressure, and the threat of their use, exert constant influence on allies and adversaries alike, though in varying degrees. In other words, there is an ever-present baseline, or background, threat. We seek to examine deviations from, or spikes in, the level of that threat.[4] When we consider a case of coercion, then, we are not talking about a sudden appearance of the threat of force. Instead, we are talking about relative changes in the threat of force—usually denoted by demonstrative uses of force, explicit threats and demands, and other overt signs. Using the 1972 Christmas bombings in North Vietnam as an example, a standard question is: Did the Christmas bombings coerce North Vietnam to negotiate terms more favorable to the United States? This is a poor and misleading proxy for the question more useful for understanding the air campaign's contribution: Did the marginal increase in force represented by the Christmas bombings increase the probability that North Vietnam would engage in behavior it would not otherwise have chosen? The value of the instrument must be measured for its contribution to the background level of pressure as well as to the spikes in the level of threat.

The uncertain meaning of success

Even if one instrument is evaluated in combination with other instruments rather than in isolation, assessing its contribution to successful coercion requires picking a baseline: What is success? Studies of coercion often pay inadequate attention to the range of goals pursued by a coercer. Moreover, they typically employ absolute, binary metrics of success in which a coercive strategy is seen as either working or failing.[5]

4 These points are discussed in Karl Mueller, "Strategy, Asymmetric Deterrence, and Accommodation," Ph.D. dissertation, Princeton University, 1991, chap. 1; and John Mueller, *Quiet Cataclysm: Reflections on the Recent Transformation of World Politics* (New York: HarperCollins, 1995), chap. 4.

5 The use of these binary metrics of success stems largely from measurement concerns. If one wishes to test certain hypotheses about coercion by correlating success with independent variables (such as type of force used or type of adversary assets threatened), then one would like to code as many cases as possible. A binary coding of success avoids the messy gray area into which many cases might fall if a nonabsolute measure were used. For an example of the binary coding of success and failure, see Walter J. Peterson, "Deterrence and Compellence: A Critical Assessment of Con-

Assessments of coercive strategies must shed these tendencies and consider a spectrum of possible outcomes.[6]

Classifying a case as a success or a failure depends on what behavior an observer thinks the coercer seeks, leading to confusion when different analyses of the same event are compared. For example, in Operation Desert Storm, the behavior sought from Saddam Husayn might have been Iraq picking up and peacefully retreating from Kuwait. Or, the goal might have simply been for Iraq to not be in Kuwait, one way or another. One observer might conclude that the air campaign was a coercive success because by the time it ended, Iraq was willing to withdraw under conditions relatively favorable to the United States.[7] Classifying the air campaign as successful coercion, however, assumes that the coalition's objective was simply an Iraqi expulsion. But was that the objective? Janice Gross Stein concludes that the air campaign represented a failed coercive strategy because she has a different interpretation of what behavior the coalition sought.[8] To Stein, the air campaign represented a failure of coercion the moment the ground war began, because coalition objectives were to induce Iraq to withdraw *without having to forcefully expel it* through the use of ground troops.

Coercers generally have multiple goals as they pursue coercive strategies, further confusing assessments of success. Since the early 1990s, the United States has sought a change in the North Korean regime, has tried to deter a conventional attack by the North on the United States' South Korean ally, has tried to induce North Korea to completely abandon its nuclear program, and has tried to halt further progress in the North's nuclear program. Although the relative priority of these goals has varied considerably, they nonetheless have remained goals through the Bush, then Clinton, and now new Bush administrations. It is possible to declare U.S. policy toward North Korea a success (no invasion occurred and the nuclear program has made at most limited progress since 1994) or a failure (Pyongyang has not ended its pro-

ventional Wisdom," *International Studies Quarterly*, Vol. 30, no. 3 (September 1986), pp. 269–294.

6 See Baldwin, "Power Analysis and World Politics," for an excellent review of how different outcomes affect the assessment of different foreign policy tools.

7 Lawrence Freedman and Efraim Karsh, *The Gulf Conflict, 1990–1991* (Princeton, NJ: Princeton University Press, 1993), pp. 380–385.

8 Janice Gross Stein, "Deterrence and Compellence in the Gulf, 1990–91," *International Security*, Vol. 17, no. 2 (Fall 1992), pp. 147–179.

gram and the current regime remains in power). Success, in this case, depends not only on discerning the effect of threats on each of these fronts but on attaching various weights of priority to them. David Baldwin's argument about economic pressure applies to coercion more broadly: "To view economic statecraft strictly in terms of securing compliance with explicit and publicly stated demands is to load the dice in favor of failure. Third parties, secondary goals, implicit and unstated goals are all likely to be significant components of such undertakings."[9]

The way in which the very issue of success is framed exacerbates this confusion. The use of absolute, binary measures—Did air attacks coerce, yes or no?—does not capture the complex and often subtle effects of coercive threats. Iraq both conceded to and defied the United States during Desert Storm: it offered a partial withdrawal from Kuwait, yet it refused to accept all U.S. demands. States seldom respond to coercive threats with a clear yes or no. Most states, when facing a coercive threat, modify their behavior, trying to placate the coercer with small changes while pursuing their own policy objectives. Syria, for example, allowed Palestinian terrorists to strike Israel from its territory from 1965 to 1967 and provided them with support and encouragement.[10] After Syria's defeat in 1967, however, Damascus became far more cautious and no longer let terrorists operate directly out of Syrian territory. Instead, it encouraged terrorists to operate out of Lebanon, a nominally independent state that eventually became a Syrian satrap. The straitjacket of binary metrics distorts the lessons that can be drawn from aggregated empirical data when cases in which a coercive instrument helped move an adversary in favorable ways but short of the coercer's maximal objectives are coded either as absolute failures or as absolute successes.

At the same time as binary metrics may bias studies of coercion, they may also overlook the detrimental effects of coercive strategies. This measurement pathology is particularly problematic once coercion is understood in more dynamic terms. Coercion carries the potential for backfire; threatening an adversary may provoke an increase in unwanted behavior rather than the desired course. The 1967 Arab–Israeli War and the 1969–1970 Israeli-Egyptian War of Attrition are frequently cited examples of inadvertent escalation resulting from coercive

9 Baldwin, *Economic Statecraft*, p. 132.

10 Avi Shlaim, *The Iron Wall: Israel and the Arab World* (New York: W.W. Norton, 1999), pp. 232–233.

threats.[11] In the first, Egypt lost a war in a humiliating defeat after grandiose promises of triumph; in the second, Israel's escalation through the use of deep air strikes provoked Soviet involvement, leaving Israel in a no-win confrontation with a superpower. In other words, coercive strategies can leave the coercer worse off than before. Yet within the binary framework, the worst outcome recognized is the null result: backfires, the hardening of adversary resistance, and other detrimental effects are coded just as if coercive threats caused no effect.

It is even possible to, in a sense, *over*coerce. Issuing a threat often increases the "audience costs" facing a particular regime, which make it more difficult for the regime to concede. Almost all leaders prefer to be viewed as strong and as resistant to foreign pressure. Public threats or the use of force challenge this preferred perception. These audience costs often lead to a disjuncture between what is best for the country as a whole and what is most advantageous for the country's leadership.[12]

At times, issuing a coercive threat may raise the audience costs so high that the stakes for the adversary leadership become truly vital and far exceed the issue in dispute. This problem of overcoercing is particularly likely when the leadership cannot control information flows and when it is highly nationalistic. Overcoercing may even lead an adversary's leadership to take risks it would otherwise avoid and to escalate a

11 See Janice Gross Stein, "The Arab-Israeli War of 1967: Inadvertent War Through Miscalculated Escalation," in *Avoiding War: Problems of Crisis Management,* Alexander L. George, ed. (Boulder, CO: Westview, 1991), pp. 126–159; and Yaacov Bar-Siman-Tov, "The War of Attrition, 1969–1970," ibid., pp. 320–341.

12 See Downs and Rocke, "Conflict, Agency, and Gambling for Resurrection." See also James D. Fearon, "Bargaining, Enforcement, and International Cooperation," *International Organization*, Vol. 52, no. 2 (Spring 1998), p. 270. The concept of audience costs is theoretically embedded in a broader frame developed by Robert Putnam and known as "two-level" games (Robert D. Putnam, "Diplomacy and Domestic Politics: The Logic of Two-Level Games," *International Organization,* Vol. 42, no. 3 [Summer 1988], pp. 427–460). For a good case study applying this framework, see John S. Odell, "International Threats and Internal Politics: Brazil, the European Community, and the United States, 1985–1987," in *Double-Edged Diplomacy: International Bargaining and Domestic Politics*, Peter B. Evans, Harold K. Jacobson, and Robert D. Putnam, eds. (Berkeley: University of California Press, 1993), pp. 233–264.

conflict in order to stay in power.[13] This last point is part of a broader one, elaborated in later chapters: sometimes the adversary sees the costs of conceding as prohibitively high—possibly made even higher by the coercive threat itself—and no amount of threatened force can compel it to bend.

Conceptually, the dependent variable in analyzing coercive threats should be understood as a marginal change in the probability of behavior. Against a fluctuating background level of threat (and blandishments, for that matter), the probability of the adversary altering its behavior is never zero. Viewing success in absolute terms, based on observed behavior, ignores this positive probability and classifies all desired behavior as successful coercion, regardless of how likely that behavior was prior to the additional coercive threat. Data limits may require a focus on observable behavior, but analysts should not forget that the true effects of coercive strategies lie in the altered—in some cases, hardened—policy preferences or decision-making calculi of the actors involved.

COERCION AS A DYNAMIC CONTEST: KEY ANALYTIC CONCEPTS

There is a strong temptation to treat coercive threats as single, discrete events with a simple, linear logic: the coercer issues a threat, and the coercee responds by resisting or backing down.[14] This view fails to capture the dynamic nature of coercion. Coercive contests are better viewed as series of moves and countermoves in which each side acts not

13 Downs and Rocke, "Conflict, Agency, and Gambling for Resurrection," p. 364. In several instances, democratic states—in the face of strong public opposition to an intervention—have escalated, in part because their governments sought to score a decisive victory and thus improve their faltering political position (Ariel Levite, Bruce Jentleson, and Larry Berman, *Protracted Military Interventions: From Commitments to Disengagement* [New York: Columbia University Press, 1992]).

14 For works that generally follow this logic, see Paul K. Huth, *Extended Deterrence and the Prevention of War* (New Haven, CT: Yale University Press, 1988); Paul K. Huth and Bruce Russett, "Testing Deterrence Theory: Rigor Makes a Difference," *World Politics,* Vol. 42, no. 4 (July 1990); and Richard Ned Lebow and Janice Gross Stein, "Rational Deterrence Theory: I Think, Therefore I Deter," *World Politics*, Vol. 41, no. 2 (January 1989), pp. 208–224.

only based on and in anticipation of the other side's moves, but also based on other changes in the security environment.

As discussed in Chapter 1, the cost-benefit equation is useful for understanding coercion in the abstract, but it often confuses the study of coercion when taken as a true depiction of state behavior. One problem is that this equation fosters static, one-sided thinking about coercive contests. It encourages analysts to think about costs and benefits as independent variables that the coercer manipulates while the adversary stands idle, recalculating its perceived interests only as the coercer makes and implements various threats.

A more accurate picture requires viewing coercion as a dynamic, two-player (or more) contest. The adversary also moves so as to alter the perceived costs and benefits associated with certain actions.[15] For example, it can divert resources from civilian to military functions to offset a coercer's attempts to undermine its defensive capacities. It can engage in internal repression to neutralize a coercer's efforts to foment instability. Rather than simply minimizing the effect of coercive threats, the adversary may try to impose costs on the coercing power. For example, it can escalate militarily or attempt to drive a diplomatic wedge between states aligned against it, perhaps convincing the coercer to back down and withdraw its own threat to impose costs.[16]

Escalation dominance

It flows from an understanding of coercion as a dynamic contest that a critical condition of successful coercion is *escalation dominance*: the ability to increase the threatened costs to the adversary while denying the adversary the opportunity to negate those costs or to counterescalate. More precisely, it is through the parties' perceptions that the coercer can achieve the escalation dominance that enables coercive strategies to succeed. Escalation dominance is more than just an absolute ability to inflict more costs on an adversary than the adversary can in-

15 Pape examines this issue briefly in his discussion of why Germany did not surrender in *Bombing to Win*, p. 256, especially n. 4. This point is also implicit in Pape's discussion of how adversaries offset coercive pressure (for a summary, see *Bombing to Win*, p. 24).

16 For an assessment of such strategies, see Daniel Byman and Matthew Waxman, "Defeating U.S. Coercion," *Survival*, Vol. 41, no. 2 (Summer 1999), pp. 107–120.

flict in return. Rather, it requires a preponderance that is relevant to every form of possible escalation: no matter where the adversary chooses to increase pressure, the coercer is always able to overwhelm the adversary in that area. Part II of this book examines key factors that affect U.S. and adversary perceptions of their respective abilities to impose, absorb, and deflect costs, and that thus also affect the U.S. ability to achieve the critical condition of escalation dominance against likely foes.[17]

The realistic possibility of nuclear weapons use poses the most vivid example of how escalation dominance can prompt adversary concessions. During the Korean War and even the Gulf War, this possibility—on one side—contributed to successful coercion. In the Korean War, the North agreed to accept talks leading to the continued partition of the country in part because of the U.S. election of President Eisenhower, who threatened the use of atomic strikes to end the conflict.[18] This threat, while probably not sufficient by itself to bring about peace, contributed to the North Korean and Chinese decision to seek a negotiated settlement. Similarly, the implied threat of nuclear use did not lead Iraq to capitulate to the United States after the invasion of Kuwait, but it may have played a role in deterring Saddam's use of chemical weapons during the conflict.[19] In both of these cases, the adversary lacked an option for matching U.S. escalation to nuclear weapons, a condition that tremendously enhanced the U.S. bargaining position.

17 George and Simons, among others, identify several valuable rules of thumb that contribute to successful coercion: the clarity of the objective, the strength and asymmetry of the parties' motivation, the sense of urgency, the strength of leadership, the level of domestic and international support, the unacceptability of threatened escalation, and the clarity of the settlement (George and Simons, *The Limits of Coercive Diplomacy*, pp. 281–286). It is our contention that the factors George and Simons point out (which are discussed throughout this book) are indeed vital. However, most of the points that they and their colleagues point to are, in fact, components of escalation dominance. That is, the strength of motivation, the need for domestic support, and so on are part and parcel of a coercer's ability to escalate and an adversary's ability to deny or to counterescalate.

18 See Mark Clodfelter, *The Limits of Air Power: The American Bombing of North Vietnam* (New York: Free Press, 1989), for a discussion.

19 James E. Baker, *The Politics of Diplomacy* (New York: G.P. Putnam's Sons, 1995), p. 359; and Iraqi News Agency Broadcasts, January 9–13, 1991, in FBIS NES-91-009, January 14, 1991.

The concept of escalation dominance was developed during the Cold War, when the specter of a nuclear exchange hung over the world, but it has always applied to conventional crises as well. Herman Kahn, in his seminal work *On Escalation*, discusses conventional scenarios and precedents, such as the bombing of population centers during World War II, alongside his comprehensive discussion of escalation scenarios involving nuclear weapons.[20] In perhaps the most thorough and valuable work on the subject, Richard Smoke demonstrates the dynamics of escalation through five pre–World War II case studies using this exploration to understand both conventional and nuclear diplomacy.[21]

The concept of escalation dominance is critical to understanding contemporary crises. One side may have a preponderance of force and few targetable weaknesses, leaving the adversary with little choice but to concede. In Bosnia and Kosovo, Operation Deliberate Force (1995) and Operation Allied Force (1999) succeeded in part because Serb leaders understood that the U.S. air strikes could increase in number and scope and inflict even greater damage on their forces and reduce their political support. The damage, combined with the Serbs' inability to respond, created intense coercive pressure.

Rather than threatening to employ higher levels of violence, coercers often threaten to maintain a steady level, utilizing the prospect of mounting aggregate costs to influence adversary decision making. Although such a strategy would be effective against a perfectly rational adversary, states and leaders facing these types of threats are often unduly optimistic about the consequences of their actions and attempt to

20 Herman Kahn, *On Escalation: Metaphors and Scenarios* (Washington, DC: Praeger, 1965), pp. 25–34. Kahn defines escalation dominance as "a capacity, other things being equal, to enable the side possessing it to enjoy marked advantages in a given region of the escalation ladder" (p. 290). Kahn's focus is on specific crisis typologies—escalation dominance allows one side to triumph because its rival cannot risk taking the next step on the ladder. We build on and broaden Kahn's concept in our work. In particular, we focus on the ability of one side to prevent the other from escalating (rather than simply being in a better position should escalation occur) as a key part of escalation dominance. In general, our concept of escalation dominance is more open ended than Kahn's—he focuses on more-specific types of crises, driven by superpower rivalries, while we examine a far broader set of contingencies.

21 Richard Smoke, *War: Controlling Escalation* (Cambridge, MA: Harvard University Press, 1977).

wait out coercive campaigns.[22] The adversary may also believe that the coercer cannot maintain the pressure. Thus, an adversary may hold out longer, simply to determine whether the coercer can sustain the punishment.

The result of a steady increase in pain is usually a long-delayed reaction, though sometimes, ultimately, a favorable one. Israeli operations against Palestinian terrorists in Jordan and Iranian support of Kurdish insurgents in Iraq took years to bear fruit. Such operations did not bring about a rapid change in the adversary's decision making and, had the Israeli and Iranian governments called them off, would have gone down in history as great failures. The Jordanian and Iraqi governments slowly, but ultimately, realized that they could not prevent the intervention and that the costs imposed might lead to their loss of power. The U.S. Linebacker II operations in Vietnam succeeded in part because the North Vietnamese perceived them as sustainable. Hanoi recognized that Washington could continue its massive air campaign in the face of a paucity of North Vietnamese air defense assets. Inversely, the failure to sustain a bombing campaign or other form of coercive pressure can hearten an adversary, convincing it that its defense is working and the other side is irresolute.[23]

At times, sudden escalation is a more effective element of escalation dominance than is sustained pressure, because the former concentrates

22 For more on such biases in decision making, see Scott Plous, *The Psychology of Judgment and Decision-Making* (New York: McGraw-Hill, 1993), pp. 15–18; Irving L. Janis, *Groupthink* (Boston: Houghton Mifflin Company, 1982); Camerer, "Individual Decision-Making"; and Daniel Kahneman and Amos Tversky, "Prospect Theory: An Analysis of Decision Under Risk," *Econometrica,* no. 47 (1979), pp. 263–291. Jack Levy highlights the importance of the "endowment effect"—a phenomenon that makes people overvalue their current possessions (and thus incur more costs or gain fewer benefits than would a perfectly rational individual)—on political decision making (Levy, "Prospect Theory," p. 89). He concludes that coercion becomes harder as a result (p. 93). Paul Pillar notes that individuals are often willing to suffer more pain as a conflict nears an end, buoyed by the belief that suffering will soon end (Paul R. Pillar, "Ending Limited War: The Psychological Dimensions of the Termination Process," in *Psychological Dimensions of War*, Betty Glad, ed. [Newbury Park, CA: Sage Publications, 1990], p. 253).

23 George H. Quester, "The Psychological Effects of Bombing on Civilian Populations: Wars of the Past," in *Psychological Dimensions of War,* Betty Glad, ed. (Newbury Park, CA: Sage Publications, 1990), p. 209.

the attention of adversary decision makers and thus more directly affects their perceptions. Sudden escalation allows the coercer to convey its point with less of the background noise that emanates from other policies and different bureaucracies. As George and Simons note, "Clarity and consistency in what is demanded help persuade the adversary of the coercing power's strength of purpose."[24] When making decisions, policy makers typically draw heavily on existing frameworks and biases and may be seeing what they want to see. Gradual changes thus are more likely to pass unnoticed.[25] Sudden escalation, in contrast, can often force decision makers to reevaluate their situation. Moreover, it creates a sense of urgency among them, which is amenable to successful coercion.[26]

As these examples make clear, the first element of escalation dominance is the ability to threaten costs. Much attention in academic and policy literature is generally devoted to this element, including the study of particular instruments for threatening or imposing costs and their direct effects on targeted regimes. Such emphasis is not surprising given that this is the element over which a coercer has the most control and that the infliction of costs is often the most visible aspect of coercive contests.

A key theme of this book is that the analytic emphasis on threatening costs must be balanced with an equal emphasis on adversary countermoves in response to threats. Countermoves are an aspect of coercive contests over which coercers have limited control, and they are often hard to study because they may be difficult to detect. Nevertheless, the study of coercion must come at the problem from both the coercer's and the adversary's perspectives.

Historically, militarily superior coercers have watched their strategies fail or backfire in the face of unexpected counterescalation or efforts that neutralized the potency of their threats. When Israel, France, and Britain attacked Egypt in 1956 following Nasser's nationalization of the Suez Canal, Egypt scuttled ships in the canal, closing it to traffic. Nasser thereby sought to stop the invading powers by fulfilling their worst fears: the closing of the waterway itself. During the Israeli-Egyptian War of Attrition (1969–1970), Israeli deep-bombing strikes

24 George and Simons, *The Limits of Coercive Diplomacy*, p. 280.

25 Plous, *The Psychology of Judgment and Decision-Making* (New York: McGraw-Hill, 1993), pp. 15–17.

26 George and Simons, *The Limits of Coercive Diplomacy*, p. 282.

proved highly effective, devastating Egyptian air defense and artillery positions and creating consternation among Egyptian leaders. Rather than concede, however, the Egyptian leadership turned to the Soviet Union for assistance. Moscow not only sent more air defense assets, it also provided Soviet crews to man them and Soviet personnel to fly counterair operations. Israel thus faced a superpower's wrath when it continued its coercive campaign, leading it eventually to accept a cease-fire that in essence hindered its command of the air over the canal zone. "And so," according to one account of the contest, "admit it or not, and despite the appearance of a draw, Israel had lost her first war."[27]

In addition to issuing counterthreats or increasing the political costs faced by the coercer, an adversary facing coercive threats may take a variety of steps to negate a coercer's ability to escalate. During the Korean War, the North Koreans lowered water levels to prevent U.S. destruction of irrigation dikes from causing widespread flood damage, and they employed quick construction brigades that specialized in rapidly repairing damaged facilities. Many governments have proven especially skilled at diverting resources from civilian uses and from less critical military activities, making it hard to escalate pressure by halting enemy military production.

There is an internal, political component to escalation dominance, at times as important as the relative capabilities of the coercer and coercee. To resist pressure, adversaries must be able to maintain domestic support, at least among key constituencies, which often requires a demonstration that they are fighting back effectively.[28] When an adversary can demonstrate to its population or elites that the coercer is backing down or that the coercer too is suffering, then the psychological impact of the pain is lessened.[29] The adversary's population and elites can hope, with some justification, that the coercive pressure will subside because the coercer cannot bear the costs of continuing to apply it.

Almost all adversaries, including the most tyrannical, emphasize in their public statements not only their country's resilience, but also the suffering that their opponent is undergoing. Even the brutal World War

27 Shimshoni, *Israel and Conventional Deterrence*, p. 170.

28 Stephen T. Hosmer, *Psychological Effects of U.S. Air Operations in Four Wars, 1941–1991: Lessons for U.S. Commanders* (Santa Monica, CA: RAND, 1995), p. 70.

29 See Quester, "The Psychological Effects of Bombing on Civilian Populations, pp. 201–214, for an example.

II Axis regimes went to great lengths to score public relations victories in the face of Allied attacks. Japan and Germany spent tremendous amounts of their scarce resources on air defense of civilian areas and conducted militarily foolish attacks that overstretched their forces in order to demonstrate that they could respond effectively. In the aftermath of the Normandy invasion, and with the Red Army only 500 kilometers from its borders, Germany devoted roughly one-third of its armaments budget to air defense, a tremendous drain on resources—but a drain considerably more understandable when the importance of "fighting back" is recognized. Similarly, Japan responded to the legendary, but operationally ineffectual, U.S. bombing effort on April 18, 1942—the Doolittle raid—by conducting punitive raids and diverting vital fighter groups for air defense. More importantly, the humiliation of the raids led Japan's leaders to attempt two major operations simultaneously, leading to the disaster at Midway.[30] Coercive strategy making requires an understanding of the internal political logic behind the coercer's and adversary's responses to escalatory threats as much as it requires an understanding of the military strengths and weaknesses of each party with respect to the other.

Pressure points

In designing coercive strategies as well as in studying them, it is critical to avoid a one-size-fits-all mentality. The potential costs to which an adversary regime is susceptible and the array of countermoves it has available will vary considerably with the type of adversary and the broader strategic context of the crisis. To threaten effectively, a coercer must first understand what the adversary values. Then the coercer must determine what it can credibly put at risk without too much cost to itself. In other words, a coercer must seek out an adversary's pressure points: those points that are sensitive to the adversary and that the coercer can effectively threaten.

Pressure points vary by regime. In a democracy, the number of people who influence decision making is vast. Successful coercion might therefore focus on the opinion of the majority or the country's eco-

30 James G. Roche and Barry D. Watts, "Choosing Analytic Measures," *Journal of Strategic Studies*, Vol. 14, no. 2 (June 1991), pp. 181–182 and 186–187.

nomic health. Authoritarian regimes have different pressure points. Against them, successful coercion often requires an elite-based strategy. Sanctions, infrastructure strikes, and other pressures that affect an entire country might fail or even backfire because they do not affect elites and nonelites the same way.

Different regimes also have different options when confronted with a coercive threat. Responses are shaped and limited by a regime's institutions, ideology, and base of support. Some may seek to rally the nation, bolstering their status by defying the coercer.[31] Others may increase repression, fearing that the coercive threats might inflame popular dissent. Not all adversaries are equally skilled, but deception, operational substitutes, and other steps to resist the damage inflicted by coercive military operations are frequently attempted.

Aside from using operational steps designed to neutralize the threat of escalation, adversaries employ political tactics to offset the coercer's military dominance. A common technique is the exploitation of civilian suffering. As discussed in Chapter 5, U.S. policy makers' apparent concern with the political risks associated with adversary civilian suffering creates adversary opportunities for exploiting collateral damage. By propagandizing suffering, adversaries may impose diplomatic and domestic political costs on coercers.

In threatening that which an adversary regime holds dear, coercers face the following difficulty: those interests that are most vital to a regime are likely to be those that the regime is best equipped for (and practiced at) protecting. Saddam Husayn, for example, has demonstrated an acute concern with his relationship to his power base and, as discussed in Chapter 3, efforts by the United States and its allies to threaten that relationship have sometimes proven successful at moving his regime's policies in directions favorable to the United States. But in addition to the difficulties inherent to engineering coercive strategies that credibly threaten to rupture that relationship, the United States and its allies must deal with the massive resources Saddam has at his disposal for protecting internal stability. To stay in power, he has systematically eliminated potential rivals, either killing them outright or transferring or demoting them to prevent them from developing an

31 For the initial, and perhaps best, work on the rally-round-the-flag effect of coercion, see Johan Galtung, "On the Effects of International Economic Sanctions: With Examples from the Case of Rhodesia," *World Politics,* Vol. 19, no. 3 (April 1967), pp. 384–388.

independent power base. The vast majority of the Iraqi people probably loathe and oppose Saddam's rule, but open dissent in areas under the Baath regime's sway is almost nonexistent. Although—indeed, because—it is such a sensitive point, elite dissatisfaction is probably the danger Saddam is most prepared to combat. The very structure of his governing apparatus centers on preserving power against a coup by members of the armed forces, Baath party, or security services.[32] For coercers, this means that it will be difficult—though perhaps nonetheless necessary—to apply pressure at this point.

This apparent paradox is reconciled by distinguishing between an adversary's *susceptibility* to coercive pressure at a particular point and its *vulnerability*.[33] A regime's decision making may be highly susceptible to certain forms of pressure, but if applying that pressure is problematic for the coercer, or the adversary regime is adept at neutralizing the pressure, the adversary will not be vulnerable to it.

THE PATH AHEAD

The discussion in this chapter on the nature of coercion and how to measure it properly forms the basis for the rest of the book. The remaining chapters, while examining specific aspects of coercive strategies and factors critical to effective U.S. coercion, all underscore the dynamic nature of coercion and, accordingly, the need to focus on escalation dominance and on the pressure points of both the adversary and the United States.

In thinking about the various cases cited throughout this book, it is important to focus on the adversary decision-making process. Moving beyond broad classifications of successful versus failed coercive strate-

32 Amatzia Baram, *Building Toward Crisis: Saddam Husayn's Strategy for Survival* (Washington, DC: Washington Institute for Near East Policy, 1998), pp. 25 and 50; and Regis W. Matlak, "Inside Saddam's Grip," *National Security Studies Quarterly* (Spring 1999), electronic version.

33 This distinction, introduced in the context of interdependence, applies more broadly to various types of pressure; see Robert O. Keohane and Joseph S. Nye, *Power and Interdependence* (Boston: Little, Brown, 1977), pp. 12–16, for its initial discussion. Keohane and Nye contrast the sensitivity of a state and its vulnerability, noting that two states that import petroleum for 35 percent of their petroleum needs are not equally vulnerable if one can easily substitute domestic sources and the other has no option other than to buy from the international market (p. 13).

gies to examinations of whether and when an adversary will be likely to choose a particular path is difficult, and the results of such a study are likely to generate more debate than consensus. Yet that is precisely the locus of debate—how and why an adversary chooses a particular path—that is critical to learning and applying the lessons of the past to future policy.

3

Coercive mechanisms

Effective coercive strategy making requires an understanding of coercive mechanisms—the processes by which the threat or infliction of costs generates adversary concessions. Mechanisms are the crucial middle link of the means-end chain of a coercive strategy. An understanding of these mechanisms helps to answer questions of why and how coercion works and in turn allows a better understand of whether and, if so, when a particular coercive strategy is more or less likely to succeed.

By examining mechanisms, we attempt to peer into the "black box" that links attempts at coercion to the desired outcomes. Against whom should the coercer try to direct the costs it threatens? Why might the threat of costs lead to concessions? Who might benefit inadvertently from coercive threats and efforts? These questions often decide the success or failure of a coercive strategy.

Consider the following. A military strike that destroys an electric grid in south Freedonia reduces quality of life for the nation. Yet the strike may mean little to the inhabitants of north Freedonia, who feel little sympathy for Freedonians to the south due to ethnic or religious differences. Freedonia's military forces may not perceive an immediate crisis, particularly if the attacks do not affect operations of existing forces. The strike may have humiliated Freedonia's leadership if south Freedonians were key regime supporters. On the other hand, leaders might see it as useful if south Freedonia were an area of unrest and rebellion. Black marketeers, who would benefit from the disruption of normal commerce, may even welcome the strike. Understanding why, and indeed whether, the Freedonian leadership might make concessions requires recognizing that simple pain inflicted on Freedonia in a general sense does not automatically translate into coercive leverage.

To sort out whether an adversary is likely to succumb to a coercer's demands, it is necessary to think about coercive mechanisms. The strike on Freedonia's electric grid could produce concessions for several reasons. The grid's destruction, if it truly humiliated Freedonia's leadership, might lead the regime to make concessions for fear that future strikes would provoke a popular revolt, an ouster by powerful elites, or a loss at the polls. Each such possibility—undermining popular morale, fomenting elite revolt, and so on—is a mechanism that the strike might trigger. Alternatively, Freedonia's leaders may care about the welfare of the country and concede to the coercer's demands in order to preserve the population from further disruptions. Or perhaps the military, though not perceiving an immediate impact on its state of readiness, might fear that continued strikes on Freedonia's infrastructure would slowly erode its strength at home and against neighboring rivals. Freedonia's leadership might concede to keep its forces strong or even to avert the resulting threat of a coup.

We use the Freedonia example to suggest that the discussion begun in Chapter 2 on how to understand successful and failed coercion is incomplete without a discussion of how policy instruments induce the desired change in behavior. Policy instruments are discussed in Chapter 4; this chapter explores the critical intermediate step between the threatened infliction of pain and the adversary's decision to change course. This chapter also highlights some of the strengths and weaknesses of various mechanisms and describes some of the conditions under which they are likely to work or might backfire. In describing these conditions, we try to look beyond the actual behavioral changes that may have taken place in various cases and to focus on whether and why adversary policy changes became more likely (or less likely) in the face of threats.

The purpose of this chapter is not to prove that certain mechanisms do or do not work. All of them have, to varying degrees, contributed to successful coercion, yet all of them have failed as well. Rather, this chapter aims to introduce the logic behind several of the more common mechanisms that military strategists and decision makers have focused on in their planning and to outline some of the problems and limits commonly associated with using them. We peer inside the black box of decision making, but we do not attempt to dissect its intricacies for any given regime. Indeed, one lesson of history is to caution against reliance on too general a blueprint of those inner workings in designing a coercive strategy. This chapter presents concepts critical to the analysis of later chapters and an understanding of the limits of U.S. (or any country's) coercive strength.

COMMONLY USED MECHANISMS

Coercers typically employ a variety of mechanisms in trying to manipulate adversary decision making. Five of the most common are power base erosion—threatening a regime's relationship with its core supporters; unrest—creating popular dissatisfaction with a regime; decapitation—jeopardizing a leadership's personal security; weakening—debilitating the country as a whole; and denial—preventing battlefield success (or political victories via military aggression).[1] All of these mechanisms, in theory, might lead an adversary to change its behavior.

These mechanisms are presented separately as ideal types in order to simplify analysis, but they overlap in practice. Viewing them first in isolation helps in understanding not only how they might be combined as part of an overall strategy, but also, as discussed in more detail in later chapters, how they might interfere with each other and destroy the effectiveness of coercive threats.

As discussed further in Chapter 4, the same coercive instrument can play on different or multiple mechanisms. Not surprisingly, coercers often try to trigger more than one mechanism simultaneously in the hopes of augmenting pressure. Air strikes, for example, might create popular dissatisfaction with a regime, decrease the country as a whole's power, and reduce the country's overall military might—unrest, weakening, and denial mechanisms, respectively.

1 In his valuable study of coercive air power, Robert Pape offers a somewhat different typology, dividing strategies into punishment, risk, denial, and decapitation. Because Pape's terms are quite evocative, we follow his terminology when possible. We use *decapitation* in a manner similar to his; we also use his term *denial*, following his general use but adding an explicit political dimension. His use of *punishment*, for us, falls under several categories, including "power base erosion," "unrest," and "weakening." His definition of risk involves the gradual escalation of damage that eventually tips the balance of costs and benefits against the adversary, leading it to concede. To us, risk is not an explicit mechanism but rather a particular application of force—the audience that suffers from the damage could be the leadership, the country as a whole, or another target. (Pape, *Bombing to Win*, p. 57.)

The impact of using different mechanisms simultaneously is often cumulative. When decision makers weigh costs, they do so in the aggregate. Freedonia's leaders may ignore a decrease in military strength or an increase in popular suffering if it is the only cost they face; together, however, these costs might be too much to bear. Thus, a combination of mechanisms may affect decision making when the triggering of individual mechanisms might fail. Mechanisms may combine in more complex ways as well. Popular dissatisfaction may only worry a particular regime when it also faces the potential wrath of key elites. Or, put slightly differently, the regime might have little to fear from those elites as long as mass public opinion remains favorable. For instance, regime decision makers might only change policy out of worry about a possible coup when they perceive fury among *both* the military officer corps *and* the masses, who might rally to support a change in regime.

At the same time, it is important to remember that many mechanisms for manipulating adversary decision making can operate in reverse, and the failure to trigger a mechanism as intended can inadvertently produce resistance to concessions. Creating popular unrest through military strikes might induce surrender if the decision-making process is susceptible to public outcry, but that supposed weakness also usually means that inadvertently bolstering public support for a regime might produce hardened defiance. And because many different inputs affect adversary decision making simultaneously, a single coercive threat can produce opposing effects on decision making. The same coercive air strikes that hinder Freedonia's own military operations and cause severe disaffection with the regime among the highest echelons of the army might cause a rally-round-the-flag effect among the population, resulting in policy paralysis—or contradictory policies—as Freedonian decision making is pulled in opposite directions.

Table 3.1 presents an overview of some more-recent attempts at coercion, indicating the various mechanisms that the coercer sought to trigger and the most salient results, both positive and negative. As the table shows, states usually seek to combine several mechanisms in a single, integrated coercive strategy. Moreover, some of the mechanisms they commonly used have received much scholarly attention (for example, denial) whereas others have received less (for example, power base erosion). The cases presented are neither a full survey of attempts at coercion (which would involve a review of almost all major foreign pol-

Table 3.1. Selected Attempts at Coercion and Associated Mechanisms

Coercer[a]	Adversary	Dates	Coercer's Goals	Coercer's Key Mechanisms[b]	Adversary's Key Mechanisms	Outcomes from Coercer's Viewpoint[c]	
						Desired	Undesired
Britain, France, Israel	Egypt	1956	Reverse Suez Canal nationalization; destroy Egyptian military threat; encourage Nasser's ouster	Power base; unrest		Partial destruction of Egyptian military strength	Nasser's popularity increased; canal remained Egypt's; tension between coercers and U.S.
Britain	Malayan guerrillas	1948–1960	Defeat Communist insurgency	[Brute force]	Unrest and denial	Guerrillas defeated	Protracted effort required
France	Insurgency in Algeria	1954–1962	Defeat pro-independence movement (FLN) and its armed forces (ALN)	[Brute force]	Unrest and denial	ALN forces devastated	Protracted conflict; large losses; political exhaustion and unrest in France; independent, FLN-dominated Algeria recognized; tension within NATO
Iran	Iraq	1974–1975	Gain Iraqi concessions over their border	Denial; power base		Iraq conceded to Iranian demands	
Iraq	Iran	1982–1988	Force Iran to halt ground offensives and aggressive stance toward Iraq	Unrest; denial; [brute force]	Unrest; [brute force]	Fear of attacks at times caused short-term de-escalation	Little or no unrest; adversary regime popularity may even have increased; led to attacks on Iraqi cities

Table 3.1. Continued

Coercer[a]	Adversary	Dates	Coercer's Goals	Coercer's Key Mechanisms[b]	Adversary's Key Mechanisms	Outcomes from Coercer's Viewpoint[c]	
						Desired	Undesired
Israel	Egypt	1969–1970	Stop Egyptian harassment along canal	Unrest; denial		Egypt temporarily moderated territorial goals; Egyptian leaders feared military losses and civilian unrest	Cairo turned to Soviet Union for additional support; Israel began to lose local air supremacy; disruptions of arms supply from U.S.
Israel	Palestinians in Jordan	1950s–1970	Stop Palestinian cross-border attacks and terrorism in general	Power base; unrest; decapitation	Unrest	Palestinian attacks eventually stopped due to Jordanian government intervention	Protracted effort required; diplomatic difficulties; exodus of the PLO to Lebanon with resultant war and instability
Israel	Lebanese Hezbollah	1982–2000	Stop cross-border attacks and terrorism in general	Decapitation; unrest	Unrest and denial	Hezbollah limited scope and scale of attacks	Attacks continued; Hezbollah grew in stature; attacks contributed to Lebanon's instability; domestic criticism of government in Israel leads to withdrawal

Table 3.1. Continued

Coercer[a]	Adversary	Dates	Coercer's Goals	Coercer's Key Mechanisms[b]	Adversary's Key Mechanisms	Outcomes from Coercer's Viewpoint[c]	
						Desired	Undesired
Israel	Palestinians in Lebanon	1970–1982	Stop cross-border attacks and terrorism	Decapitation; unrest; weakening	Unrest	Palestinians limited attacks	Protracted effort required; Palestinians at times gained in stature; contributed to Lebanon's civil war; led to Israeli invasion and quagmire
NATO	Serbia	1999	Accept Rambouillet accords	Denial; power base; unrest	Denial; unrest	Eventual acceptance of accords	Long and brutal ethnic-cleansing campaign
Russia	Chechen guerrillas	1994–1996	Crush independence movement	Weakening; decapitation; denial; [brute force]	Denial; unrest		Heavy military and civilian losses; terrorist attacks in Russia; hardened support for secession; de facto secession agreement; reinter-vention necessary in 1999
United States	Cuba and USSR	1962	Force Soviets to withdraw missiles from Cuba	Weakening[d]		Soviets withdrew missiles	U.S. withdrew Jupiter missiles from Turkey
United States	Dominican Republic	1961–1962	Oust corrupt oligarchy	Power base; decapitation		New government took power	

Table 3.1. Continued

Coercer[a]	Adversary	Dates	Coercer's Goals	Coercer's Key Mechanisms[b]	Adversary's Key Mechanisms	Outcomes from Coercer's Viewpoint[c]	
						Desired	Undesired
United States/ Britain[e]	Germany	1943–1945	Use bombing to reduce German desire and ability to continue war	Weakening; unrest; [brute force]		Brute force damage aided Allied military victory, but morale damage had little impact on surrender decision	Considerable casualties, bomber losses
United States	Haiti junta	1994	Oust Cedras regime in favor of Aristede	Decapitation; power base; unrest		Junta leaders stepped down	
United States	Iran	1987–1988	Secure free flow of oil	Weakening; denial	Denial	Iran limited attacks on tankers	Occasional Iranian attacks continued
United States	Iraq	1990–1991	Remove Iraq from Kuwait and devastate Iraqi heavy forces	Power base; unrest; denial; decapitation; [brute force]	Unrest	By Jan. 1991, Iraq was willing to remove forces	Massive effort required; Baghdad refused maximal U.S. demands
United States	Iraq	1991–present	Compel Iraqi compliance with UN resolutions	Power base; decapitation; denial; weakening	Unrest (directed at U.S. allies)	Iraq grudgingly accepted inspections and refrained from regional aggression	Protracted effort required; strained U.S.-regional relations; limited compliance

Table 3.1. Continued

Coercer[a]	Adversary	Dates	Coercer's Goals	Coercer's Key Mechanisms[b]	Adversary's Key Mechanisms	Outcomes from Coercer's Viewpoint[c]	
						Desired	Undesired
United States	North Korea	1993–1994	Compel North to abandon nuclear program and to allow International Atomic Energy Agency access; stop nuclear program; deter attack on South Korea	Weakening	Weakening[f]	North Korea refrained from continuing nuclear program but did not abandon it; no attack on South	Large inducements required, including diplomatic and economic concessions; possibility of a "demonstration effect" outside North Korea
United States[g]	North Korea and China	1950–1953	Reduce Communists' desire and ability to continue war	Denial; weakening; [brute force]		Communists agreed to armistice after recognizing a military victory was impossible	Protracted, bloody effort required; U.S. did not achieve maximal goals
United States	Laotian guerrillas	1960–1973	Stop NVA from transiting Laos	Denial			Protracted effort required; limited impact on flow of arms
United States	Libya	1986	End Libyan support for terrorism	Decapitation; power base		May have enhanced credibility with allies regarding counter-terrorism	Temporary surge in Libyan-supported terrorist attempts
United States[h] (Rolling Thunder)	North Vietnam	1965–1968	Compel North to stop supporting guerrillas in South	Denial; weakening	Denial; unrest		Protracted effort required; little impact; PRC and Soviet aid to North increased

Table 3.1. Continued

Coercer[a]	Adversary	Dates	Coercer's Goals	Coercer's Key Mechanisms[b]	Adversary's Key Mechanisms	Outcomes from Coercer's Viewpoint[c]	
						Desired	Undesired
United States (Line-backer I and II)	North Vietnam	1972	Bring about cease-fire	Denial; weakening	Denial; unrest; [brute force attempt to invade South with conventional forces]	Hanoi agreed to a temporary cease-fire	Protracted effort required; U.S. scaled back goals
United States/NATO	Bosnian Serb forces (Deny Flight)	1993–1994	Reduce scope and scale of Balkan conflict	Denial		Helped contain conflict and ensure humanitarian relief	Incomplete compliance undermined NATO credibility; conflict continued
United States/NATO	Bosnian Serb forces (Deliberate Force)	1995	Compel Serbs to accept cease-fire	Denial		Serbs sought negotiated agreement	
United States/UN	Somali factions	1993	Stop interference with humanitarian aid	Denial; decapitation	Unrest; denial	Secured flow of aid	Brute force attempt eventually failed; increased support for anti-U.S. factions; led to early U.S. withdrawal

Notes to Table 3.1:

[a]The distinction between coercer and adversary is often arbitrary, as both sides try to coerce each other. This column lists the coercer as the ostensibly stronger power or, when in doubt, the one most actively trying to change the status quo. At times the "coercer" used brute force far more than coercion—we examine such instances both to measure the effectiveness of the instruments in question and to assess the adversary's counters to brute force, which generally were coercive in nature.

[b]Although coercers at times attempted to use many mechanisms, not all of them worked equally or even had a positive effect. In many instances, the coercer's use of force fell into the "brute force" part of the coercion-to-brute-force spectrum; in ambiguous cases, both brute forces and the possible mechanisms are listed.

[c]The focus here, as in the rest of the book, is on the U.S. (or nominally stronger power's) perspective.

[d]The threat of nuclear attack on the Soviet heartland would, of course, also threaten the Soviet power base, leadership, and population. This classification is described later in this chapter, in the section on weakening.

[e]The Allied bomber offensive and other operations against Germany are arguably seen not as cases of coercion but as cases of brute force.

[f]North Korea used its possible acquisition of a nuclear weapon—which would enable it to inflict massive punishment on its foes—to force concessions from the United States and South Korea.

[g]Like operations in World War II, operations in Korea arguably fall more on the brute force than on the coercion end of the spectrum.

[h]Although the Vietnam conflict in general falls into the brute force part of the force-to-coercion spectrum, particular elements of it—such as several of the air campaigns against North Vietnam—can be treated as coercive in nature, though they must be judged against the backdrop of the overall war.

icy standoffs among states) nor a representative sample. The list is designed to illustrate actual attempts to use various mechanisms, focusing on prominent cases of military coercion that involve the United States or offer important lessons relevant to the U.S. position today.

An analysis of the various mechanisms must consider two basic questions: Does the mechanism in question affect decision making in the way that the coercer desires? And can coercers successfully trigger the mechanism? Some mechanisms only rarely produce the desired outcome; others have proven more reliable but are difficult to trigger. The following discussion explores these questions for the five mechanisms on which we focus.

Power base erosion: threatening a regime's relationship with key supporters

Coercers may attempt to prompt concessions by threatening to undercut the adversary leadership's support among its power base. A regime's power base consists of the select group of individuals whose support is necessary for the regime to maintain political control. Economic power, political access, a position in the military, and other factors usually make some individuals more important than others to a country's decision makers. If a coercer can threaten a regime's grip on power, the leadership may concede to avoid losing control or, if it proves recalcitrant, may be swept away and replaced by a more compliant regime.[2] Thus, a regime's relationship with its power base is often a key adversary pressure point.

The identity of the power base varies by regime. In a democracy, core constituencies can include elected representatives of the party in power, key civic leaders, and others who shape and express public opinion. In authoritarian regimes, it is often the military, the security services, key tribes, certain ethnic groups, or others who control the intimidation and cooptation necessary to keep a regime in power.[3] Saddam's Iraq, Milosevic's Serbia, and other recent adversary states are

2 See Kirschner, "The Microfoundations of Economic Sanctions," p. 42, for a discussion of some of these points.

3 Not all autocratic regimes are unpopular. The governments of Adolph Hitler, Ayatollah Khomeini, and imperial Japan are only a few examples of dictatorial regimes that enjoyed a significant degree of popular support.

(or were) run by small cliques of individuals who wield disproportionate power over their countries' politics and economies.[4]

A leadership's power base helps it stay in power, but this dependence creates for the coercer a potential pressure point for altering adversary decision making. The same groups of individuals that are vital to a regime's survival—the ones that control the enforcement and cooptation levers essential for repressing and buying the goodwill of the population—can also topple the regime. Threats to a power base can therefore lead a regime to concede, both because elites force the leadership to change its policies (either by using their clout to demand change or by replacing the existing leadership) or because the leadership fears elite criticism and concedes to avoid a further threat.[5] Not surprisingly, internal security is of overriding concern to many states in the developing world.[6] Thus, they often behave cautiously when faced with a threat to their grip on power.

This last point raises the apparent policy paradox introduced in the previous chapter: in general, adversary regimes that depend on a narrow power base, and are therefore sensitive to disruption of relations with that base, are likely skilled or at least practiced at countering any threat from that group. Regimes faced with threats of a coup, for instance, frequently do not hesitate to purge the intelligence services, officer corps, or other security institutions. Indeed, they may do so regularly. Regimes in Saudi Arabia, Syria, and elsewhere in the world have attempted to "coup proof" their governments through overlapping se-

4 For a review of the importance of the Iraqi elite, see Baram, *Building Toward Crisis*. For general accounts of Milosevic's concern with political support, see Franklin Foer, "Slobodan Milosevic: How a Genocidal Dictator Keeps Getting Away with It," *Slate*, June 20, 1998, http://www.slate.com (accessed on March 11, 1999); and Misha Glenny, *The Fall of Yugoslavia* (New York: Penguin Books, 1993), pp. 32–33 and 60–70. An account of Milosevic as a diplomatic tactician can be found in Richard Holbrooke, *To End a War* (New York: Random House, 1998).

5 A leadership's fears are often difficult to demonstrate, as there is no observed action to monitor and the leaders' motivations are often opaque to outsiders.

6 See Mohammed Ayoob, "The Security Problematic in the Third World," *World Politics,* Vol. 43, no. 2 (January 1991), pp. 257–283; and Stephen David, *Choosing Sides: Alignment and Realignment in the Third World* (Baltimore, MD: Johns Hopkins University Press, 1991).

curity services, politicization of the military, and other measures.[7] Power base support is often a point of great susceptibility, but not necessarily vulnerability, for developing countries.

U.S. attempts to coerce Saddam's Iraq since the Gulf War illustrate some potential benefits and pitfalls of a strategy that seeks to target a regime's key supporters. Saddam's power base is narrow. He relies on the support and loyalty of family members, select tribes, Baath party officials, and military officers.[8] Maintaining their support is Saddam's overriding focus. As Amatzia Baram argues, "Throughout his career . . . whenever Iraq's foreign interests clashed with perceived domestic security interests, the latter always prevailed. Insofar as internal security is concerned, Saddam Husayn has never taken any chances."[9]

Fear of dissatisfaction within his power base—a fear that U.S. planners sought to play on—contributed substantially to Saddam's willingness to make concessions in the immediate aftermath of the Gulf War, suggesting the potential effectiveness of power base approaches. The U.S.-led coalition sought to compel Iraq to fulfill various UN resolutions that called for Baghdad to detail and eliminate its WMD programs. In response to Iraq's harassment of UN inspectors and refusal to cooperate, the United States and Britain (and at times France) threatened bombing campaigns several times in 1991 and 1992.[10] Iraq backed down as a result of these threats, and Saddam showed himself extremely sensitive to U.S. threats of force as he accepted inspectors and made limited declarations.[11] Although he later proved he could

7 For an excellent review, see James T. Quinlivan, "Coup-proofing: Its Practice and Consequences in the Middle East," *International Security*, Vol. 24, no. 2 (Fall 1999), pp. 131–165.

8 Ofra Bengio, "How Does Saddam Hold On?" *Foreign Affairs,* Vol. 79, no. 4 (July/August 2000), pp. 94–101.

9 Baram, *Building Toward Crisis,* p. 2.

10 The United States used its military presence in the region, which it occasionally bolstered, to back up threats. During a standoff in March 1991, the United States sent the carrier *America* to the Gulf as an escalation option—a particularly potent threat given the large U.S. ground presence in Iraq itself and along its borders at that time. In September 1991, President Bush sent combat aircraft and Patriot missile batteries to Saudi Arabia after Iraq temporarily detained 40 UN inspectors. In these cases, Washington apparently was weighing a graduated bombing campaign to force Iraqi compliance.

11 Nevertheless, Baghdad still continued its deception campaign, hiding its weapons and claiming that any known stocks and systems were destroyed

weather a limited U.S. bombing campaign, U.S. credibility—in terms of both resolve and capabilities—was high in the days following Desert Storm, and Saddam's position at home was at its lowest ever. The combination of military defeat, popular and military rebellions, political isolation in both the Arab and international context, and a comprehensive economic embargo created massive fissures in Saddam's power base. Saddam was unsure of the loyalty of key tribes and military forces, and the near-collapse of his regime in 1991 served as a vivid reminder that another major military clash with the U.S.-led coalition could prove disastrous. Tensions within Saddam's extended family, coup plots in the upper echelons of Iraqi security services, unrest among key tribes, and other pressures made Saddam extremely cautious about confronting the United States again.[12]

At times, a power base can be turned against a leadership, leading to its removal (though such a result is arguably more akin to brute force than to coercion). The United States engineered a coup against the Diem regime in Vietnam and facilitated a coup in Chile using coercive pressure (alongside direct covert action) to create the conditions that would facilitate a military takeover. The United States, along with other members of the Organization of American States (OAS), imposed sanctions and diplomatically isolated the Trujillo government of the Dominican Republic in 1960. Sanctions on sugar, the Dominican Republic's leading product, hurt the middle-class and wealthy supporters of the regime. Dominican business and military elites—angered by the pain of sanctions and inspired by the international consensus against Trujillo—worked together to assassinate him.[13]

It is difficult to target threats and military attacks so as to produce particular effects on key power elite groups, and attempts to influence adversary policy this way can easily backfire. Dictators generally possess more-effective and more-precise tools for shaping popular unrest in

during the war. Iraq's continuing recalcitrance suggests that it is highly committed to retaining a WMD capacity and would resume its programs were inspections ended.

12 Sarah Graham-Browne, *Sanctioning Saddam: The Politics of Intervention in Iraq* (London: I.B. Tauris, 1999), pp. 192–198; and Baram, *Building Toward Crisis,* p. 4.

13 For a discussion of the Dominican Republic, see Kirschner, "The Microfoundations of Economic Sanctions," pp. 56–63. The new regime, of course, also had its problems, leading to continued confrontations with the United States until 1965.

their country than coercers do. Coercive strategies that rely on generating elite or power base dissatisfaction with adversary policies of resistance are particularly liable to generate conflicting political pressures within the adversary decision-making system. Instead of generating elite consensus in favor of the leadership backing down, coercive threats may inadvertently heighten the internal political fears the adversary leadership associates with capitulation. Moreover, properly threatening a leader's relationship with his power base can be tricky, in part because weakness at the domestic level offers negotiating strength at the international level. If a leader's grip on his power is in jeopardy, he may have less room to compromise or concede in the face of coercive threats. A leadership in trouble at home can quite credibly vow to hold out despite mounting costs if it becomes clear that backing down will result in its downfall.[14] NATO attacks against Serbia in 1999 were designed in part to foster elite discontent with the Milosevic regime, though NATO simultaneously sought to erode popular support for Milosevic.[15] Several of Serbia's top generals were placed under house arrest, testifying to Milosevic's sensitivity about possible loss of political control during the conflict.[16] However, at least in the short term, the pressure from the military and other elite cliques that supported Milosevic and saw the profitability of that support endangered by his defiance of NATO appeared to be offset by inflamed nationalist passions among other segments of the population.

The various examples in this chapter expose a key implication for designing coercive strategies using a power base approach: because concessions entail a political price for a regime, the pain of continued resistance must offset this additional price as well as the initial level of regime commitment. Coercive pressure may make it more difficult

14 See Putnam, "Diplomacy and Domestic Politics," passim, for a discussion.

15 General Klaus Naumann, who chaired NATO's military committee, declared that NATO's intention was "to loosen [Milosevic's] grip on power and break his will to continue" (as quoted in Michael R. Gordon, "NATO Plans Weeks of Bombing to Break Grip of Serb Leader," *New York Times*, April 1, 1999, p. A1).

16 Steven Brill, "War Gets the Monica Treatment," *Brill's Content* (July/August 1999), pp. 103–104.

politically for a government to make concessions, as that government may be charged with "giving in" to foreign influence.[17]

The Israeli experience with Hezbollah and the Palestine Liberation organization (PLO) within Lebanon illustrates how regimes targeted with coercion often cannot make concessions without losing domestic reign. The costs of acquiescence to an outside power's demand can be prohibitively high, especially in noninstitutionalized democracies where a compliant regime may fear for its very survival. In the early 1970s, the PLO had few high-value targets in Lebanon. More important, Israeli military strikes actually helped PLO recruitment by demonstrating the PLO's commitment to the struggle against Zionist Israel. If the PLO refrained from attacks, other Palestinian groups would gain recruits. Any leadership concessions to the Israelis were fiercely criticized and often caused a loss of popular support.[18] Thus, the Israelis risked obtaining concessions that would be meaningless, as rivals quickly denounced them. The situation is similar for any group that relies on resistance to attract new members: concessions may destroy the group more effectively than the coercer could ever hope to do.

Indeed, the high cost of concessions may produce a backlash rather than simple failure. Just as coercive threats or strikes can risk buttressing an adversary state leadership's stature at home and abroad, they can inadvertently increase the support a nonstate organization receives from sympathetic international and local sponsors. Israeli strikes helped the Lebanese Hezbollah attract more money from abroad;[19] they also provoked a nationalist backlash, strengthening Hezbollah within the Lebanese community. Israeli military activity and withdrawals from parts of Lebanon in response to Hezbollah violence further bolstered

17 For an argument along these lines, see T. Willett and M. Jalaighajar, "U.S. Trade Policy and National Security," *Cato Journal,* Vol. 3, no. 3 (1983), pp. 717–728.

18 Defiance of coercive threats also provides a way for radicals within a nonstate group to show their disapproval of the dominant group. The PLO often was cautious in its dealings with Israel. More-radical groups, such as the Popular Front for the Liberation of Palestine and smaller splinter groups used their defiance of Israel to embarrass the PLO, hoping to force the PLO's leadership to choose between kowtowing to Israel and the loyalty of their own supporters.

19 Kenneth C. Schow, "Falcons Against the Jihad: Israeli Airpower and Coercive Diplomacy in Southern Lebanon," master's thesis, School of Advanced Airpower Studies, 1995.

the movement's reputation.[20] Over time, Hezbollah's claim to be the leading force of resistance to Israel became its source of legitimacy; continued resistance was necessary even if the coercer backed down.

Unrest: creating popular disaffection

At times, an undermining of elite support for an adversary regime is too difficult to implement or may not be sufficiently menacing to force concessions. In such cases, coercers may instead or also try to put pressure on the adversary's civilian population as a whole or on major segments of that population. Such efforts are a blunt instrument—many are punished to change the minds of a few. The hope is that pressure placed on a country's population may "trickle up" and prompt decision makers to concede. Unrest strategies frequently fail, however, because the population cannot sufficiently influence decision making or because the coercive threat backfires, increasing popular support for defiance.

In theory, popular disaffection can lead a regime to concede for a number of reasons. Regime leaders may care about the well-being of the population (an issue discussed later in this chapter) and therefore direct policy away from options likely to result in suffering among the population. Or, particularly in regimes where there is considerable popular input into decision making, civilian suffering may be of great political concern to the leadership: decision makers may avoid unpopular policies—or ones they anticipate will lead to a loss of support—so as to maintain power. Alternatively, the population may rise up in response to the coercive pressure, threatening to remove the leadership unless it gives in to the coercer's demands. Or civilian suffering may undermine the adversary's capacity to fight. For example, worker absenteeism may increase along with military desertions among the rank and file, which might cause adversary decision makers to see the likelihood of military victory declining (again, this issue is discussed in more detail later). Like threats directed at a regime's power base, threats of popular disaffection can lead a regime to concede even if the level of popular unrest or suffering is low. A regime may fear that popular unrest will grow in the future and thus concede even when the immediate threat it faces is limited.

20 Magnus Ranstorp, *Hizb'Allah in Lebanon: The Politics of the Western Hostage Crisis* (New York: St. Martin's Press, 1997), pp. 38–39.

Punishment of civilians is a commonly used strategy of coercion, especially where the risks or practical barriers of brute force solutions or attacks directed at the adversary's military or power base are high. In medieval and early modern Europe, where conquest was typically achieved one city at a time, siege methods of warfare harnessed the threat of starvation of city residents to compel garrisons to open their gates to opposing armies. In more-recent times, coercers have bombed enemy populations, embargoed their economies, and otherwise tried to increase the suffering and misery of adversary populations in order to force leaders to surrender.[21]

Historically, coercive attempts to foment popular unrest have yielded uneven results. Sometimes such efforts have made important contributions to an adversary's decision to concede, while other times they have produced the opposite reaction. The Israeli-Egyptian War of Attrition provides one example of a coercive unrest strategy bringing about favorable changes in adversary decision making, at least in the short term. In January 1970, after roughly six months of limited attacks in the canal zone, Israel attacked military and military-related industrial targets deep within Egypt in order to ensure that the Egyptian populace and elite felt the war and recognized that Egypt was losing. As Yaacov Bar-Siman-Tov notes, "Israel's political aims in deciding on in-depth air raids were to get the Egyptians to end the War of Attrition by threatening to weaken or overthrow Nasser's regime."[22] Israel intended the raids to humiliate Egyptian President Nasser before the Egyptian people, who would then overthrow him or at least press his regime to end the war. Nasser rightly believed that Israel sought to overthrow him and tried to shield those Egyptians most immediately affected by evacuating roughly 750,000 people to other parts of the country. High losses in the conflict, combined with a lack of any major military success, risked popular disgruntlement and led Nasser to come to the bargaining table. The war was hardly a strategic success for Israel—the end result was internationalization of the canal dispute and Israel's loss of com-

21 Matthew C. Waxman, "Siegecraft and Surrender: The Law and Strategy of Cities as Targets," *Virginia Journal of International Law*, Vol. 39 (1999), pp. 353–423.

22 Yaacov Bar-Siman-Tov, *The Israeli-Egyptian War of Attrition, 1969–1970: A Case-Study of Limited Local War* (New York: Columbia University Press, 1980), p. 120.

mand of the air, both serious drawbacks—but the mechanism of fostering unrest to force concessions did, to a degree, succeed.[23]

The Iraqi regime also exploited the mechamism of popular unrest in its eight-year war with Iran beginning in 1980. Both countries attacked each other's population centers to undermine morale and force concessions. The attacks initially failed, instead bolstering popular support for the war.[24] After several years of limited and inconclusive raids, Iraq stepped up its attacks in 1987, using newly acquired long-range Scud missiles that could directly strike Tehran, Iran's capital and largest city.[25] These attacks were more sustained and effective than previous attacks had been, and Iranian popular morale plummeted as a result.[26] Several million Iranians fled Tehran and other major cities in the face of

23 Bar-Siman-Tov, *The Israeli-Egyptian War of Attrition*, pp. 117–138 and 179–180; Dupuy, *Elusive Victory*, pp. 366–372; and Shimshoni, *Israel and Conventional Deterrence*, p. 16. Because of Nasser's fears of instability from air strikes, he sought Soviet assistance in improving Egypt's air defense in order to neutralize the Israeli Air Force attacks. This increased the military difficulty of Israel's strategy and forced Israel to risk a confrontation with Moscow—a tremendous geopolitical risk. Nasser successfully internationalized the dispute and cost Israel local air superiority, both grievous losses. Nasser thus gained politically from the conflict despite the "defeat" of his military forces.

Pape codes the War of Attrition as a failure for coercion, noting that Egyptian civilian vulnerability was low, that Israel's attacks were aimed at military targets, and that probably fewer than 4,000 Egyptian civilians died as the result of the attacks (Pape, *Bombing to Win*, p. 352). Pape overlooks, however, the large number of evacuees and the deliberate Israeli tactic of bombing military targets near civilian areas—a tactic designed to foster unrest while striking militarily important targets.

24 James A. Bill, "Morale vs. Technology: The Power of Iran in the Persian Gulf War," in *The Iran-Iraq War: The Politics of Aggression*, Farhang Rajaee, ed. (Gainesville, FL: University of Florida Press, 1993), p. 200.

25 S. Taheri Shemirani, "The War of the Cities," in *The Iran-Iraq War: The Politics of Aggression*, Farhang Rajaee, ed. (Gainesville, FL: University of Florida Press, 1993), pp. 37–38 provides a year-by-year listing of missile and air attacks on Iranian cities. Shemirani's data show a dramatic increase in missile attacks in 1987–1988, though air attacks had peaked several years earlier.

26 Anthony H. Cordesman and Abraham R. Wagner, *The Lessons of Modern War, Vol. II: The Iran-Iraq War* (Boulder, CO: Westview Press, 1990), pp. 364–368; and Thomas L. McNaugher, "Ballistic Missiles and Chemical Weapons: The Legacy of the Iran-Iraq War," *International Security*, Vol. 15, no. 2 (Fall 1990), p. 5.

the attacks. Speculation that Iraq might use chemical weapons heightened the Iranians' fear. Iranians did not rise up or lose their will to fight, but genuine concern about the populace and fear of losing political support for the revolution in general propelled Iran's decision makers to consider concessions. Iraq's attacks on Iran's population thus contributed to Iran's decision to concede—an inclination further reinforced by Iran's losses on the battlefield and lack of political support from other powers.[27]

The Chechen insurgents' 1994–1996 use of terrorism and violence to coerce Russia to allow a de facto secession is yet another example of an unrest strategy, this time a very low-technology strategy conducted by a small power against a much more militarily powerful state. A series of daring Chechen strikes into Russia proper, including the taking of Russian hostages, increased popular disgruntlement in Russia and the sentiment that the game was not worth the candle. In June 1995, Chechen guerrilla leader Shamil Baseyev raided the Russian town of Budennovsk, taking more than 1,000 civilians hostage in a hospital and leaving over 100 dead, an event that turned many Russian citizens against the war.[28] The Chechen insurgents also used their attacks (and obvious survival) as "proof" that Moscow was not meeting its war aims of crushing the insurgency—a denial strategy.[29] Again, Moscow's failure to win a political or military victory contributed to its decision to make concessions, but growing popular resistance to the war was also a major factor.

Public reaction to coercive threats is extremely unpredictable, however, and a recurring historical lesson has been that attempts to force an adversary's hand by targeting its populace's will to resist often fail or backfire. One problem is that the pain inflicted sometimes fails to produce the intended unrest. Instead, the coercive campaign may raise the cost of compliance for the adversary leadership by provoking a hostile public backlash against the coercer. Russian attempts to bomb the Chechens (and earlier, in the 1980s, the Afghans) into submission simply led to unified defiance, as residents who had formerly favored peaceful solutions—or fighting each other—joined others to expel the

27 McNaugher, "Ballistic Missiles and Chemical Weapons," p. 15.

28 Benjamin S. Lambeth, "Russia's Air War in Chechnya," *Studies in Conflict & Terrorism*, Vol. 19, no. 4 (Winter 1996), p. 374.

29 Gail W. Lapidus, "Contested Sovereignty: The Tragedy of Chechnya," *International Security*, Vol. 23, no. 1 (Summer 1998), p. 21.

invader. In these instances, an unrest strategy increased pressure on leaders not to concede.

A leader's defiance in the face of a coercer's attempts to cause civilian hardships may enhance that leader's stature even in the absence of military success. Egyptian President Nasser lost the Suez War but attained more popularity than ever by his defiant stance toward Israel, France, and Britain. As Donald Neff notes about the attacks on Egypt:

> The bombings, though carefully kept away from civilian targets, were nonetheless having the same counterproductive result that they had had in London during the Nazi aerial war. They were stiffening civilian resolve and morale. During the rest of the crisis, Nasser was greeted by shouts repeating his defiant motto as he drove through Cairo streets.[30]

Leaders may gain politically despite their countries' overall suffering and losses.

Many historical uses of air power to foster unrest demonstrate the related difficulties coercers face when seeking to trigger this mechanism. After World War I, some air power theorists speculated that aerial bombardment could induce social and political collapse. Italian air power advocate Giulio Douhet speculated:

> [W]e need only envision what would go on among the civilian population of congested cities once the enemy announced that he would bomb such centers relentlessly.... How could a country go on living and working under this constant threat, oppressed by the nightmare of imminent destruction and death?[31]

British Air Force planning during the interwar years emphasized the morale effects that strategic bombing might have on enemies in future conflicts, inducing them to surrender and thus alleviating the costly stalemate of the previous conflict.[32]

These prophecies were not borne out by Allied strategic bombing attacks in World War II, however. The United States almost totally destroyed Japan's largest cities, particularly vulnerable because of their many wooden buildings, through air raids. Over 900,000 Japanese

30 Donald Neff, *Warriors at Suez* (New York: Simon & Schuster, 1981), p. 393.

31 Giulio Douhet, *The Command of the Air*, Dino Ferrari, trans. (Washington, DC: Office of Air Force History, 1983), pp. 20–22.

32 For a review of British thinking, see Phillip S. Meilinger, "The Historiography of Airpower: Theory and Doctrine," *The Journal of Military History*, no. 64 (April 2000), pp. 480–482.

civilians died from air attacks.[33] Germany suffered almost as much, with 40 percent of its major urban areas destroyed.[34] Allied bombing killed over 300,000 German civilians and injured another 780,000. Over 1.8 million Germans lost their homes. Yet the regimes were not toppled. As the most comprehensive postwar survey of the bombing concluded, "Under ruthless control [the German people] showed surprising resistance to the terror and hardships of repeated air attack, to the destruction of their homes and belongings, and to the conditions under which they were reduced to live."[35] This conclusion was reiterated in the official British history of the air campaign: "The cardinal error of intelligence was the description . . . of the German people as exhausted, disaffected and liable to panic and revolt when, in reality, . . . they were vigorous, calm, stoical and loyal."[36]

The World War II experience, the most comprehensive attempt to use air attacks on civilians to force the adversary to concede, offers evidence that air strikes trigger effects that might cause popular unrest—just not enough or not in ways to trigger the appropriate mechanisms for altering adversary decision making. Postwar studies of air attacks indicate that allied air strikes produced feelings of anger, fear, and apathy among victims. Sustained bombing disrupted the rhythms of daily life in Japan and Germany; damage to the transportation and civil infrastructure made life far more difficult.[37] The effects were real but often marginal. The revolts, uprisings, and paralysis predicted by Douhet and others did not materialize. One survey of Germans by the U.S. military indicates that towns that were not bombed were almost as supportive of accepting an unconditional surrender as those that were bombed.[38] Al-

33 Pape, *Bombing to Win*, p. 129. In part these attacks stemmed from a lack of precision. Despite the hopes of theorists, bombing accuracy was poor, and large targets such as urban areas were the only targets that bombers could be sure of hitting.

34 Pape, *Bombing to Win*, pp. 128 and 254–255.

35 This conclusion, taken from the United States Strategic Bombing Survey commissioned after the war, is described in Mark Clodfelter, *The Limits of Air Power*, p. 9.

36 Charles Webster and Noble Frankland, *The Strategic Air Offensive Against Germany*, Vol. 1 (London: H.M. Stationary Office, 1961), pp. 26–29.

37 Irving L. Janis, *Air War and Emotional Stress: Psychological Studies of Bombing and Civilian Defense* (Santa Monica, CA: RAND, 1951).

38 Bombings did have a larger impact on morale when their level exceeded the expected level—thus, the massive firebombing of Dresden did under-

though air strikes on Japanese cities did lower Japanese morale, they neither induced nor created the probability of an uprising.[39] Air Marshall Harris, who orchestrated the British bombing effort, conceded after the war: "The idea that the main object of bombing German industrial cities was to break the enemy's morale proved to be wholly unsound."[40]

Many regimes can ignore popular sentiment in formulating their policies. Neither the Nazi regime nor imperial Japan regularly consulted with the populace through elected bodies or less formal means. Most authoritarian regimes share this characteristic. They face few institutional mechanisms through which a disgruntled population could change regime behavior. Even in democratic states, leaders are often able to control information, place items on the popular agenda, and otherwise dominate decision making.[41]

Populations may have little choice but to suffer quietly if they oppose a policy. And when coercive operations threaten—whether wittingly or unwittingly—to foster popular instability, target regimes often are well-prepared and skilled at maintaining order. If widespread domestic unrest appears likely, many regimes will increase police presence, use mass arrests, and even execute potential opposition members in order to preserve their power.[42] It was relatively easy for the Nazis and the militarist government in Japan to crush any popular opposition before it became serious. During Operation Allied Force, Milosevic shut down independent newspapers and radio stations inside Serbia and used state-run television to stoke nationalism. The threat of popular unrest is therefore not a pressure point for most authoritarian regimes.

mine morale. Subsequent bombings that were less destructive, however, had little effect as popular expectations adjusted. (Quester, "The Psychological Effects of Bombing on Civilian Populations," p. 205.)

39 United States Strategic Bombing Survey, *The Effects of Strategic Bombing on Japanese Morale* (Washington, DC: Government Printing Office, June 1947), p. 21.

40 Arthur Harris, *Bomber Offensive* (London: Greenhill Books, 1990), p. 78.

41 Downs and Rocke, "Conflict, Agency, and Gambling for Resurrection," p. 362.

42 See Ian Lustick, "Stability in Deeply Divided Societies: Consociationalism Versus Control," *World Politics,* Vol. 31, no. 3 (April 1979), pp. 325–344, for a review of the use of force to control unrest.

The historical difficulties of fine-tuning the effects of coercion on adversary popular politics, and thus on adversary regime decision making, highlight some of the methodological points of the previous chapter, including the need to shed the binary framework in thinking about whether coercive threats succeed or fail. Military strikes and other coercive threats may erode adversary popular support or inflame nationalist passions, or both. Analyzing possible outcomes as either a "yes" or a "no" obscures the potential for threats aimed at popular attitudes and behavior to backfire, hardening adversary resistance and alleviating coercive pressure, or even to split the population, with some segments becoming more supportive of the regime and others opposing it.

The value of unrest, moreover, is best appreciated when the additive and synergistic effects of different coercive mechanisms are recognized. The Chechens, Israelis, and Iraqis did not use manipulation of adversary public opinion as their sole means of forcing concessions from, respectively, Russia, Egypt, and Iran. Rather, they used the threat of unrest in combination with military denial (discussed later in the chapter) to raise the adversary costs of continuing the fight.

Decapitation: threatening the leadership's personal security

In addition to threatening the well-being of elites and the populace as a means of influencing adversary decision making, coercers can try to menace the lives of the adversary leadership itself. In some respects, this is the most direct method of influencing adversary policy choices, as it imposes threats on the decision makers themselves rather than manipulating the fortunes of others in the hope of moving decision makers' policy preferences.

Decapitation strategies can bring about the desired behavioral changes in several ways. Actual assassination can bring to power a different individual or regime that may change policy, though a successful attack on a president or dictator, of course, would generally fall into the brute force category of strategies. During the Cold War, some U.S. nuclear warfare planners considered whether a first strike might be capable of disabling the enemy's retaliatory force by eliminating Soviet leaders in their bunkers.[43] The threat of a leadership attack, however,

43 Freedman, *The Evolution of Nuclear Strategy*, p. 393.

might intimidate enemy leaders into making concessions even if an actual attack failed or was never carried out. This latter phenomenon is purely coercive. And even the successful execution of a leadership attack can have truly coercive effects as well, because such an attack might spur the replacement leadership to adopt more-conciliatory policies than would otherwise have been chosen.

Although coercers seldom publicly acknowledge assassination attempts or even their consideration of assassination as an option, threats to adversary leadership figures are not uncommon. Indeed, the norm against assassination may be in decline.[44] During the Gulf War, the United States used the threat of decapitation to augment its conventional military campaign. Although fear of decapitation did not coerce Saddam Husayn to leave Kuwait in accordance with U.S. demands, the threat to Saddam himself seems to have played a role in convincing Iraqi leaders not to use chemical or biological weapons during the conflict. Iraq probably considered WMD use during the war. Baghdad had large stockpiles of biological and chemical weapons, had used chemical weapons against Iran and Kurdish villagers, and had deployed chemical weapons in the theater of operations. But Saddam refrained from using them this time around. In a meeting with Iraqi Foreign Minister Traqi Aziz, Secretary of State James Baker had warned that the United States would hold the persons who used WMD individually responsible and would punish them accordingly.[45] U.S. officials also deliberately used vague but ominous language to describe their response to WMD use, suggesting the possibility of massive punishment to reinforce the decapitation strategy.[46]

Decapitation threats are often used by nonstate groups as a means of influencing their adversaries' behavior. Several radical Palestinian

44 Ward Thomas, "Norms and Security: The Case of International Assassination," *International Security*, Vol. 25, no. 1 (Summer 2000), p. 126.

45 The *Manchester Guardian Weekly* reprinted the Bush letter to Saddam that was conveyed at the Baker-Aziz meeting (*The Manchester Guardian Weekly*, January 20, 1991, p. 21). See also Rick Atkinson, *Crusade: The Untold Story of the Persian Gulf War* (Boston, MA: Houghton Mifflin, 1993), p. 87; and Baker, *The Politics of Diplomacy*, p. 359.

46 As with most coercive strategies, two mechanisms—in this case, decapitation and weakening—were involved. Saddam probably refrained from using WMD in response to the combination of the hint of a nuclear threat and the threat to his personal status in Iraq.

groups, for example, have used the threat of assassination to extort money and support from Arab leaders, particularly those in the Persian Gulf. The Abu Nidal organization obtained millions of dollars by threatening officials and diplomats from Saudi Arabia and the United Arab Emirates. Regime officials supported the radicals financially and tempered their diplomatic condemnation of the radicals' actions because limited concessions preserved their personal security.[47]

Despite their apparent directness, assassination threats have not historically proven very successful for coercive purposes, because the lives of leaders are seldom a pressure point.[48] Israel has assassinated a host of Palestinian terrorist and political leaders, but these efforts have done little to stem the long-term conflict—Israel's attacks have sometimes disrupted military operations, but its foes' commitment to violence has remained strong.[49] Israel has also assassinated several leaders of the Lebanese Hezbollah, but their successors have proved equally committed to the struggle. Similarly, in 1996, when Russian forces finally killed Chechen President Dzhokhar Dudayev after repeated attempts, Chechen fighters did not let the loss of their leader deter them from continuing their rebellion against Russian forces.

Part of this poor record is explained by the fact that for some leaders, the threat of assassination from abroad is far less likely or credible than the immediate, and often lethal, costs of backing down in the face of coercion.[50] Authoritarian systems (and civil wars in particular) often

47 Yossi Melman, *The Master Terrorist: The True Story Behind Abu Nidal* (New York: Adama Books, 1986), pp. 96–97; and Daniel L. Byman and Jerrold D. Green, *Political Violence and Stability in the States of the Northern Persian Gulf* (Santa Monica, CA: RAND, 1999).

48 For a review, see Franklin L. Ford, *Political Murder: From Tyrannicide to Terrorism* (Cambridge, MA: Harvard University Press, 1985); and Murray Clark Havens, Carl Leiden, and Karl M. Schmitt, *The Politics of Assassination* (Englewood Cliffs, NJ: Prentice-Hall, Inc., 1970).

49 Hanan Alon, *Countering Palestinian Terrorism in Israel: Toward a Policy Analysis of Countermeasures* (Santa Monica, CA: RAND, 1980).

50 The difficulty of credibly threatening successful decapitation, however, is not universal. Syria's Hafez al-Asad has, to a degree, used this strategy successfully in Lebanon. Asad's government has assassinated a number of communal leaders, such as Druze Leader Kamal al-Jumblatt in March 1977, to intimidate other groups into falling into line. The presence of roughly 30,000 Syrian troops and a massive intelligence network—to say nothing of a demonstrated willingness to kill rivals of all sorts—lend

bring to the fore highly committed individuals. The hardened attitudes of the Hezbollah and Chechen rebel leaders tend to be the rule, not the exception. Some leaders also are personally committed to their policies and ideologies and prefer to risk death rather than make concessions.[51]

In addition to its limited chances of success, assassination can create tremendous political complications and unintended consequences for the coercing power. In 1997, the Israeli Mossad bungled an attempt to kill a Hamas leader in Jordan. In response to Jordan's outrage, Israel released Hamas's spiritual leader as a concession, strengthening the movement Israel sought to weaken. On January 5, 1996, Israel killed Yahya Ayyash, a Hamas terrorist who had orchestrated a series of attacks on Israel. Not only did the Hamas not stop its attacks, but Ayyash's martyrdom led the Hamas to respond brutally, launching several attacks that killed dozens of Israelis and contributed to the electoral defeat of the Peres government.

Decapitation also raises thorny ethical and international legal issues that limit its use, though these constraints remain ill defined, and the way in which decapitation strikes are viewed at home and abroad is likely to depend on many contextual factors, such as whether they occur in peacetime versus wartime and the extent to which an adversary leader has been demonized.[52] In the United States, Executive Order 12333 prohibits "assassination," though this term is subject to differing interpretations.[53] U.S. decision makers may also be especially inclined to avoid decapitation strategies for fear of eroding international norms against assassinating political figures, in part because they fear that U.S. officials might become more vulnerable as well. Rather than imposing

Syria both more capabilities and more credibility than most coercing states enjoy in this regard.

51 Stephen Hosmer, *Operations to Remove Enemy Leaders* (Santa Monica, CA: RAND, forthcoming).

52 Louis R. Beres, "The Permissibility of State-Sponsored Assassination During Peace and War," *Temple International and Comparative Law Journal*, no. 5 (Fall 1992), pp. 231–249. Some commentators argue that the United States may kill enemy military officials, including leaders such as Mohammar Qaddafi, as part of self-defense (see Patricia Zengel, "Assassination and the Law of Armed Conflict," *Military Law Review*, no. 134 [Fall 1991], pp. 145–146).

53 A survey of international and domestic law bearing on U.S. assassination policy is found in Michael N. Schmitt, "State-Sponsored Assassination in International and Domestic Law," *Yale Journal of International Law*, no. 17 (Summer 1992), pp. 609–685.

strict barriers on the mechanism's use, these types of constraints generally impose additional costs on the coercer that must figure into the policy calculus like any other costs.

Weakening: debilitating the country as a whole

Instead of focusing on individuals or the elite of an adversary's population, coercion can involve the destruction of a range of infrastructure, industrial, communications, and other targets that make up a country's economic strength and social cohesion. The weakening mechanism targets the entire country with the threat of pain. Of course, the country as an entity does not make decisions, but individual leaders, elites, or the population may decide to make or force concessions to avoid further pain to the country.

There are several reasons why leaders may make concessions when their country as a whole is suffering. Leaders may respond to a weakening campaign because their power base or the population in general cares about the well-being of the country. In such cases, the causation of the weakening mechanism becomes one step removed and thus more difficult: coercers must be able to inflict enough general costs that specific audiences take the steps necessary to change regime policy or to cause it to be changed. If the coercer's strategy relies on indirectly rupturing power base support or provoking popular unrest by weakening the country as a whole, the same factors that affect those mechanisms, discussed earlier in this chapter, will generally apply (i.e., the process could be understood in terms of the power base or unrest mechanisms rather than as a separate mechanism). However, leaders may care about the overall strength of the country and the well-being of the populace independent of the pressure placed on them from their constituencies, whether due to a genuine concern for the suffering of their people or to other ambitions that require a strong regime.

The threat of nuclear punishment generally relies on the weakening mechanism.[54] Though a devastating nuclear strike would, of course, affect the population, the leadership, the military, and the power base of

54 The U.S. policy of massive retaliation, the dominant strategy during the Cold War, clearly relied on the weakening mechanism. However, the policy of "flexible response" was more of a denial strategy, while at times the United States considered using nuclear weapons as part of a decapitation strategy.

a country, it is conceptually much simpler to think of such a strike as affecting the country as a whole for two reasons: it would wreak such devastation that normal policy-making processes would be wiped away, and all constituencies are likely to react strongly to a nuclear threat.

At the other end of the spectrum, though, weakening comes into play in economic statecraft. The British behavior in the 1956 Suez crisis, during which the United States successfully used financial pressure to coerce Britain to end its campaign against Nasser's Egypt, illustrates how the weakening mechanism can compel concessions. During the crisis, the United States threatened to refuse the British government access to additional funds to prop up its currency, raising the specter of a British economic crash. The Eden government had relatively little domestic support for the Suez mission among the British populace. Rather than see the country as a whole weakened, Prime Minister Eden ended the invasion. He recognized that a withdrawal of U.S. support would be disastrous for Britain and made concessions to avoid this scenario, even though the collapse of the Suez campaign sped the demise of his government.[55]

For many coercive standoffs, however, the rather simple model offered by Eden's Britain is complicated by the disconnect between a country and its leadership. Many autocratic governments care little about the well-being of the country as a whole. In Eden's place, they would have accepted an economic crisis and continued with the war. The general effort to weaken a country does not usually directly or immediately affect an ongoing military campaign or a regime's domestic priorities. Moreover, governments have proven skilled at diverting resources from civilian projects and from less-critical military activities to their priorities, making it harder to use general punishment to force them to concede. Governments also can manipulate pressure, using any resulting shortages or problems to punish political opponents while ensuring that loyal followers are relatively unaffected. In such cases, the weakening mechanism is of little value.

At times, the punishment is simply too diffuse; the pain inflicted does not match the potential benefits (measured in ideological terms, political terms, and so on) of continued resistance. Or the pain and threatened pain may be so diluted that they fail to create mass protest or to disrupt the regime's relations with its power base. In sum, attempts to use the

55 Neff, *Warriors at Suez,* pp. 409–410.

weakening mechanism often fail because they do not directly affect adversary pressure points.

Denial: preventing military and political victory

Another common mechanism linking coercive threats to altered adversary decision making is that of rendering impotent an adversary's strategy for winning a crisis or conflict. The above four mechanisms primarily involve imposing costs, but denial centers on preventing a foe from gaining the desired benefits of resistance. According to Pape, "Denial strategies seek to thwart the enemy's military strategy for taking or holding its territorial objectives, compelling concessions to avoid futile expenditures of further resources."[56] Denial works when adversary leaders recognize that they cannot gain benefits and will continue to pay costs if they do not concede.

Denial in coercion is not the same as denial in war. Coercive denial hinges on the perception that benefits will not be achieved; denial by warfighting rests on making that perception a reality. A denial strategy at times blurs with brute force, as both usually seek to defeat an adversary's military, but while coercive denial focuses on convincing an adversary that future benefits are unattainable, conventional warfighting focuses on physically stopping an adversary regardless of what its leadership believes. In practice, this distinction is one of degree: if the attack focuses on demonstrating to the adversary that it cannot succeed, then the attack falls into the coercion realm; if the attack focuses on preventing the adversary from succeeding, then the attack is brute force.

History offers strong support for the proposition that an adversary is likely to come to the negotiating table when it sees its strategy for victory being thwarted. Pape, in his study of coercive air power, makes a convincing case that bombing, when directed at fielded forces, can yield success—as long as those forces are essential to victory. On the other hand, if the forces attacked are not necessary for an adversary to gain victory, air strikes accomplish relatively little.[57] Pape's argument on air power can easily be extended to a broader argument about coercion: coercive strategies are more likely to succeed when the coercer can hinder an adversary's strategy for victory.

56 Pape, *Bombing to Win*, p. 69.
57 See Pape, *Bombing to Win*, passim.

The use or sponsorship of guerrilla warfare to exhaust a foe can be a form of denial. In 1974, Iran provided considerable funding, arms, and a haven to Kurdish guerrillas battling Iraq in order to place pressure on Baghdad. Baghdad had long sought to dominate the Kurdish north, using scorched-earth methods and population transfers alongside a counterinsurgency campaign to crush the Kurdish fighters. Iraq in 1975 recognized, after over a year of unsuccessful fighting, that it could not defeat Kurdish insurgents as long as they had Iran's backing. Moreover, the continued unsuccessful campaign threatened to weaken the Baath regime's support among the Iraqi elite. Because Baghdad foresaw that it would not be able to gain victory, it agreed to Iran's demands about their contested border.[58]

The key to successful denial is to defeat the enemy's actual strategy for victory, not simply to stop conventional military operations. As Pape argues, for denial to be effective, "the coercer must exploit the particular vulnerabilities of the opponent's specific strategy."[59] To force an adversary to recognize a military stalemate or defeat, denial campaigns often attack military production, interdict supplies to the battlefield, shatter enemy air defenses, disrupt communication and command, and defeat fielded forces.[60]

The degree to which these efforts are effective depends on the nature of the adversary and its strategy. Pape argues that Operation Rolling Thunder in Vietnam, as well as the U.S. interdiction efforts in Laos and during the Korean War, failed in large part because the resource needs of the adversary's fighters were limited.[61] Although the United States devastated the transportation grid and hindered throughput, the fact

58 Shahram Chubin and Charles Tripp, *Iran and Iraq at War* (Boulder, CO: Westview Press, 1988), pp. 13–20; and Phebe Marr, *A Modern History of Iraq* (Boulder, CO: Westview Press, 1985), pp. 232–233.

59 Pape, *Bombing to Win*, p. 30.

60 Robert Pape, "The Limits of Precision-Guided Air Power," *Security Studies*, Vol. 7, no. 2 (Winter 1997–1998), p. 97.

61 Operation Rolling Thunder sought to systematically target the enemy's economic assets. The goal was to destroy the North's war-making capability, which in turn would lead the insurgency to collapse. Rolling Thunder destroyed 65 percent of the North's oil storage capacity, 59 percent of its power plants, 55 percent of its major bridges, and thousands of vehicles and rail cars. Almost 90 percent of the targets were transportation related—the strikes hindered movement, but they did not affect infiltration. (Clodfelter, *The Limits of Air Power*, pp. 100 and 134.)

that the guerrillas and soldiers required relatively few supplies allowed them to use the degraded transportation network effectively.[62] In contrast, Operation Linebacker in Vietnam succeeded because the North Vietnamese had switched to a conventional military strategy. U.S. air power proved highly effective at cutting off the supplies and infrastructure necessary for conventional operations. After failing to sustain conventional operations in the South, Hanoi realized that military success depended on removing the United States, particularly the U.S. Air Force, from the conflict.[63]

Some adversary strategies are difficult to counter through denial. In 1993–1994, North Korea sought to reinvigorate its nuclear program in order to gain both defensive advantages and coercive leverage over its neighbors. Denial was not a viable option for compelling Pyongyang to abandon its nuclear program, as the United States and its allies lacked the ability to disrupt the North's means of attaining its goal—a well-developed technical infrastructure for producing a nuclear device. In theory, the United States could have used force to destroy the scientists, engineers, and technical infrastructure, but it lacked both the intelligence necessary to target those individuals and assets and, equally important, the political support at home and in the region for such drastic and unprecedented preemptive attacks.

Denial strategies often become more and more similar to a brute force approach because of the adversary's response. In response to the successful denial of one of its strategies of victory, an adversary may shift to another strategy, and then another if the second fails. Thus, the coercer may find itself trying to counter multiple enemy strategies for victory, leading it to escalate to the point that its actions are not distinguishable from brute force efforts.

In some cases, adversaries may be willing to pay the price of military defeat to score a political victory, in which case military denial becomes more difficult to harness for coercive pressure. Consider Egyptian

62 Mark Clodfelter argues that air power was ineffective when North Vietnam was employing a guerrilla strategy but effective when North Vietnam used conventional military operations: "Because of revamped American political objectives and the North's decision to wage conventional war, Linebacker proved more effective than Rolling Thunder in furthering U.S. goals in Vietnam" (Clodfelter, *The Limits of Airpower*, p. 148). See also Pape, *Bombing to Win*, pp. 193–194.

63 Pape, *Bombing to Win*.

President Anwar Sadat's ambitions in the 1973 Yom Kippur War with Israel. Sadat recognized that in a drawn-out battle, his forces were no match for Israel's. He successfully used surprise, however, to score impressive short-term gains. Although Israel eventually defeated Egypt's forces, Cairo's initial successes and the considerable Israeli losses gave Sadat increased credibility at home and focused increased international attention on the Middle East. Both these factors helped Sadat negotiate with Israel successfully and regain the Sinai through diplomacy. Israel did not, and indeed could not, produce the desired concessions simply by defeating Egypt's fielded forces.

Similarly, Saddam Husayn's 1997–1998 challenge of the UN weapons inspection regime proved frustrating to the United States and its allies. Despite their overwhelming military superiority, the U.S.-led coalition had few options for using that superiority so as to credibly threaten to deny Saddam's ability to achieve his political ambitions with respect to WMD development. From autumn 1997 through the end of 1998, Saddam blocked United Nations Special Commission (UNSCOM) inspections on numerous occasions. He probably intended to speed the lifting of sanctions and, more important, to demonstrate to his supporters that he remained defiant.[64] Saddam's strategic objective was not only to get the sanctions lifted, but to do so in a way that would reinforce his prestige at home and abroad. In essence, he could demonstrate to his power base that the WMD programs they favored remained intact while forcing the end of sanctions. The United States responded by increasing its military forces in the region and threatening strikes if Iraq refused to comply with its demands. A series of deals, breaches, U.S. threats of air strikes, and new deals and compromises ensued, resulting in, initially, a watered-down inspection regime and, eventually, the complete collapse of the inspections process in December 1998.

Although Saddam did not succeed in getting the sanctions lifted, the United States and its allies failed to restore an inspections regime. Military denial, in this instance, was not a practical choice for policy makers, because Saddam's strategy for victory relied on creating a crisis over inspectors' access, a difficult strategy to counter through military means. Conceivably, the United States and its allies could have offered military protection to the inspectors, "denying" Saddam the ability to

64 Baram, *Building Toward Crisis*, p. 79.

expel them and forcing him to attack coalition forces to hinder inspection activities. Yet this would have required a massive effort—one calling for large numbers of ground troops—for which there was little allied support. In addition, such protection still would not have forced Iraq to cooperate with the inspectors, which was essential for them to gain a full accounting of Iraq's weapons programs. Indeed, the use of air strikes or other military measures might even have aided Iraq's political strategy, adding to Saddam's prestige and leading to squabbling among coalition members.

Denial may take time. It is not enough for an adversary strategy to fail—adversary decision makers must recognize that their strategy is failing and that the coercer can continue the pressure as long as necessary. Before they accept defeat, they usually try to hold out until they are sure that the coercer can sustain the pressure. In addition, they often step up their counter-coercion in hopes of forcing the coercer to halt the denial campaign.

SECOND-ORDER COERCION

The five commonly used coercive mechanisms involve direct pressure on the adversary insofar as they are directed at groups, individuals, or military forces within the adversary itself. At times, however, a coercer may have only minimal direct leverage or may lack sufficient information to use its leverage effectively, leaving only the option of indirect pressure: leverage with a third party that can influence the adversary. Although a third-party approach is generally ignored by analysts of coercion, it is common in diplomacy. The United States, for example, may have little influence with North Korea when it attempts to convince it to stop its WMD development or refrain from selling missiles to rogue states. Yet Washington can, and does, press China to use its more extensive influence with Pyongyang to push North Korea to make concessions.

Indirect coercion, of course, requires far more effort than indirect diplomacy. Coercion through a third party requires the coercer to induce or compel the third party to become a coercer itself (or to use brute force) against an adversary. Because third-party coercion requires coercion or suasion to work twice, the problems facing coercers generally multiply. The coercer must be able to shape the behavior of the third party in such a way that the third party's response will effectively shape the adversary's will in accord with the coercer's overall objectives.

A useful illustration of successful indirect coercion is Israel's attacks on Palestinians in Jordan during the 1950s. Israeli policy recognized that Palestinian terrorism could not be stopped directly by Israeli actions and that a third-party host was better positioned to control activities from within its territory. As Moshe Dayan declared about Israel's policy in the early days of the state's existence:

> We cannot guard every water pipeline from explosion and every tree from uprooting. We cannot prevent every murder of a worker in an orchard or a family in their beds. But it is in our power to set a high price on our blood, a price too high for the Arab community, the Arab army, or the Arab government to think it worth paying. We can see to it that the Arab villages oppose the raiding bands that pass through them, rather than give them assistance. It is in our power to see that Arab military commanders prefer a strict performance of their obligation to police the frontiers rather than suffer defeat in clashes with our units.[65]

Israel relied on third parties—Arab military commanders—to restrain movements that Israel itself could not stop. After several years of unsuccessful Israeli attempts to stop infiltration, which led to about 100 casualties a year from 1951 to 1954, Israeli reprisals in the 1950s succeeded in forcing the Jordanian government to stop Palestinian raids. Israeli reprisals against refugee camps and villages in Jordan provoked local demonstrations against the Jordanian government, which the people felt was failing to protect them.[66] King Hussein became militantly anti-Israel in his public diplomacy, but at the same time he ordered the army to crack down on any infiltration in order to prevent domestic unrest. After 1954, infiltration fell dramatically. Israeli raids had threatened King Hussein's quest for national integration, prompting him to seek the *status quo ante*.[67]

Jordan once more became a key base of Palestinian operations after the 1967 Arab-Israeli War. Plagued by Palestinian cross-border attacks

65 As quoted in Bar-Joseph, "Variations on a Theme," p. 152.

66 Israel primarily struck at Arab military objectives instead of towns and villages after attacks on Palestinian civilians in Jordan led to condemnation in Israel, the United States, and elsewhere (Benny Morris, *Israel's Border Wars, 1949–1956* [Oxford: Clarendon Press, 1997], pp. 274–276).

67 Shimshoni, *Israel and Conventional Deterrence*, pp. 37–51; and Morris, *Israel's Border Wars*, pp. 100–101.

from refugee camps in Jordan both before and after that war, Israel engaged in retaliatory strikes against Palestinian militants in Jordan and, at times, Jordanian villagers and the soldiers protecting them. This failed to stem Palestinian terrorism, because the high commitment of the Palestinians made them reluctant to give in to Israeli pressure. In addition, the Israeli attacks raised support for the militants among both the Palestinian community at large and the more radical states in the Arab world, increasing funding and recruiting for the militants.

Because Israeli retaliation led Palestinian groups to stay well armed and active, it damaged the credibility of the Jordanian government in the eyes of its own populace. Amman could not keep order in its own country, despite trying to police its borders more effectively—efforts that angered the Palestinians but did not satisfy the Israelis. Thus, Israel's operations again raised the specter of unrest in Jordan, as local guerrillas became more active, better armed, and highly critical of the Hashemite regime. Because Hussein greatly feared internal unrest and sought to integrate Palestinians into a larger Jordanian national identity, the Israeli attacks threatened to impose unacceptable costs. Hussein, while outwardly professing defiance of Israel, instructed his army to crack down on Palestinian cross-border operations. When the Palestinian militants turned against the regime and undermined his control over Jordan, Hussein ordered his army to suppress all Palestinian guerrillas, leading to a bloody battle in 1970 that forced the Palestinian guerrillas to flee to Lebanon.[68]

As this example demonstrates, for a strategy such as Israel's to work, the third party (in this case, Jordan) must have the necessary leverage to act as a coercer itself—a condition that may be missing. That is, the third party must have influence over the ultimate target and must have the potential willingness to exercise that influence in ways that accord with the primary coercer's ultimate objectives. In the early 1970s, Israel tried a strategy similar to that employed in Jordan in the 1950s and 1960s in order to force the Lebanese government to crack down on the PLO. The Lebanese government, however, was not strong enough to crush the Palestinians. In response to Israeli attacks, Maronite Chris-

68 See Shimshoni, *Israel and Conventional Deterrence*, pp. 37–51, and Morris, *Israel's Border Wars*, pp. 100–101, for information on 1950s operations. See Dupuy, *Elusive Victory*, pp. 378–381, for information on the Palestinian guerrillas and the crisis in Jordan in 1968–1970; also see Shlaim, *The Iron Wall*, pp. 232–234 and 298–299.

tian officers led the Lebanese army into clashes with Palestinian commandos. But by 1969, the army was forced to retreat and give the PLO de facto military autonomy in the so-called Cairo agreement. The Palestinians continued their operations with little interference. Indeed, the end result was a disaster for Israel, as other groups, such as the Shi'a, formed militias because they were convinced that the government was too weak to protect them. This contributed to the collapse of the Lebanese state and the proliferation of anti-Israel militant groups.[69]

CONCLUSION

There is no best mechanism for successful coercion. The ideal mechanism (or combination of mechanisms) varies according to the vulnerabilities of the regime and the particulars of the crisis in question. There are many ways to force a regime to change its behavior, but even the most historically effective mechanisms can backfire or work only in certain circumstances. What worked against Iraq in 1993 may fail against Serbia in 2001, or even against Iraq in 2001.

When triggered simultaneously, several mechanisms may reinforce each other, helping to achieve escalation dominance by increasing the overall degree of pressure on an adversary and cutting off adversary countermoves. However, various effects of threats on key groups and institutions within the adversary political system can also combine in unpredictable or counterproductive ways, alleviating coercive pressure or adding to the costs associated with concessions.

The discussion of mechanisms in this chapter suggests that successful coercion may not always be possible. As Schelling observed in *Arms and Influence*: "Coercion by threat of damage also requires that our interests and our opponent's not be absolutely opposed. . . . Coercion requires finding a bargain, arranging for him to be better off doing what we want—worse off not doing what we want—when he takes the threatened penalty into account."[70] In some cases, the perceived costs of giving in are so dreaded that virtually no military threat will compel the adversary to bend. Pape argues that the reason Germany did not surrender to the Allies was that German leaders feared occupation by Russia and the likely vengeance for atrocities committed by Germany in

69 Dilip Hiro, *Lebanon: Fire and Embers* (New York: St. Martin's Press, 1992), pp. 81–110.

70 Schelling, *Arms and Influence*, p. 4.

the East. Thus, the massive bombing campaign against Germany, as well as continued *Wehrmacht* battlefield defeats, could not sway a German leadership that saw continued punishment and likely defeat as preferable to occupation.[71] The German case may be extreme—it is not clear whether, by the end of the war, the German leadership had even a remotely plausible theory of victory—but it illustrates that coercion can be impossible under certain circumstances.

The importance to coercive strategy making of identifying proper mechanisms for a particular crisis has tremendous implications for selection of the proper instrument, the focus of the following chapter. When choosing among air strikes, sanctions, diplomatic pressure, or other means of inflicting costs, policy makers must remember that the best choice depends on identifying the most appropriate mechanism, which requires an understanding of the adversary regime and its particular vulnerabilities. At times, coercion is best done indirectly, using another state or actor that has more influence over the adversary. At best, failure to properly understand an adversary may cause the instrument to work less effectively than it otherwise would have. At worst, the instrument may backfire, leaving the coercer even farther from its goals.

71 Pape, *Bombing to Win*, p. 310.

4

Coercive instruments

Effective coercive strategy making calls for an understanding of the tools of the trade. Coercion, in practice, requires that abstract notions of costs, benefits, and mechanisms be translated into concrete policies. The choice of instrument to be used depends on instrument effectiveness, costs to the coercer, and the overall political context. The wrong choice can lead to failure or counterproductivity.

The range of coercive instruments is vast. Xenophon writes of the Spartans devastating the countryside around Athens and blockading the city, reducing it to starvation in order to force the Athenians to tear down their walls, shrink their navy, change their constitution, and fall in line with Spartan foreign policy.[1] In the Middle Ages and the Renaissance, the Vatican placed entire nations under interdiction in order to force their leadership to comply with its demands. The British empire relied on "gunboat diplomacy" to enforce its will on its colonies. During the Cold War, both the United States and the Soviet Union threatened to use their nuclear arsenal during several crises. Since the end of the Cold War, the United States has bombed Serbia, killed militia members in Somalia, supported sanctions on Iraq, issued diplomatic demarches on subjects ranging from trade disputes to narcotics trafficking, and utilized a host of other means to threaten adversaries with costs.

This chapter surveys some key strengths and weaknesses of the instruments often used by the United States and other major powers to in-

1 For an interesting review, see Anna Missiou-Ladi, "Coercive Diplomacy in Greek Interstate Relations," *The Classical Quarterly*, Vol. 37, no. 2 (1987), pp. 336–345.

crease pressure on adversary elites or populations, deny an adversary victory, or otherwise impose the threat of pain. In so doing, it attempts to answer the question of how coercive costs are actually levied. The chapter focuses on several major coercive instruments: air strikes, invasions and land grabs, the threat of nuclear retaliation, economic sanctions and political isolation, and support for insurgencies. It examines the mechanisms they may trigger and the reasons they may be attractive to policy makers. It also explores how the instruments work in combination, offering both additive and synergistic benefits (and, at times, drawbacks) to the coercer. Although the chapter emphasizes to instruments heavily featured in U.S. foreign policy, it also draws on the experience and perspective of other states.

AIR STRIKES

Coercion by the United States and its allies today commonly features air strikes—indeed, air strikes sometimes seem to have become the military instrument of first resort. In the last several years, the United States has used air strikes against Milosevic's Serbia, terrorist bases in Afghanistan, and (repeatedly) Saddam Husayn's Iraq. The United States increasingly uses air strikes as its chief instrument rather than as a supplement to other forms of pressure.

Air strikes are attractive to policy makers for several reasons. First, air strikes can inflict damage along the entire coercion-to-brute-force spectrum, ranging from precise attacks on a few, select targets to total devastation of an adversary's cities. Because of this range, air strikes can be, and have been, used to trigger all of the mechanisms discussed in Chapter 3. They are also useful for escalation, enabling policy makers to vary the amount of damage they inflict according to their needs. This versatility makes air strikes a common choice for policy makers, even though air strikes have historically not proven effective in triggering some mechanisms.

Air strikes are particularly attractive to policy makers as a tool in low-stakes contests, because they allow the coercer to escalate without becoming irrevocably involved or paying high political costs at home. In Eliot Cohen's words, "Air Power is an unusually seductive form of military strength, in part because, like modern courtship, it appears to offer gratification without commitment."[2] In such cases, U.S. policy makers seek to keep down the extent of U.S. involvement in order to minimize the costs—both financial and human—of intervention. If adversaries lack sophisticated air defenses, air strikes can be employed with little risk of large numbers of casualties for the coercer. The United States bombed Libya with only two casualties; the far more massive Persian Gulf War, along with its ten-year campaign (to date) to contain and coerce Iraq, has resulted in only 148 casualties. In Operation Allied Force, NATO waged a 78-day war against Serbia while sustaining zero battlefield casualties, an astounding figure. Israeli leaders have shifted toward using air strikes against Hezbollah for similar reasons.[3]

The increasing precision of air strikes has made them even more attractive in recent years because it has given policy makers some control—or the illusion of control—over the level of pain actually inflicted. Until the advent of precision bombing toward the end of the Vietnam War, targets could only be destroyed by air with massive collateral damage. The improved accuracy of modern air power has allowed policy makers in some cases to keep enemy civilian casualties and collateral damage at relatively low levels by historical standards. In Kosovo, civilian casualties resulting directly from NATO air attacks numbered roughly 500, and between 1,200 and 2,300 Iraqi civilians probably died during the Gulf War—a fraction of the civilian deaths in Vietnam, Korea, and other wars.[4]

2 Eliot A. Cohen, "The Mystique of U.S. Air Power," *Foreign Affairs*, Vol. 73, no. 1 (January/February 1994), p. 109.

3 The United States lost fewer than one soldier per 3,000 who fought in the Gulf War, an amazing ratio even when compared with those of other overwhelming victories. This ratio was less than a tenth of Israel's loss ratio during the 1967 Six Day War and less than a twentieth of the ratio for German attacks on Poland and France (Stephen Biddle, "Victory Misunderstood: What the Gulf War Tells Us About the Future of Conflict," *International Security*, Vol. 21, no. 2 [Fall 1996], p. 142).

4 On Iraq, see John G. Heidenrich, "The Gulf War: How Many Iraqis Died?" *Foreign Policy*, no. 90 (Spring 1993), pp. 108–125; and Middle East Watch, *Needless Deaths in the Gulf War: Civilian Casualties During the Air Campaign and Violations of the Laws of War* (New York: Middle East Watch, 1991). On Kosovo, see Human Rights Watch, "Civilian Deaths in the NATO Air Campaign," Vol. 12, no. 1 (February 2000), http://www.hrw.org/reports/2000/nato/index.htm.

These figures do not include civilian deaths from the degradation of civilian infrastructure caused by the air strikes, however. The disabling of dual-use infrastructure can have enormous reverberating health and other adverse effects throughout the civilian population—effects that may be difficult to anticipate and plan for and that are unlikely to command the same public attention as direct bomb damage. Not surprisingly, coercive strategy makers have at times attempted to harness these ripple effects, as well as the direct destructive effects, to alter adversary decision making.

Air power and coercive mechanisms

As noted, one of air power's greatest advantages as a coercive instrument is that it can potentially trigger many of the mechanisms identified in Chapter 3. We examine air power in more detail than we do the other instruments because of its growing prominence in U.S. foreign policy—a prominence explained in part by its perceived versatility.

Air strikes and denial

One of air power's most important functions—and one that is increasingly practical given continuing advances in intelligence and precision strike capabilities—is threatening an adversary with defeat or otherwise preventing it from achieving its military objectives. Against a state adversary seeking to impose its regional ambitions via armed aggression, air power can play a key role in threatening to deny that adversary fulfillment of its designs before they become a fait accompli.

The air arm's flexibility and versatility make it well suited for denying an adversary the perceived fruits of military operations. Air power can be used to disrupt command and control of adversary forces or otherwise strike with the *potential* to devastate. In Operation Deliberate Force, NATO air strikes knocked out Bosnian Serb command and communications facilities with relatively little risk of allied or Bosnian Serb civilian casualties. Because of the strikes, Bosnian Serb commanders would have had far more difficulty directing their forces, making them easier prey for their Croat and Muslim foes. These strikes enabled NATO to place considerable military pressure on the Serbs without causing large amounts of suffering.

Modern air power—at least as employed by capable air forces such as those of the United States, Britain, Australia, and Israel—can effectively prevent or hinder certain types of operations, particularly those involving considerable mechanized forces and large logistics efforts and conducted in relatively open terrain. Desert Storm demonstrated this capability vividly, when U.S. air power disrupted parts of two Iraqi corps before they even engaged U.S. ground forces near Khafji. The small Iraqi force that did capture the empty town was then easily isolated and destroyed by coalition ground and air forces. During the Linebacker operations in Vietnam, the North Vietnamese discovered that they could not sustain large-scale conventional operations given the damage done by the U.S. bombing campaign. Hanoi found itself unable to accomplish its objectives on the battlefield.[5]

But air power is far from omnipotent, and its ability to deny an adversary military victory is severely checked in certain contexts. Enemy military forces, especially light infantry units, fighting in mountainous, urban, or jungle terrain can often camouflage their movements, making it difficult to strike them.[6] In addition, as elaborated in Chapter 8, terrorist organizations and other substate foes often provide few military targets to destroy or interdict. Their reliance on low-technology communications also inhibits air power's ability to paralyze their operations.

Not all military *strategies* are susceptible to denial by air power, either. Guerrilla armies in particular have few fielded forces to strike and do not engage in large-scale maneuvers that are easily targeted. The Chechen fighters, for example, tried to avoid massing their forces and used terrain to hide their movements from air strikes. Their strategy was premised on playing defense and engaging Russia in a costly and prolonged conflict on the ground.

Air power may actually become less visibly effective for coercion in the future even as its capabilities increase. It is precisely because of the potency of air power as a tool of denial that adversaries facing modern

5 Pape, *Bombing to Win*, pp. 195–210; and Clodfelter, *The Limits of Airpower*, pp. 166–173. As one British military expert, Sir Robert Thompson, noted: "You cannot refuel T-54 tanks with gasoline out of water bottles carried on bicycles" (as quoted in Clodfelter, *The Limits of Airpower*, p. 167).

6 For ways to improve this capability, see Alan Vick, David T. Orletsky, John Bordeaux, and David A. Shlapak, *Enhancing Air Power's Contribution Against Light Infantry Targets* (Santa Monica, CA: RAND, 1996).

air power are likely to adopt strategies that neutralize air power's advantages. Any attentive adversary is likely to avoid playing to the strength of the United States. Of course, the phenomenon masks the great achievements of U.S. air power in taking adversary options off the table both before and during crises.

When air power is used for denial, it is generally directed against fielded forces or other deployed assets, but it can also be used to trigger other denial variants. U.S. interwar air power theorists posited that air attacks on adversary infrastructure and industry would compel surrender—essentially a denial approach that relies on disrupting industrial might rather than military forces directly. During the 1920s and 1930s, instructors at the U.S. Air Corps Tactical School (ACTS) taught that attacks on critical production nodes could paralyze an adversary by halting its war production. If its ability to wage war was destroyed, the foe would soon surrender.[7]

During World War II, U.S. strategists expected that the bomber offensive would bring Germany's ability to sustain the war to a halt without devastating the entire country. (The British school, in contrast, believed that air strikes would disrupt Germany's will to fight.) In Germany, the bombing prevented production from increasing far beyond then-existing levels. In Japan, bombing decreased morale and led to tremendous absenteeism, in addition to wreaking direct destruction on the industrial base.[8] This weakening, however, failed to induce the surrender of either power.

Threatening a regime's relationship with its power base

The United States and other powers have also used air strikes effectively to threaten an adversary regime's relations with its power base, though the impact has at other times been negligible or even backfired. Air strikes can kill important backers of a regime, target the assets of praetorian guards or other elite units, destroy backers' personal prop-

7 Meilinger, "The Historiography of Air Power," pp. 476–479. This strategy blurs with brute force, as the ACTS argued that the enemy would not wage war in large part because it could not do so effectively.

8 R. J. Overy, *The Air War, 1939–1945* (New York: Stein and Day, 1980), p. 123; Overy, *Why the Allies Won*, p. 126; and United States Strategic Bombing Survey, *The Effects of Strategic Bombing on German Morale*, pp. 16–27.

erty, and otherwise place pressure on key supporters. Such strikes may turn elites against a regime or foster concern among decision makers.

Air strikes or threats of them directed at Saddam Husayn's power base have in several instances contributed to Iraqi concessions. As noted in Chapter 3, Saddam made repeated concessions to the United States and its allies in the immediate aftermath of the Gulf War. He allowed UN inspectors to explore his WMD programs, accepted the de facto exclusion of his forces from much of his country, and abided by restrictions on his military activities—all because he feared further humiliation before his power base. These concessions occurred in response to U.S. threats and limited force carried out through cruise missile attacks and air strikes aimed at regime intelligence and security assets.[9] Air power was used in this case against a backdrop of other threats, including the threat of continued economic sanctions, but it was the primary instrument of force.

Many regimes and the power structures within them have proven quite resilient in the face of air strikes, however, making it difficult to extract concessions from the air. During the December 1998 Desert Fox bombings of Iraq, the United States struck Iraqi command and control centers and the barracks of elite forces, particularly the Republican Guard and the Special Republican Guard. In three days of intense bombing, the strikes killed several leaders and over 1,000 elite troops. The intention of the strikes was to increase troop disaffection with Saddam's regime and promote a coup.[10] The strikes did increase unrest and disaffection with the regime but did not produce a regime change; nor did Saddam make serious concessions regarding UN inspections, the nominal purpose of the air strikes. In this instance, the costs of backing down in the face of U.S. pressure outweighed the dangers of continued strikes—or perhaps Saddam concluded that the United States would not sustain its attacks beyond a few days.

The 1986 air raids on Libya produced similar limited results. In response to Libyan support for terrorism, the United States launched Operation El Dorado Canyon: air strikes on Mohammar Qaddafi's command center, a naval special operations training school, a military

9 See Daniel Byman, Kenneth Pollack, and Matthew Waxman, "Coercing Saddam Hussein: Lessons from the Past," *Survival* (Autumn 1998), Vol. 40, no. 3, pp. 127–152.

10 Dana Priest and Bradley Graham, "Airstrikes Take a Toll on Saddam, U.S. Says," *Washington Post*, January 9, 1999, p. A14.

portion of the Tripoli International Airfield, air defense facilities, and the barracks of elite troops.[11] The United States hoped that the El Dorado Canyon bombings would provoke the Libyan military to overthrow the regime. If anything, however, these raids appear to have strengthened Qaddafi vis-à-vis his rivals.[12] He used the strikes to play on nationalism and draw people to him.

Threatening decapitation through air strikes

Air strikes can also be used to directly threaten the security of adversary leadership. They appear to be an attractive option for decapitation threats because they offer a means of striking otherwise unreachable individuals. Most leaders are protected by elaborate security networks and a close ring of bodyguards. An assassin is not likely to get through these forces, but an air strike can bypass them.[13]

Despite its public claims to the contrary, the United States has repeatedly tried to kill enemy leaders through air strikes. These efforts include the bombing of Qaddafi's residence during Operation El Dorado Canyon, Gulf War attacks against Saddam's residences and command bunkers with super-penetrator munitions,[14] cruise missile attacks in 1998 on terrorist camps in Afghanistan thought to house Osama bin Laden, and NATO attacks in 1999 against Slobodan Milosevic's residence and command sites during Operation Allied Force.[15]

11 To minimize the possibility of civilian casualties and collateral damage, F-111 pilots operated under strict engagement standards that prevented four of the nine F-111s sent against the command center from dropping their ordnance (Tim Zimmerman, "Coercive Diplomacy and Libya," in *The Limits of Coercive Diplomacy*, Alexander George and William E. Simons, eds., (Boulder, CO: Westview Press, 1994), pp. 213–215.

12 Hosmer, *Operations to Remove Enemy Leaders*.

13 For an argument along these lines, see Warden, "Employing Air Power in the Twenty-First Century," pp. 57–82; and John A. Warden III, "The Enemy as a System," *Airpower Journal,* no. 9 (Spring 1995), pp. 40–55. Warden's emphasis is as much on brute force as on coercion; that is, on using a successful attack to paralyze an adversary as much as to induce changes in its behavior.

14 Michael Gordon and Bernard Trainor, *The Generals' War: The Inside Story of the Gulf War* (Boston, MA: Little, Brown, 1994), pp. 314–315.

15 For a discussion, see Hosmer, *Operations to Remove Enemy Leaders*.

Decapitation, or the effective threat of it, requires both superb intelligence to locate the leader in question and the ability to strike that location with great precision. With advances in precision in recent years, one hurdle has been largely overcome. During World War II, the prospects of an air raid successfully targeting a particular individual, especially a well-protected individual, were slim to none. In April 1996, a Russian Su-25 successfully bombed Chechen resistance leader Dzhokhar Dudayev after he gave away his location by using a cell phone. In the 1980s and 1990s, Israel used helicopter attacks to assassinate Hezbollah leaders. With today's precision capabilities, the limiting technical factor on decapitation strikes for the United States comes from intelligence, not the accuracy of delivery.

These advances have spawned a back-and-forth contest that pits an adversary's deception and protection measures against new technological developments. "Bunker buster" munitions and real-time intelligence are used to go after previously unreachable targets. Adversary leaders, in response, have cloaked their movements, used doubles to confuse intelligence, and dug deeper and better-protected shelters in order to negate these advances.[16] In sum, it remains difficult to target an individual, requiring superb intelligence and remarkable precision in ordnance delivery—a rare combination, even for countries with powerful, modern air power capabilities.

For coercive purposes, the increased feasibility of assassination from the air masks a deeper problem: air strikes on leaders can kill, but they seldom can coerce. An air strike can certainly shake a foe. The El Dorado Canyon attacks on Qaddafi unnerved him and increased his paranoia. The U.S. air strikes on Saddam during the Gulf war forced Saddam into hiding, reportedly causing him to be anxious and to lose weight.[17] But these effects did little to make measurable changes in these leaders' policies. Nor did bin Laden, Milosevic, Hezbollah and Chechen leaders, and other targets of assassination make dramatic changes in their policies. In the end, air strikes appear to offer little value for coercion when they are used to threaten a leader's personal security.

16 Pape, *Bombing to Win*, pp. 79–88.
17 Hosmer, *Operations to Remove Enemy Leaders*.

Population attacks and damage to the country as a whole[18]

Since its advent, air power has been used coercively—and often indiscriminately—as an instrument for attacking enemy populations, the objective being both to trigger unrest and to threaten weakening of nations. Air strikes are attractive in these respects because they allow a coercer to largely bypass an enemy's fielded forces and strike directly at the enemy's population or industry.

Many original theorists of air power believed that an adversary would be forced to concede, or even surrender, due to the destruction wrought by air strikes on the civilian population.[19] Attacks on civilians would produce terror and riots, leading to social chaos and, eventually, economic and political collapse. Writing in 1921, Giulio Douhet, one of the pioneers of air power, evoked the devastation of such attacks:

> Within a few minutes some 20 tons of high-explosive incendiary and gas bombs would rain down. First would come explosions, then fires, then deadly gases floating on the surface and preventing any approach to the stricken area. . . . By the following day, the life of the city would be suspended. . . . What could happen to a single city in a single day could also happen to ten, twenty, fifty cities. . . . In short, normal life would be impossible in this constant nightmare of imminent death and destruction. . . . A complete breakdown of the social structure cannot but take place in a country subjected to this kind of merciless pounding from the air. The time would soon come when, to put an end to the horror and suffering, the people themselves, driven by the instinct of self-preservation, would rise up and demand an end to the war.[20]

As air power developed, this argument seemed even more plausible. Zeppelin raids and other air attacks in World War I had underscored Douhet's predicted psychological terror, leading others to take up his arguments.[21]

18 These ideas are drawn in part from Alan Vick, "Catalyst for Rebellion? Air Campaigns and Civil Unrest in Three Wars," unpublished manuscript, 1998.

19 For a view on the vulnerability of adversary economies as a possible source of coercive leverage, see Warden, "The Enemy as a System," pp. 50–51.

20 Douhet, *The Command of the Air*, pp. 58–59.

21 Phillip Meilinger, "Trenchard, Slessor, and Royal Air Force Doctrine Before World War II," in *The Paths of Heaven: The Evolution of Airpower Theory,* Phillip Meilinger, ed. (Maxwell Air Force Base, AL: Air University Press, 1997), p. 43.

World War II is widely viewed as disproving Douhet and similar thinkers. The World War II case is problematic for drawing general lessons, however, because the stakes for all parties and the demands of the Allies—unconditional surrender—were so high. As noted in Chapter 3, in lesser conflicts with less committed foes, fear of population attacks contributed to leaders' decisions to make concessions. In both the Iran-Iraq War and the 1969–1970 War of Attrition between Israel and Egypt, air (and missile) strikes on military and population targets—and the leaders' resulting fear of popular unrest—along with defeats on the battlefield, helped push Tehran and Cairo to the negotiating table. These results suggest that air strikes to produce unrest can be effective but are seldom decisive.

Although the United States is not likely to conduct massive area bombing in the future, it still may use air power to trigger unrest. During the 1990–1991 Gulf War, the U.S.-led coalition relied on precision bombing to create popular disquiet. The air campaign was not primarily, or even largely, directed at creating unrest, but unrest was one of the many goals for which the United States used air power. A study of the Gulf air war noted that U.S. strategists sought to weaken Saddam's grip on power by debilitating Iraqi morale and society, though by means short of inflicting massive civilian suffering.[22] Air planners deliberately sought to bring the war home, disrupting electricity and transportation to undermine morale.[23] The United States also dropped leaflets on Iraq that called for the population to rise up against Saddam.[24]

The effort produced some success at the operational level, insofar as many of the targets were effectively destroyed or damaged. However, this destruction did not translate into the desired effects on Saddam's decision making—he continued to resist coalition demands. By the standards of World War II, suffering during the Gulf War was not substantial. Iraqi morale probably decreased, but it did not paralyze Iraqi society or prompt massive unrest.[25] The additional suffering inflicted

22 Thomas A. Keaney and Eliot A. Cohen, *Gulf War Air Power Survey (GWAPS): Summary Volume* (Washington, DC: Government Printing Office, 1993), p. 43.

23 Most of these attacks had a brute force purpose—decreasing Iraq's ability to wage war—that overshadowed their coercive ambitions.

24 Hosmer, *Operations to Remove Enemy Leaders*.

25 Hosmer, *Psychological Effects of U.S. Air Operations in Four Wars*, p. 54.

on the Iraqis was moderate compared to what they had suffered during the Iran-Iraq War and from Saddam's depravations, and the danger posed was far less than that from the internal security services. Any incentive to rise up was weak, and the consequences of rising up were considerable.

In recent years, the United States has shied away from using air strikes to engender popular unrest or overall weakening of an adversary where doing so might cause human suffering on a massive scale. The result has not been abandonment of strategies that rely on these mechanisms but a crafting of those strategies that emphasizes precision military strikes in an effort to carefully regulate destructive effects. U.S. policy makers try to walk a line between creating pressure on the adversary leadership to relent and curbing civilian damage and injury.[26] Concerns about adversary civilian casualties, as well as a growing recognition that these casualties often backfire and harden adversary resolve, have led air planners to focus on holding down potential levels of collateral damage. So, for instance, during the Gulf War air campaign, the United States sought to degrade Iraq's electric power capacity primarily for direct military effect, but also knowing that doing so would cause civilian deprivations and thereby apply further pressure on Saddam.[27] In doing so, however, U.S. air forces tried to destroy Iraqi transmission stations, which can easily be rebuilt, while avoiding generators, which take more time to repair. Perhaps partly as a result of Gulf War criticism, Yugoslavia's major electric power infrastructure was a politically sensitive target in the 1999 Kosovo air campaign and was struck only after NATO leadership decided to escalate strategic air attacks.[28] As discussed in Chapter 6, Washington's unwillingness to inflict casualties may have emboldened adversaries, reducing the credibility of the U.S. threat to increase future costs.

26 Matthew C. Waxman, *International Law and the Politics of Urban Air Operations* (Santa Monica, CA: RAND, 2000), pp. 25–42.

27 Barton Gellman, "Allied Air War Struck More Broadly in Iraq," *Washington Post*, June 23, 1991, p. A1.

28 Michael R. Gordon, "NATO Air Attacks on Power Plants Pass a Threshold," *New York Times*, May 4, 1999, p. A1.

Air power and coercive strategy making

A major debate today among policy makers, analysts, and academics is whether air power alone can compel adversary concessions in major disputes.[29] In part, this is a false debate, because the threat of air strikes never exists in a vacuum. As explained in Chapter 2, there are always background threats—possible ground war options, nuclear scenarios, and so on—that weigh on adversary decision makers, and air strikes may not only add to these background threats but magnify them. The better approach is to ask how and under what conditions the use or threat of air strikes contributes to coercive strategies. We return to this question later in our examination of U.S. domestic politics and the future of U.S. coercion.

INVASIONS AND LAND GRABS

Many countries, particularly those lacking large and proficient air forces, rely heavily on ground forces to coerce. The United States, though increasing its reliance on air power, also maintains the world's most capable ground forces, which occasionally are used to threaten invasion or augment other coercive instruments.

The use or threat of ground troops can trigger several mechanisms that might lead to adversary concessions. First, the possible occupation of valuable territory, along with the devastation inherent to most land

29 The leading academic work on the use of air power as a coercive instrument is Pape, *Bombing to Win*. See also Pape's "The Air Force Strikes Back: A Reply to Barry Watts and John Warden," *Security Studies*, Vol. 7, no. 2 (Winter 1997–1998), pp. 200–214, and "The Limits of Precision-Guided Air Power." For the best critique of Pape, see Mueller, "Denial, Punishment, and the Future of Air Power." Other valuable works on the use of air power include Cohen, "The Mystique of U.S. Air Power"; Stuart Peach, ed., *Perspectives on Air Power* (London: The Stationary Office, 1998); Robert F. Futrell, *Ideas, Concepts, Doctrine: Basic Thinking in the United States Air Force* (Maxwell Air Force Base, AL: Air University Press, 1989); Phillip S. Meilinger, ed., *The Paths to Heaven: The Evolution of Airpower Theory* (Maxwell Air Force Base, AL: Air University Press, 1997); and Phillip S. Meilinger, *Ten Propositions Regarding Air Power* (Washington, DC: Air Force History and Museums Program, 1995).

campaigns, can impose costs on the country as a whole, inducing concessions through general weakening. Second, the threat of a defeat on the ground might embarrass an adversary's leadership and humiliate its military forces, threatening to unhinge the leadership from its power base. Third, a ground-based strategy can be used for denial, demonstrating that the adversary cannot hope to gain its objectives through continued resistance. The possible use of ground forces is a potent threat and, if credible, reinforces other instruments by highlighting the potential for escalation.

The line between brute force and coercive use of invasions and land grabs is often blurry. Once force is actually used to seize territory, the volitional element of an adversary's concessions is often limited. This haziness is most common when the coercer's demands involve withdrawal from disputed geographic areas, as was the case in the Gulf War. During Desert Storm, brute force eclipsed coercion as the U.S.-led coalition forcibly expelled the Iraqi army from Kuwait. At times, however, a state will invade and conquer territory to force concessions in other regions or over other issues. In May 2000, for example, Ethiopia sent troops deep into parts of Eritrea, leading Eritrea to withdraw its troops from territory along their border in the disputed Zalambessa area. In this case, force was used to extract concessions, whereas in the Gulf War, force was used to remove troops from the territory in dispute.

The use of ground forces as a primary coercive instrument is rare today for the United States because of the tremendous effort that sustained ground operations usually require. Compared with air power, ground forces raise the risk of heavy friendly casualties and are therefore viewed by U.S. policy makers as a far more costly option. Ground forces provide policy makers with less flexibility in that they can strike only those targets located relatively near to where they are based, which limits their value as an instrument of escalation and their ability to strike key pressure points. Ground forces also often require more time to deploy than do air forces. In crises that require a quick response, they are often unsuitable altogether.[30] Finally, ground forces take more time to extract than do air and naval forces and are generally vulnerable

30 During Operation Allied Force, some pundits called for ground forces to prevent or quickly stop the Serb ethnic cleansing. However, even a rapid deployment of ground forces would have taken weeks if not more, particularly if heavier forces were included.

during extraction. In short, they often require too high a price for their use in low-stakes contests.

However, the threat of a ground invasion may be sufficiently potent to carry coercive weight even when the likelihood of the invasion coming to pass seems slight. In 1999's Operation Allied Force, the threat of NATO ground forces—though ambiguous—helped convince Milosevic to meet NATO demands over Kosovo. NATO considered (and took several steps to prepare for) a ground campaign, a consideration that featured heavily in the decision making of both NATO and Serbia.[31]

A decision to use ground forces in Kosovo had not been reached by the end of the air campaign, though by then momentum for a ground intervention was growing.[32] But the possibility of ground forces was sufficiently plausible to influence Milosevic's calculus. A ground invasion, even if the preponderance of the evidence available to Milosevic suggested it was unlikely, threatened to take away the very objective—Serbian control of the Kosovo province—of his policy. Still more frightening to Milosevic was the fact that a ground war might lead to the occupation of other parts of Serbia. Serbia's stationing of forces along likely attack routes and its efforts to fortify against a ground attack show that the ground threat was of sufficient concern to leadership to affect important resource allocation decisions.[33]

Just as the threat of air strikes must be considered in the context of simultaneous threats (even if unlikely or in the background), the threat of ground invasions—like those debated during Operation Allied Force—must be analyzed in the context of ongoing air attacks and other pressures. Recall from Chapter 2's discussion of synergies that the in-

31 General Wesley Clark, the Supreme Allied Commander who ran the war, argues that NATO ground troops posed an implicit threat that contributed to Milosevic's decision to capitulate, even though NATO leaders refused to issue any explicit threats of ground assault ("Interview: General Wesley Clark," *Jane's Defence Weekly*, July 7, 1999).

32 Carla Anne Robins and Thomas E. Ricks. "NATO Weighs Plan for Bigger Kosovo Force," *Wall Street Journal*, May 19, 1999 (electronic version); Thomas E. Ricks, David Rogers, and Carla Anne Robbins, "NATO to Reconsider the Issue of Ground Troops in Kosovo," *Wall Street Journal*, April 21, 1999 (electronic version); and Rowan Scarborough, "Apaches Were Sent to Scare Serbs," *Washington Times*, May 21, 1999, p. 1.

33 Michael R. Gordon, "NATO Says Serbs, Fearing Land War, Dig in on Border," *New York Times*, May 19, 1999, p. A1.

creasing intensity of NATO air attacks would have amounted to a softening up of Serbian forces before a ground push, thus providing NATO with the potential for launching a ground campaign at less cost to itself and more cost to the Serbs. Viewing the crisis dynamically, Milosevic's most obvious counter to a NATO ground campaign and the biggest deterrent to its launch—inflicting heavy casualties on NATO forces—was far less viable in the face of the air supremacy that NATO would have enjoyed and the destruction of assets that would have resulted from allied air strikes had Serbia massed its conventional forces to repel an invasion. Surely Milosevic remembered that in the Gulf War, coalition air attacks did not prompt Saddam Husayn's quick surrender but did facilitate a coalition rout once the ground assault was launched. Had NATO threatened a ground invasion by massing troops, Milosevic would have faced the unpleasant choice of leaving his forces dispersed and allowing NATO to roll through his territory or concentrating his forces to meet the ground threat, leaving them vulnerable to destruction by air.

THE THREAT OF NUCLEAR ATTACK

Although the threat of a large-scale nuclear strike is a potentially powerful coercive tool, it has very limited applicability in today's world for most major powers. Many of the dynamics of nuclear threats (and other types of WMD threats, such as those involving chemical and biological weapons) that the United States and possible adversaries could pose are further elaborated in Chapter 8.

It is hard to match the threat of nuclear attack with the mechanisms outlined in the previous chapter because almost any nuclear use would threaten considerable destruction to the adversary's civilian population, key elite groups, leadership, military, and country as a whole. The size and lethality of the U.S. arsenal make it exponentially more destructive than the massive U.S. conventional arsenal. This is also the case with nuclear-armed adversaries. Even a country with a limited arsenal could kill millions of Americans—far more than in all U.S. wars combined—if it chose to use nuclear weapons against U.S. cities. Smaller nuclear devices, while still devastating when compared with conventional weapons, could also be used to destroy a government complex where a regime's leadership resided, a city where many regime elites lived, critical infrastructure targets, and so on. Nuclear weapons are therefore often seen as an instrument for triggering the weakening mechanism, because they are indiscriminate in their damage to the country, but elite and leadership fears in the face of nuclear threats also could help to produce concessions, at least in theory.

For coercive purposes, the problem with nuclear weapons is that they are *too* devastating. The incredibly destructive power of nuclear weapons makes them difficult to use, or even to threaten to use, for the limited aims common to coercion. This devastation limits their value as an escalatory instrument, because policy makers cannot use them to ratchet up pressure slowly or inflict limited costs. The United States never solved the question of how to use nuclear weapons strictly to augment compellence during the Cold War.[34] In the post–Cold War world, the likely massive casualties, the strong international norm against nuclear use, and other concerns (discussed further in Part II) all reduce the chance of the United States credibly brandishing the nuclear threat. In short, the use or threat of WMD carries massive potential costs for the coercer itself.

During the height of the Cold War, both the United States and the Soviet Union generally avoided explicit nuclear threats. Indeed, both superpowers usually took steps to defuse lesser crises for fear that they would escalate into nuclear confrontations, though the threat of nuclear surprise attack or escalation always operated in the background.[35] Credibility for nuclear use was highest when the United States and its allies were already involved in a massive conventional effort or when the crisis involved a foe with its own nuclear arsenal. During the Korean War, the North agreed to accept talks leading to the continued partition of the country in part due to President-elect Eisenhower's threat to use nuclear weapons to end the conflict—a threat whose credibility was increased by the already massive U.S. conventional campaign.[36]

34 Fred M. Kaplan, *The Wizards of Armageddon* (Stanford, CA: Stanford University Press, 1991), p. 371.

35 For example, both the United States and the Soviet Union took steps to negotiate a cease-fire to the 1973 Yom Kippur War between Israel and Egypt, fearing it could escalate and drag them both in.

36 A caveat is in order here. In 1952, the memory of the atomic bombing of Japan was fresh, and Moscow lacked the ability to retaliate against the United States. Both factors aided the credibility of the U.S. threat.

Perhaps the most well-documented case of a nuclear threat influencing adversary decision making is the Cuban missile crisis of 1962. As the confrontation over Cuba unfolded, U.S. intelligence informed the Kennedy administration that Soviet nuclear forces were in a poor state of preparedness and that the United States could, if necessary, launch a devastating nuclear first strike with low probability of a Soviet response. Moreover, the proximity of Cuba to the United States and the long-standing U.S. effort to isolate and overthrow Castro underscored the credibility of U.S. threats. Nuclear dominance allowed President Kennedy to stake out a demanding public profile, as he knew that the costs of escalation would weigh more heavily on Moscow.[37] Ultimately, Soviet leaders publicly backed down and removed their missiles from Cuba—a widely credited triumph for the Kennedy administration.[38]

The end of the Cold War has diminished the greatest threat to U.S. interests, leaving in its wake a host of lesser concerns and adversaries. Because of the devastation inherent in nuclear use, few conflicts today would justify even consideration of a nuclear strike. Nuclear weapons are now most plausibly considered as options for responding to a WMD attack or WMD threat by an adversary.[39] As noted in the previous chapter, the United States threatened the Iraqi leadership during the Gulf War with unspecified massive punishment—a deliberately vague threat meant to encompass nuclear use—if it used chemical weapons against U.S. forces or U.S. allies. Iraqi defectors subsequently reported that this threat was a major factor in Iraq's decision not to use chemical weapons.[40] Iraq ultimately chose not to use chemical weapons—despite

37 A. A. Fursenko and Timothy Naftali, "*One Hell of a Gamble*": *Khrushchev, Castro, and Kennedy, 1958–1964* (New York: Norton, 1998); George and Simons, *The Limits of Coercive Diplomacy*, p. 125; and John Lewis Gaddis, *We Now Know: Rethinking Cold War History* (New York: Oxford University Press, 1997), p. 247.

38 For a review of the crisis, see Gaddis, *We Now Know*, pp. 260–280.

39 For arguments on the importance of using nuclear threats to deter opponents today, see Richard N. Haass, "It's Dangerous to Disarm," *New York Times*, December 11, 1996, p. A21; David C. Gompert, "Rethinking the Role of Nuclear Weapons," *Strategic Forum*, no. 141 (May 1998), pp. 1–4, and David Gompert, Kenneth Watman, and Dean Wilkening, "Nuclear First Use Revisited," *Survival*, Vol. 37, no. 3 (Autumn 1995), pp. 27–44.

40 Scott Sagan criticizes these reports, arguing that Saddam may have used the nuclear threat to drum up sympathy for his cause, that Saddam had a

its repeated use of them in earlier wars, despite the advantages that chemical weapons might have brought it on the Gulf War battlefield, and despite the fact that it was involved in a major war that was perhaps putting the regime's very survival at stake.[41]

Although its immediate relevance to minor crises, or even major regional ones, is usually limited, the prospect of nuclear use always functions in the background. Adversary leaders know there is a limit to their escalation: if they pose a truly massive or horrific threat to the United States or another nuclear-armed power, that power could respond with nuclear weapons. Gauging the impact of such a background threat is difficult, as it operates on the outer edges of a country's possible behavior rather than affecting day-to-day decision making. Nevertheless, the presence of nuclear weapons means that adversaries have a tremendous interest in ensuring that they do not threaten U.S. interests to the point that nuclear use might be considered. As with so many other forms of coercive pressure, the implicit threat of nuclear strikes influences what an adversary does *not* do as much as, if not more than, it influences what the adversary does.

SANCTIONS AND INTERNATIONAL ISOLATION

Although sanctions and international isolation do not involve military means—the primary focus of this book—they are often used to re-

domestic interest in saying that nuclear weapons (as opposed to a threat to his continued rule) led to his choice, and that Saddam took actions such as destroying the Kuwaiti oil fields despite similar threats (Scott Sagan, "The Commitment Trap: Why the United States Should Not Use Nuclear Threats to Deter Biological and Chemical Weapons Attacks," *International Security,* Vol. 24, no. 4 [Spring 2000], p. 95). We disagree with Sagan's argument for several reasons. We feel it is not likely that defectors would cite the nuclear threat *after* they had left Kuwait if that threat were simply for domestic consumption. And the fact that Saddam destroyed the oil fields simply indicates that the letter containing the threat was not enough on this score, because Saddam believed WMD use would provoke a more serious response, or because several other official U.S. government statements on WMD in other venues reinforced the letter in question, or both. In addition, it is logical that the threat to regime stability and the threat of nuclear retaliation acted in tandem.

41 Baker, *The Politics of Diplomacy*, p. 359; and Iraqi News Agency Broadcasts, January 9–13, 1991. The threat of a decapitation strike, as discussed in Chapter 3, also influenced the Iraqi regime.

inforce military threats and, like military attacks, can impose tremendous costs on, and deny benefits to, an adversary. An examination of their impact is useful for highlighting broader points about coercion and coercive strategy making and for casting in sharp relief important attributes of military threats.

Sanctions

Sanctions are generally characterized as efforts to place economic pressure on an adversary. They can involve restrictions on a country's imports, boycotts of its exports, punishment of particular firms, aid cutoff, or an embargo of a country's entire trade. Their primary function is to create pressure by weakening the entire country and creating broad, popular discontent, but they may also be used to apply pressure more precisely against a regime's power base, for example, by targeting financial assets. Either way, coercers try to create a "fifth column" that will then push the government to change its policies.[42] During war, sanctions also serve brute force purposes, cutting off the flow of arms, spare parts, and training to a foe and decreasing its industrial output and available capital.[43]

The pain inflicted by sanctions depends on the coercer's ability to block the adversary's alternative economic channels. Unlike some of the other coercive instruments described in this chapter, sanctions almost always require the cooperation of major powers and neighboring states, some of which may be hostile to the coercer or friendly to the adversary. If the adversary can replace the capital, markets, aid, or other affected items with relative ease, sanctions will have little effect. All else being equal, the more powers involved in implementing sanctions, the more effective they will be.

42 Zachary A. Selden, *Economic Sanctions as Instruments of American Foreign Policy* (Westport, CT: Praeger, 1999), p. 6.

43 In recent years, talk has shifted to imposing financial sanctions more and trade sanctions less—a strategy far more feasible given efforts to track financial flows as part of the U.S. counternarcotics strategy. It is too soon to evaluate this shift. However, as countries and leaders become more enmeshed in the international financial system, and as the ability to track money increases (a possibility, though hardly a certainty), the impact of financial sanctions will likely grow.

The United States, its major allies, and the UN have frequently turned to sanctions in recent years—so much so that sanctions have become a leading instrument of coercion. Since its founding, the UN has imposed sanctions on Afghanistan, Angola, Haiti, Iraq, Liberia, Libya, Rwanda, Sierra Leone, Somalia, South Africa, Rhodesia, Sudan, and Yugoslavia (both before and after its breakup).[44] Washington has directed unilateral sanctions at China, Cuba, Iran, Iraq, Libya, Nicaragua, North Korea, and a host of others, its coercive goals including stopping support for foreign guerrillas, ending WMD production, and preventing human rights abuses. A leading study of the use of sanctions between 1914 and 1990 reviewed 115 cases of sanctions. Their use has increased since the end of the Cold War; the 1990s saw over 50 uses of sanctions.[45]

U.S. and allied policy makers' recent proclivity toward sanctions stems from several sources. Jonathan Kirschner argues that major powers regularly use sanctions to affect low-stakes contests in which the risks and costs of using force are too high.[46] One of the greatest advantages of sanctions, from the viewpoint of a policy maker, is that their cost to the coercer is quite low. The coercer may lose trade or investment opportunities, but the downside risks of employing sanctions are relatively modest and predictable, particularly when compared with those of using military force.[47] Although most sanctions take time to work (if they work at all), many of today's crises lack the urgency of Cold War crises, making sanctions more suitable. The spread of market economies since the fall of the Soviet Union may also have increased the

44 "Fitting Sanctions," *Jane's Defence Weekly*, May 3, 2000 (electronic version).

45 See Jean-Marc F. Blanchard and Norrin M. Ripsman, "Asking the Right Question: *When* Do Economic Sanctions Work Best?" *Security Studies*, Vol. 9, no. 1–2 (Autumn 1999–2000), pp. 219–253; and Gary Clyde Hufbauer et al., *Economic Sanctions Reconsidered*. For a review of economic instruments, see Baldwin, *Economic Statecraft*. See also Lisa Martin, "Credibility, Costs, and Institutions: Cooperation on Economic Sanctions," *World Politics,* Vol. 45, no. 3 (April 1993), pp. 406–432; and Stephanie Lenway, "Between War and Commerce: Economic Sanctions as a Tool of Statecraft," *International Organization,* Vol. 42, no. 2 (Spring 1988), pp. 397–426.

46 Kirschner, "The Microfoundations of Economic Sanctions," pp. 32–33.

47 Baldwin, "The Sanctions Debate and the Logic of Choice," pp. 80–107.

exposure of regimes to economic punishments from abroad. It is therefore not surprising that sanctions are attractive to policy makers.

Sanctions are more effective when many international partners implement them, but they can also be imposed unilaterally with comparatively little domestic or international fallout, despite the human suffering to which they often contribute.[48] Indeed, they often serve to demonstrate that a government is acting decisively even when it has no intention of further escalation. British Prime Minister David Lloyd George reportedly said that the sanctions the League of Nations imposed on Italy in 1935 for attacking Abyssinia "came too late to save Abyssinia, but just in the nick of time to save the [British] Government."[49] Sanctions are also relatively easy to apply to a wide range of issues, especially nonmilitary disputes. In contrast to military force, sanctions are seen as an acceptable response to human rights violations, narcotics trafficking, and other problems that do not typically have a major military dimension.[50]

A sanction's degree of severity can be varied, which makes sanctions useful for escalation. As Kirshner notes, the term *sanctions* covers a very broad category of instruments. Sanctions can be placed on aid, assets, finance, trade, and money, all to different effect.[51] Restrictions on investment, for example, can hinder the development of new commerce, targeting potential entrepreneurs and perhaps eroding support for regime decision makers among key elite groups. Sanctions that are narrow, confined to one sector of the economy, can target particular audiences, but their overall impact is likely to be more limited than that of broad trade sanctions, which are very blunt instruments. Policy makers can tailor sanctions to fit particular coercive strategies and to suit other political exigencies. The United States has placed restrictions on investment and trade with Iran in order to punish Tehran for supporting terrorism. And it has also imposed sanctions on specific Russian companies that have passed sensitive technologies to Iran.

48 See John Mueller and Karl Mueller, "Sanctions of Mass Destruction," *Foreign Affairs,* Vol. 78, no. 3 (May–June 1999), pp. 43–53, for a condemnation of the devastating humanitarian impacts of sanctions.

49 As quoted in Selden, *Economic Sanctions as Instruments of American Foreign Policy*, p. 7.

50 Baldwin, "The Sanctions Debate and the Logic of Choice," p. 95.

51 Kirschner, "The Microfoundations of Economic Sanctions," pp. 47–48.

Many scholars have criticized the overall effectiveness of sanctions.[52] Pape, for example, claims that "economic sanctions have little independent usefulness for pursuit of noneconomic goals."[53] Indeed, sanctions are easy to undermine or counter. But sanctions present even deeper problems for coercive strategy making. As Kirshner posits: "The greatest challenge to sanctions often comes not from the failure of such measures to have an economic effect, but from the failure of that economic effect to translate into the desired political outcome."[54]

Sanctions' ineffectiveness has many causes. During the Cold War, the imposition of sanctions by one side was often offset by an increase in aid by the other.[55] The United States, the major source of exports for Batista's Cuba, cut off trade after Castro took power—a potentially devastating blow. The Soviet Union, however, provided massive aid and offset the loss of Cuba's main market. Today, the United States still finds its efforts undermined by other states willing to fill economic spaces created by U.S. sanctions. Targeted states can also counter the political costs of sanctions by whipping up nationalism. People often accept deprivation in the name of their nation.[56] Sanctions that disrupt trade increase smuggling and may also encourage import substitution, creating constituencies at home that even favor the continuation of sanctions.[57]

Sanctions often have at most a limited impact because money is the ultimate fungible asset. If sanctions are designed to cut off trade to one segment of the economy or to stop the flow of arms to a region, regimes can often use any remaining revenues to offset the pain of sanctions. These efforts can include using the black market to gain the goods in question, diverting investment from unsanctioned sectors to sanctioned ones, using regime assets to placate those hurt directly by sanctions, or

52 For critiques of sanctions, see Pape, "Why Economic Sanctions Do Not Work"; Robert A. Pape, "Why Economic Sanctions *Still* Do Not Work," *International Security*, Vol. 23, no. 1 (Summer 1998), pp. 66–77; and T. Clifton Morgan and Valer L. Schwebach, "Fools Suffer Gladly: The Use of Economic Sanctions in International Crises," *International Studies Quarterly*, Vol. 41, no. 1 (March 1997), pp. 27–50.

53 Pape, "Why Economic Sanctions Do Not Work," p. 93.

54 Kirschner, "The Microfoundations of Economic Sanctions," p. 41.

55 Mueller and Mueller, "Sanctions of Mass Destruction," p. 49.

56 Pape, "Why Economic Sanctions Do Not Work," pp. 106–107.

57 Seldon, *Economic Sanctions as Instruments of American Foreign Policy*, p. 20.

otherwise blunting the impact of sanctions. The Panamanian regime, for example, reacted to a U.S. cutoff of the flow of dollars by paying less important supporters (such as government employees) with a cash substitute while ensuring that the armed forces remained well paid.[58] Sanctions are likely to be more effective when they can leverage existing costs, such as by strengthening rivals to a government, undermining a regime's other international goals, or otherwise imposing political costs that go beyond the immediate economic pain inflicted.[59]

The Iraq experience

The Iraq experience with sanctions merits a close look because it highlights both sanctions' tremendous human and political impacts and their often limited, but nevertheless significant, coercive value. The UN initially imposed sanctions on Iraq as a pressure tactic following the Iraqi invasion of Kuwait. Once the Gulf War ended, the rationale for maintaining sanctions ostensibly shifted to Iraq's WMD programs, though the common perception at the time was that sanctions would continue as long as Saddam remained in power. Under UN Security Council Resolution 687, Iraq was to eliminate all its missile systems, WMD, and associated infrastructure for sanctions to be lifted.[60] The UN also oversaw Iraq's purchases, thereby impeding Baghdad's ability to obtain arms or technologies related to its WMD programs.[61]

The United States supported sanctions to accomplish several goals, including some that are noncoercive. Washington hoped that sanctions would increase dissatisfaction with Saddam's regime, both among the populace at large and within his power base. In addition, Washington believed that Saddam would make concessions to avoid the overall weakening of his country. Finally, sanctions decreased Iraq's military capabilities by denying Saddam access to WMD technologies and conventional military imports. Although this decrease in capabilities

58 Kirschner, "The Microfoundations of Economic Sanctions," p. 52.
59 Blanchard and Ripsman, "Asking the Right Question," pp. 222–224.
60 UN Security Council Resolutions 661, 665, 666, and 678 set the stage for Resolution 687, approving and elaborating on the use of an economic or trade embargo and UN monitoring until Iraqi forces withdrew from Kuwait. Resolution 687 is the basis of post-war sanctions.
61 Mueller and Mueller, "Sanctions of Mass Destruction," p. 49.

largely served brute force purposes, it also offered limited coercive denial benefits by hindering any aggression that Iraq might consider.[62]

Sanctions have been criticized, often quite severely, on humanitarian grounds.[63] Dennis Halliday, the UN official who coordinated the oil-for-food program in Iraq, contends that over 500,000 Iraqi children have died as a result of sanctions.[64] In *Foreign Affairs*, F. Gregory Gause acidly argues that "American policy makers need to recognize that the only 'box' into which sanctions put Iraqis is coffins."[65] The debate over sanctions on Iraq typifies the general debate over sanctions' human cost. John and Karl Mueller note that economic sanctions "may have contributed to more deaths during the post–Cold War era than all weapons of mass destruction throughout history."[66]

Even if the humanitarian impact of sanctions is overstated (or the responsibility for their continuation unduly placed entirely on the sanctioning powers), the political damage stemming from U.S. support for

62 See Daniel Byman and Matthew C. Waxman, *Confronting Iraq: U.S. Policy and the Use of Force Since the Gulf War* (Santa Monica, CA: RAND, 2000), p. 33, for a discussion of U.S. discomfort with sanctions despite their benefits.

63 Critics of sanctions' humanitarian impact in the Iraq case, however, often overlook the oil-for-food program and its countervailing humanitarian effects (or potential effects if properly implemented). While sanctions remain comprehensive, Iraq is allowed to sell oil to purchase food, medicine, and other necessities. This arrangement offsets, in theory at least, much of the suffering of innocent Iraqis. (Anthony Cordesman and Ahmed Hashim, *Iraq: Sanctions and Beyond* [Boulder, CO: Westview Press, 1997], p. 148.)

64 Other UN estimates suggest that Iraq's infant mortality rate more than tripled as a result of sanctions (F. Gregory Gause III, "Saddam's Unwatched Arsenal," *Foreign Affairs*, Vol. 78, no. 3 (May/June 1999), p. 58; and Mueller and Mueller, "Sanctions of Mass Destruction," p. 49). Robert Pape uses the figure of 567,000 in his critique of sanctions (Pape, "Why Economic Sanctions *Still* Do Not Work," p. 76).

65 Gause, "Saddam's Unwatched Arsenal," p. 56.

66 Mueller and Mueller, "Sanctions of Mass Destruction," p. 43. Perhaps it is because instant imagery of bomb victims can be powerfully emotive that collateral damage appears to affect public perceptions more strongly than human suffering from resource deprivations caused by infrastructure attacks or economic sanctions. Mueller and Mueller speculate that "[s]ome of the inattention [to loss of Iraqi lives] may . . . be due to the fact that, in contrast to deaths caused by terrorist bombs, those inflicted by sanctions are dispersed rather than concentrated, and statistical rather than dramatic" (p. 47).

sanctions is real and has hurt the U.S. position in the Arab and Muslim world. Saddam has successfully attributed the collapse in the Iraqi standard of living to sanctions rather than to his regime's policies. By manipulating the access of the media and aid organizations, the Iraqi regime has created a perception throughout the world that thousands of Iraqi children are dying each month as a result of sanctions, ignoring the Baath regime's own activities and the countervailing impact of the oil-for-food arrangement. This perception has generated considerable opposition to sanctions among U.S. allies. In the Arab world, which includes the people of many Gulf allies, sanctions are seen as cruel and senseless, a tool that starves innocent Iraqi children while doing little to Saddam. The perception has also contributed to regional, and to a limited extent U.S. public, disaffection with U.S. policy.[67] These political costs have made it more difficult for the United States to enlist or maintain allied support for military attacks on Iraq, undermining escalation dominance when crises flare.

Given this price, how effective are sanctions in their ostensible purpose: stopping Iraq's WMD development? Clearly, they have not led Saddam to abandon his WMD ambitions. Citing UNSCOM reports that Iraq still retains a good-sized WMD program, Gause argues that while sanctions do impede Iraq's WMD programs, they do so only to a limited extent.[68] But this criticism uses a false baseline, one that underestimates the benefits of sanctions. The true baseline should be Iraq's probable WMD status if sanctions had never been imposed. Most experts estimate that without sanctions, Iraq would have long ago produced several nuclear weapons and an even more extensive biological weapons program.[69] By this standard, the sanctions' impact is considerable. However, this effect is one of brute force, not coercion. Saddam's regime still is committed to building a WMD program; it just has fewer means for doing so.

Yet this restriction of Iraq's WMD programs—and the related impact of sanctions in reducing Iraq's conventional capabilities—does yield benefits of a coercive sort. Ten years after the Gulf War, Iraq's military

67 Byman and Green, *Political Violence and Stability in the States of the Northern Persian Gulf*, p. 27.

68 Gause, "Saddam's Unwatched Arsenal," p. 57.

69 Michael Eisenstadt, *Like a Phoenix from the Ashes? The Future of Iraqi Military Power* (Washington, DC: The Washington Institute for Near East Policy, 1993), p. 39.

remains obsolescent, with key systems in poor repair. Renewed aggression is therefore less likely, and Iraq's capacity to withstand or counter military attacks is weakened. Iraq's air defense has not been able to shoot down coalition aircraft, despite several years of attempts after December 1998. Through sanctions, the United States and its allies have shifted Iraq from considering conventional or WMD-based aggression and facilitated their own use of air strikes or other, more forceful means of coercion.

Are sanctions effective in undermining the regime? Or in squeezing Saddam by angering his key domestic supporters? In general, sanctions have actually strengthened Saddam's grip on power. His regime controls Iraqi food stockpiles and uses them to bolster the regime's control.[70] He has successfully exploited sanctions, using the money he controls through the black market to shore up support among elites, particularly in the military and the secret police. Like despots before him, Saddam has shifted part of the burden of sanctions from his regime to the Iraqi people, particularly those who oppose his rule.[71] The Iraqi experience illustrates the difficulty of targeting sanctions at an authoritarian regime's pressure points. Those with the guns eat first, so the regime and its cronies are often the last to suffer while minority groups and the powerless pay the greater price.[72] Autocratic regimes may be susceptible to sanctions, but their actual vulnerability to them is typically limited.

This discussion suggests that the impact of sanctions is best understood by examining their contribution to U.S. objectives in combination with other instruments rather than in isolation.[73] In the case of Iraq, sanctions' ostensible purpose is to press Iraq to abandon its WMD programs and to remove the current regime—two goals that have met with limited and no success, respectively. Pressure from the sanctions, however, was part of what compelled Saddam to accept weapons inspections in the first place. If weapons inspectors enjoyed any successes

70 Cordesman and Hashim, *Iraq*, p. 143.

71 Gause, "Saddam's Unwatched Arsenal," p. 57. This problem of shifting the impact of sanctions from elites to the people in general is common (see Pape, "Why Economic Sanctions Do Not Work," p. 93).

72 Pape, "Why Economic Sanctions Do Not Work," p. 107.

73 For an attempt to assess various components of U.S. policy toward Iraq in combination, see Daniel Byman, "After the Storm: U.S. Policy Toward Iraq Since 1991," *Political Science Quarterly*, Vol. 115, no. 4 (Winter 2000–2001), pp. 493–516.

(and clearly they did), then sanctions deserve at least some of the credit.[74] And regardless of their coercive effect, sanctions have served a brute force purpose by augmenting containment and hindering Iraq's ability to acquire weapons and technology that could help it build up conventional and unconventional forces.

Evaluating sanctions as a coercive instrument is trickier than it may seem at first. Like the critics of air strikes discussed in Chapter 2, the critics of sanctions wrongly view them as instruments used in isolation and evaluate them with a false, binary view of their effectiveness.[75] An isolated view understates their additive and synergistic effects; a binary evaluation misses how they contribute to changes in behavior (even, at times, making concessions less likely). As the Iraq example illustrates, sanctions can contribute to a broader coercive strategy even though by themselves they may not produce success. In addition, sanctions critics often take the declared or maximal goals of the imposing regime at face value, neglecting how sanctions serve secondary goals or are used to signal commitment and credibility, which are necessary to back up other forms of pressure.[76] Meanwhile, though, sanctions advocates often fail to appreciate that the political and diplomatic fallout from a sanctions policy may complicate coercive strategy making by eroding allied and public support for a hardline stance.

Political isolation

Political isolation can contribute to coercion, particularly when it augments more muscular instruments, but in general its impact when used alone is limited. Political isolation is used more frequently than

74 Rogers, "Using Economic Sanctions to Control Regional Conflicts," p. 60.

75 Pape, for example, explicitly notes that he is not examining whether economic pressure can enhance force (Pape, "Why Economic Sanctions Do Not Work," p. 92).

76 David Rowe, for example, uses the commonly criticized "failure" of an oil embargo on Rhodesia as an example of this problem. He notes that while the oil embargo did not directly bring majority rule to Rhodesia—its explicit purpose—it did demonstrate British commitment to this goal, aiding London's diplomacy in general and helping to keep the British commonwealth secure. (David M. Rowe, "Economic Sanctions Do Work: Economic Statecraft and the Oil Embargo of Rhodesia," *Security Studies,* Vol. 9, no. 1–2 [Autumn 1999–Winter 2000], pp. 283–285.)

any other form of coercion. States constantly exchange diplomatic demarches; resolutions that condemn narcotics trafficking, terrorism, human rights abuses, and other unwanted behavior; and other forms of political protest. Such efforts to politically isolate invariably accompany any use of military force. The United States has tried to isolate Saddam's Iraq, post-revolutionary Iran, Milosevic's Serbia, Cedras's Haiti, Panama's Noriega, and other opponents as part of its overall campaign to coerce these regimes.

Political isolation is attractive to policy makers for several reasons. First, it is a low-cost tool. When compared with air strikes or even sanctions, it demands little and carries little risk. Second, political isolation is often a necessary condition for more-forceful types of pressure. Gaining international and domestic support for military strikes, for example, is difficult if the adversary maintains close relations with the coercer's allies or other major states, or maintains an image of legitimacy among the coercer's domestic constituencies.

The more-direct and more-immediate costs imposed by isolation, however, matter only insofar as the elites or populace of a country care about their international reputation. This is not always insignificant. Many analysts credit international pressure as a source of the South African regime's decision to end apartheid.[77] Yet for some regimes, such as those of Iraq and North Korea, the goodwill of the international community has never been a goal of the leadership, elites, or population in general. Isolation by itself seldom touches a pressure point. Indeed, international opprobrium can strengthen a regime. The revolutionary regime in Iran, for example, tried to use international outrage over its policies as proof of its revolutionary bona fides and as a means to deflect growing popular concern over the country's stagnating economy.

Because of its limited capacity to impose direct and immediate costs, political isolation often seems a mere slap on the wrist. Indeed, diplomatic demarches, UN resolutions, and other forms of political pressure are often used as a substitute for, rather than an augmentation of, more-forceful diplomacy when the coercer lacks a willingness to escalate.

But isolation can play a major role in offsetting an adversary's strategy for victory, particularly by neutralizing the adversary's options for counter-coercion. Many (if not most) adversaries rely on their military forces to achieve their ambitions, and political isolation does little to

77 See Lindsay Michie Eades, *The End of Apartheid in South Africa* (Westport, CT: Greenwood Press, 1999).

negate that military capability directly. However, if an adversary can disrupt a coalition arrayed against it, forge a new alliance with a foe of the coercing power, or otherwise raise the political stakes, it may push the coercer to back down and withdraw its threat. Political isolation can block these countermoves.

Isolation of Serbia during the Kosovo campaign—when combined with an air campaign and the threat of a ground invasion—played a key role in Milosevic's decision to concede. Serbia attempted and failed to win Russian support for its cause.[78] If Serbia had won strong Russian support, it would have gained a means of resistance and diplomatic escalation. The price to NATO of continued war in Kosovo would have meant alienating a great power on the edge of Europe. Initially, Russia pressed NATO to end the bombing as a prelude to a diplomatic settlement and, even in late May 1999, publicly touted its opposition to NATO.[79] Milosevic probably looked at Russia's rhetorical support and condemnation of the NATO campaign as an indication that Moscow would champion Belgrade's cause in the international arena. But while Russia opposed NATO's air war and complicated the subsequent occupation of Kosovo, it never sided firmly with Serbia. As the bombing campaign continued, Russian envoy Viktor Chernomyrdin even acted as NATO's de facto envoy, pressing Milosevic to yield to NATO.[80] The timing of Milosevic's capitulation suggests the importance of this factor: NATO had long offered conditions similar to those ultimately accepted by Milosevic, but Russia's lack of support had not been clear until this point. Lieutenant General Michael Jackson, NATO's commander in Kosovo, concluded that Russia's decision to back NATO's position on June 3 "was the single event that appeared to me to have the greatest significance in ending the war."[81] A key lesson is that an instrument may have immense use for coercion when

78 Posen, "The War for Kosovo," pp. 51–52.
79 See Viktor Chernomyrdin, "Impossible to Talk Peace with Bombs Falling," *Washington Post*, May 27, 1999, p. A39.
80 David R. Sands, "U.S. and Russia Patch Up Relations," *Washington Times*, June 25, 1999, p. A1.
81 As quoted in Andrew Gilligan, "Russia, Not Bombs, Brought End to War in Kosovo Says Jackson," *London Sunday Telegraph*, August 1, 1999, p. 1. General Wesley Clark also refers to Serbia's "isolation" as a major factor in Milosevic's ultimate decision to concede ("Interview: General Wesley Clark").

combined with other instruments—even though its immediate, visible impact seems negligible—because it may cut off adversary countermoves.

SUPPORT FOR AN INSURGENCY

Backing an insurgency is another common means of placing coercive pressure on an adversary.[82] During the Cold War, the United States supported Tibetans fighting Chinese communists, tribal groups in Laos during Vietnam, the Nicaraguan contras, the Afghan *mujahedin*, and the Kurds in Iraq from 1972–1975 (among many others), all in an attempt to coerce pro-Soviet regimes. The Soviets likewise supported proxies around the globe. In the years preceding and immediately following the collapse of the Soviet Union, Russia worked with opposition minorities in Georgia and Moldova, giving them military aid to resist central government control.[83] In the developing world, Rwanda has

82 Support for an insurgency can serve other goals as well. It can be used to defeat a foe through brute force, make an occupation more costly, or tie down adversary forces—all of which hinder a foe's overall power and effectiveness, as well as producing limited coercive benefits. Insurgencies by themselves can seldom topple a regime through outright military victory, as adversary leaders almost always outgun insurgent forces. Moreover, the same formidable security apparati that guarantee the leader's personal security also maintain superb intelligence, making it difficult for insurgents to organize in new areas and attract defectors. The best result is often a bloody standstill, with no hope of victory by either side. Nevertheless, the pain that insurgencies inflict can be so overwhelming that adversary regimes are forced to make concessions. For a review of counterinsurgency doctrine, see D. Michael Shafer, *Deadly Paradigms: The Failure of U.S. Counterinsurgency Policy* (Princeton, NJ: Princeton University Press, 1988).

83 Information on Russian involvement in the conflicts in Georgia and Moldova is meager. See "Georgia: Against the Odds," August 14, 1993, and "Georgia: Tricked and Abandoned," October 2, 1993, *The Economist*, for reporting on Russian involvement in the fighting in Abkhazia and South Ossetia. For Moldova, see V. Solonar, "Hatred and Fear on Both Banks of the Dniester," *New Times International*, no. 14 (April 1992), pp. 8–9; and William Crowther, "Moldova After Independence," *Current History*, no. 93 (October 1994), pp. 342–347. Information on the conflict in Abkhazia (Georgia) is extremely scarce. A description of the issues and the region's politics can be found in Neal Ascherson, *Black Sea* (New York: Hill and Wang, 1995), pp. 244–256.

recently supported fighters in Congo, Pakistan backs militants in Indian Kashmir, and Iran supports opposition movements in Iraq, all with the purpose of placing coercive pressure on rival regional powers.

During the Cold War, insurgents were often used to weaken hostile governments and as a potential stalking horse for the supporting power. Since the end of the Cold War, the use of insurgencies has remained an inviting approach. Although the Cold War rivalry that led the United States to back anticommunist movements is gone, U.S. casualty sensitivity has prompted planners and policy makers to seek strategies that avoid putting U.S. personnel directly in harm's way. An insurgency offers a threat on the ground that costs the United States relatively little in terms of lives or dollars.

Some coercive strategies exploit insurgencies to deny adversaries military victory. The United States provided money, training, and weapons—including sophisticated and easy-to-use Stinger missiles—to the Afghans. U.S. assistance strengthened the *mujahedin* considerably and made it difficult for the Soviet Union to pacify the country. The protracted struggle ultimately spurred Moscow to pull out its forces.[84]

The cost of waging internal war can create unbearable popular and elite pressure on a regime to make concessions. Although the United States wanted to change the Sandinista regime in Nicaragua, U.S. training, funding, and equipping of the contras during the 1980s were primarily intended as coercion: to force Managua to stop supporting revolutionaries in El Salvador and elsewhere in Central America.[85] Even though the contras lacked the heavy equipment and forces to defeat the Sandinistas in battle, their continued viability—and the human, monetary, and diplomatic costs of war—eventually forced the Sandinista leadership to make major concessions.[86] The simultaneous decline in Soviet support also increased incentives to come to the bargaining table. In August 1987, the Sandinistas agreed to a peace

84 For overviews, see Robert M. Gates, *From the Shadows* (New York: Simon and Schuster, 1996), pp. 183–374; and Peter W. Rodman, *More Precious Than Peace* (New York: Charles Scribner's Sons, 1994), pp. 197–221 and 324–357.

85 George Shultz, *Turmoil and Triumph* (New York: Scribner's, 1993, p. 426). This effort complemented the Contadora diplomatic process, which sought similar ends. The idea was that the United States would abandon its support for the contras if the Sandinistas would agree to stop supporting insurgency and to remove foreign advisors from their country.

86 Hosmer, *Operations to Remove Enemy Leaders*.

plan: in exchange for an end to U.S. support for the contras, Managua would cut ties to the Soviets and hold elections (in which they were ultimately defeated).

Support for insurgencies can, like other coercive instruments, backfire by strengthening an adversary regime's hand. Foreign involvement in an insurgency can at times delegitimate the movement, allowing an unpopular regime to tap nationalism and brand its enemies traitors in the pay of foreigners. Iraq's support for the Mujahedin-e Khalq (MEK), an Islamic and Marxist organization opposed to the clerical regime in Iran, is but one example of the dangers of supporting an insurgency. Although the MEK often proved successful on a tactical level, killing leading regime figures and otherwise disrupting politics in Iran, its ties to Iraq discredited the movement and enabled the clerical regime to strengthen its control over Iran in the name of combating terrorism. The regime emerged stronger from its confrontation, less likely to bow to Iraqi pressure.[87]

Like sanctions, support for insurgencies often carries political and diplomatic costs for the coercer, and the political price of achieving escalation dominance even with a successful insurgency may be high. U.S. support for the contras, for example, generated criticism at home and abroad because of their often-poor human rights record. The U.S. Congress placed limits on funding and on the types of activities the United States could support and required the Reagan administration to sacrifice considerable political capital to get even limited aid through.

Unlike the control offered by some of the other instruments discussed in this chapter, control over insurgencies is likely to be indirect and incomplete. Hence, the effects of strategies based on insurgency support may be wildly unpredictable in the medium and long term. Although the *mujahedin* and the United States worked together during the Cold War, Afghanistan has proven a haven for terrorists since the Soviet departure, many of whom operate against the United States and its allies. In Kosovo, the Kosovo Liberation Army (KLA) was in many ways a very unattractive ally for NATO, with many of its leaders linked to un-

87 For more on MEK operations against the regime and how the regime responded by consolidating its power, see Ervand Abrahamian, *The Iranian Mojahedin* (New Haven, CT: Yale University Press, 1989), pp. 206–223.

democratic ideologies and the drug trade.[88] NATO's goal of creating regional stability also required that the KLA's strength not swell so much that it undermined post-operation political settlement efforts. NATO therefore had to walk a careful line of providing enough support to prop up the KLA against Serbian forces but not fortifying the KLA so much that it would become an aggressor once a NATO-Serbian agreement was reached. (Indeed, the latter scenario has to some degree occurred since the end of the air war.)

In contrast to precision air strikes or even sanctions, support for insurgencies often has a long-lasting impact, in addition simply to political and diplomatic fallout, that goes beyond the immediate crisis. The coercer often does not control the insurgency that it funds or arms, which can lead to unintended brutalities or the spread of a civil war. The coercer may pull out its backing, but the insurgency it created can live on.

COMBINATIONS

Coercers seldom rely exclusively on one instrument at a time. Coercive instruments may complement each other and, as noted in Chapter 2 and earlier in this chapter, some of them always provide an implicit, background threat even if the probability that they will be unleashed is seen as low by the adversary.

Also as previously mentioned, combining coercive instruments offers both additive and synergistic effects. Air strikes and sanctions, for example, together can threaten more pain than the simple sum of what they threaten individually. And that combined threat may become even more potent if combined with, say, support for an insurgency, even if the insurgency is quite weak. In such a case, the adversary might find itself with its hands tied by sanctions, unable to defend itself indefinitely from both air attacks and internal disorder, and, with its resources spread thin, powerless to threaten escalation of its own.

The successful NATO coercion of the Bosnian Serbs in 1995 illustrates the powerful impact of combining coercive instruments. For several years, the Bosnian Serbs had ignored UN ultimata, continuing their war against Croats and Bosnian Muslims. The region had long suffered

88 Chris Hedges, "Kosovo's Next Masters?" *Foreign Affairs*, Vol. 79, no. 3 (May/June 1999), pp. 24–42.

from a range of economic sanctions that limited its trade and access to foreign goods, particularly military supplies. These sanctions fostered popular disgruntlement in Serbia and Serb-populated parts of Bosnia, though not enough to change regime policy. In September 1995, NATO launched Operation Deliberate Force, a series of limited attacks on Bosnian Serb command and control assets and infrastructure targets. NATO's air strikes not only hurt the Bosnian Serbs directly, but also posed the risk that Bosnian Muslim and Croat forces would make further advances at the Serbs' expense. Recent Muslim and Croat battlefield successes, particularly the Croat offensives against the Serbs in western Slavonia and in the Krajina, forced the Serbs to consider that defiance of the UN might lead to defeat at the hands of their enemies rather than just to further air strikes. U.S. air strikes complemented the local military balance and exposed vulnerabilities in Serb defensive capabilities.[89]

NATO's coercive threats may have also served the Serb leadership, helping it reduce the otherwise possibly prohibitive audience costs of concessions. Bowing to the will of the hated and despised Croats and Muslims would have carried tremendous political risks for Serb leaders. Caving in the face of pressure from the world's only superpower and its European allies was both more understandable and more acceptable.

By itself, the damage Deliberate Force inflicted was limited, particularly when compared with the costs the Serbs incurred as part of their overall campaign against Croatia and Bosnia. U.S. air strikes, however, left Serb forces open to attacks by Croat and Muslim forces—a ground threat that was augmented by a deliberate U.S. policy of overlooking violations of sanctions on military transfers to Croatia and Bosnia. As one post–Deliberate Force analysis concludes: "Hitting communication nodes, weapons and ammunition storage areas, and lines of communication took away Serb mobility and did not allow them to respond to

89 Although the use of air power to augment indigenous forces is rare, its frequency may increase in the coming years. Because air power is a relatively low-cost, low-casualty option for the United States, and because air power's effectiveness is magnified greatly when combined with ground operations, the mix of U.S. air and local allies' ground forces will prove attractive. Local allies will become more effective fighters due to U.S. air support, while the United States will not risk large numbers of casualties or long-term commitment.

. . . offensives elsewhere in Bosnia."[90] The result was a formidable coercive punch.

The bombing of North Korea during the Korean War also highlights the synergistic effects of using several coercive instruments simultaneously. Pape argues that the risk posed by the U.S. atomic arsenal, not strategic bombing, was what pushed Pyongyang to the bargaining table.[91] But separating the nuclear from the strategic bombing threats for analytic purposes loses track of how these two, in tandem, reinforce each other. Air power destroyed North Korean and Chinese fielded forces and logistics and demolished North Korean industrial complexes. North Korea and China did retain the ability to continue military operations, but U.S. air attacks made doing so more costly. When combined with the threat of atomic strikes, the costs of continuing fruitless conventional operations increased further. The combination of these instruments—industrial bombing and nuclear threats—may have been greater than the sum of the parts: escalating conventional air attacks may have bolstered the credibility of U.S. atomic threats by showcasing Washington's willingness to devastate North Korea's population and industrial base.[92] Had the United States not escalated with its conventional forces, the credibility of the nuclear threat would have been low.

Because of the additive and synergistic effects of the various instruments, rating their relative values is difficult if not impossible. Was it the continuing, if limited, pain of air strikes that forced Serb leaders to come to the negotiating table in 1995? Or was it the Croat and Bosnian ground offensives? Both, of course, entered into Serb calculations to some degree. And what was it that affected Chinese and North Korean decision making? Losses inflicted by the U.S. Army and Marines on the battlefield? the pain of strategic bombing? or the threat of nuclear use? All three played a role, each adding to and reinforcing the other.[93]

90 Michael O. Beale, "Bombs over Bosnia: The Role of Airpower in Bosnia-Herzogovina," master's thesis, School of Advanced Airpower Studies, 1997, p. 37.

91 Pape, *Bombing to Win*, pp. 141–142.

92 See Robert F. Futrell, *The United States Air Force in Korea, 1950–1953* (Washington, DC: Office of Air Force History, 1983), for a detailed account of the air campaign in Korea. A superb account of Chinese decision making is Bin Yu, "What China Learned from Its 'Forgotten War' in Korea," *Strategic Review* (Summer 1998), pp. 4–16.

93 It is often difficult for the coercer to correctly focus its threat because the military instruments available are not capable of precisely communicating

At times, to be sure, combining instruments can also undermine coercive pressure: the addition of one instrument may disrupt the potency or credibility of other, simultaneous threats. If a coercive strategy depends heavily on political isolation or allied backing for military actions, supporting an insurgency may prove counterproductive. Many states that would support the isolation of a rogue regime may oppose fomenting rebellion because of the additional suffering involved in fueling a civil war, because of their own opposition to the insurgency in question, because of broader concerns about regional stability, or because they fear it will encourage restive minorities of their own. Backing an insurgency thus might result in a loss of allied support critical to maintaining comprehensive sanctions or conducting air strikes. Or imposing sanctions might undercut regional support for the use of force if their humanitarian effects erode diplomatic support for aggressive coercion policies—as they seem to have in the case of Iraq. Of course, coercive strategies are just one facet of foreign policy, so some compromises may be necessary—even if they diminish coercive pressure—to align coercive threats with broader foreign policy goals.

CONCLUSION

Assessing a coercive instrument alone offers insights into its value for coercion, but the conclusion reached must take into account the fact that various weak or limited instruments, when used together, can play important roles in coercive strategies. There is no best coercive instrument. The optimal choice depends on the alternatives available to the coercer, the nature of the adversary, and possible synergies and additive effects.

This chapter's focus on the coercive effectiveness of various instruments should not obscure the fact that policy makers usually consider more than sheer effectiveness when making decisions about which instrument to use. As David Baldwin argues, the stakes involved and the

the coercer's intentions. For example, because civilian and military targets are often collocated, a bomb on a military headquarters may be viewed as an attempt to encourage members of the military to carry out a coup, a way to deny military victory, or, if the attack kills numerous civilians, an attempt to create popular unrest. The same attack could plausibly be intended to trigger several coercive mechanisms, and the adversary might miscalculate the threat it faces if it resists further.

costs of the instrument to the coercer also determine which (if any) instrument is chosen.[94] As discussed further in Part II, domestic politics and coalition concerns usually shape all aspects of a coercive strategy. The instrument that might be most effective at targeting adversary pressure points is often discarded because its use would find little support among the coercer's citizens, policy elite, and allies or might involve too many risks or sacrifices on the part of the coercing power.

Many coercive instruments can also serve brute force purposes, and policy makers often strive to coerce and diminish their adversary simultaneously. Air strikes against military forces, for example, may convince an adversary that it cannot gain victory—a coercive effect. But they may also degrade an adversary's overall offensive and defensive capabilities, making it easier to defeat them even if the adversary leadership will not concede—a brute force effect. This chapter focused on the coercive impact of various instruments. Policy makers, however, also must take into account the brute force impact of these instruments when judging their overall value for foreign policy.

Coercing powers must also recognize when it is appropriate *not* to use an instrument. As noted throughout Part I, an instrument can fail, and it can also backfire. Policy makers must recognize that while coercive instruments are usually additive or even synergistic in their effects, at times the use of one instrument may undermine the effectiveness of another. The undermining can be immediate—continued sanctions on Iraq make it harder to generate support for allied air strikes in the region—or it can be more insidious. And the failure of an instrument in one instance can undermine the credibility of similar threats in the future.

94 Baldwin, "The Sanctions Debate and the Logic of Choice," p. 90.

Part Two

The Context of Coercion Today

The context of coercion today

To be successful, coercive strategy making must recognize the context in which a strategy will operate. Part I discussed how to begin thinking about coercion. Successful coercion, however, depends on far more than simply understanding the nature of success, the instruments used, and the coercive mechanism that will be triggered. Analysts and policy makers must also recognize the constraints facing the United States and its allies when they conduct coercive military operations in the world today.

The nature of the post–Cold War world is a topic of constant dispute, and one that will not be resolved in this book. Nevertheless, the current era has several salient characteristics. First, the domestic political factors that shape and limit U.S. policy differ from those of the Cold War era. Second, the United States almost always conducts operations as part of a multinational coalition rather than unilaterally. Third, many of the U.S. operations are humanitarian and involve confrontations with nonstate actors. Fourth, the United States may face a WMD-armed opponent, but the threat from that opponent is likely to differ significantly from the threat once posed by the Soviet Union. An appreciation of each of these factors must be integrated into coercive strategy making.

The unity of purpose that shaped the U.S. public and elite's perspectives on intervention during the Cold War is largely absent today. Until the fall of the Berlin Wall in 1989, U.S. interventions from Guatemala to Korea—to say nothing of regular standoffs over Berlin—commanded general support in the name of containing international communism and countering Soviet power. Absent such an overriding goal, the U.S. domestic consensus has fragmented. Most confrontations involve humanitarian concerns as well as traditional, national strategic ambitions, but they tend to be viewed as lower-stakes contests, leading to significant restrictions on the types of missions and levels of force used to carry them out. Adversaries often exploit perceived U.S. hesitation and limited resolve to halt campaigns.

The United States often pursues coercive strategies as part of a multinational coalition, and that places U.S. decision makers in a dilemma. On the one hand, coalition building enhances the potency and credibility of coercive threats by shoring up domestic political support, combining military and economic resources from various coalition members, and helping to isolate the adversary. On the other hand, coalition building may erode that potency and credibility, as decision makers try to accommodate the sometimes conflicting priorities of various coalition members with respect to the use of force. To the extent that coalition maintenance is critical, or is seen as critical through the adversary's eyes, to overall U.S. strategic interests, coalition busting becomes a tempting countermove for adversaries.

During the 1990s, the United States intervened on a number of occasions for humanitarian reasons, sending troops to the Balkans, northern Iraq, Somalia, and elsewhere to succor refugees, feed the hungry, and otherwise alleviate suffering. These crises have their own dynamics. U.S. resolve is often limited at best, while many of the warlords and communal militias on the ground are highly motivated; and the United States often strives to maintain impartiality, limiting its ability to respond to potential threats. Moreover, the United States typically confronts nonstate actors in these crises, which are often harder to target and less likely to implement any agreements than are state actors. As a result, U.S. decision makers may have difficulty forging domestic and international consensus behind the use of force, which limits the available military options, whereas the adversary may have great incentive to turn to or escalate the use of force.

Humanitarian intervention represents the low end of the spectrum, but the United States also needs to rethink the strategic context at the high end. Although the threat of nuclear annihilation has receded, many regional adversaries are acquiring (or may soon acquire) a range of nuclear, chemical, and biological weapons. Such WMD may give adversaries a means for countering the vast U.S. conventional superiority and offsetting U.S. regional influence. Indeed, the greater the margin of U.S. conventional superiority, the larger the incentive for potential adversaries to acquire WMD. Regional adversaries, in contrast to the Soviet Union during the Cold War, may use WMD to back up regional aggression as well as to deter the United States. There will also be other key distinctions between these adversaries and the Soviet Union—for example, different size arsenals and different types of command and control arrangements. In contrast to many of the other possible post–Cold War crises, a WMD-related crisis would involve a high-stakes mission. Nevertheless, adversaries may still feel they can manipulate U.S. domestic and allied sentiment to halt or reverse a coercion campaign.

The following discussion of domestic politics, coalitions, mission types, and adversary capabilities is only a first step. Narcoterrorism, the spread of disease, the difficulties of globalization, and other present and emerging challenges are shaping the use of force and will continue to do so in the future. This book does not address many of the emerging challenges. Nevertheless, the following discussion provides a useful starting point for understanding how the more timeless factors identified in Part I must be understood in today's world.

5

Domestic politics and coercion

The U.S. political process creates tight constraints on military threats and operations—constraints that may significantly offset the United States' vast military superiority over any rival. U.S. adversaries are frequently authoritarian regimes that exercise strong control over their legislatures, judiciary, and press and prevent challenges to their authority through a mixture of political suasion and repressive tactics. Adversary regimes have typically created closed societies that maximize political freedom of action for leaders and minimize political accountability to others. By contrast, political leaders in the United States contend with domestic political pressures, constitutional and legal restrictions, and media scrutiny, all of which increase the need for U.S. leaders to justify their uses of force.

Domestic political pressures, especially those stemming from sensitivity to U.S. military casualties and to adversary civilian suffering, restrict military options. These sensitivities are not lost on adversaries. Believing that the U.S. public harbors these sensitivities—and that U.S. policy making is heavily influenced by public attitudes and concerns—adversaries may discount the credibility of U.S. military threats. And once U.S. military threats are carried out or military intervention begins, adversaries are likely to adopt counterstrategies designed to exploit perceived U.S. public attitudes.

A common theme running through debates about U.S. public support for military operations concerns the relationship between public sensibilities and national strategic stakes. According to the prevailing view, the public prefers, for example, multilateral action over unilateral action but is more willing to go it alone if vital U.S. interests are directly threatened. Similarly, the public is sensitive to U.S. casualties and civilian suffering brought about by U.S. actions, but that sensitivity declines as stakes rise. Many empirical studies, as well as common sense, support this view.

Yet this view sometimes overlooks a critical point: most U.S. crises have recently been, and will continue to be in the near future, relatively low-stakes (as compared to, say, the Persian Gulf War or U.S.-Soviet flare-ups at the height of the Cold War). Moreover, while this view recognizes that public pressure affects the conduct and outcome of each operation, it fails to appreciate that an operation's outcome informs the public and creates expectations about the way conflict is and will be handled by U.S. and allied forces. The lessons of Vietnam and Lebanon influenced the U.S. approach to the Gulf War, just as surely as allied operations in Bosnia and Kosovo will influence the U.S. approach in the next crisis. There is a feedback cycle in which military operations affect future political pressures that then in turn affect military operations.

Of course, sometimes U.S. public policy preferences will facilitate rather than undermine coercive threats. In considering military operations against Iraq in the years since the Gulf War, for example, U.S. administrations have seen high public support for robust U.S. responses to Iraqi provocations. For example, when President Clinton launched Operation Desert Fox in December 1998 in response to Iraqi intransigence over weapons inspection, about three-quarters of the public approved,[1] and if anything, the Clinton administration was more often criticized for not threatening or for using too little force.[2] Often, however, policy preferences limit forceful options, and perceptions abroad of U.S. policy preferences may cause observers to doubt U.S. resolve to resort to those options. As elaborated in the following sections, the challenge U.S. policy makers often face in building coercive strategies that are in line with public policy preferences and attitudes is how to use instruments to proper effect within the tight constraints generated by those preferences and attitudes.[3]

1 Marjorie Connelly, "Wide U.S. Support for Air Strikes," *New York Times*, December 18, 1998, p. A26.

2 Byman and Waxman, *Confronting Iraq*, pp. xv–xvi.

3 In speaking about domestic politics and public sensitivities, we mean to include both mass politics as well as the views of the policy elite. Of course, the views of elites and the public at large often diverge on many issues, including those related to the use of force. Often, elite consensus matters much more for initial decision making, while gaining the support of the public at large is necessary only when operations are costly or risk large

An appreciation of how domestic political constraints affect U.S. military threats is critical to understanding the mixed U.S. success record in recent decades and the problems the United States will face in the coming ones. This chapter focuses on three sets of constraints on U.S. coercion: the need to justify force, casualty sensitivity, and sensitivity to adversary civilian suffering. Each set limits U.S. decision makers' choices of coercive mechanisms and instruments. In addition, adversaries often exploit these constraints, further reducing the United States' ability to threaten or apply force.

JUSTIFYING FORCE

The U.S. public generally insists that any coercive military operation be fought for a purpose that it can agree with and support. Discussion often focuses on whether that purpose should be framed in terms of morality or of national interest. Recent experience, however, suggests that this dichotomy is false: the public typically insists on both and fails to distinguish between the two in many cases.[4]

Even coercive campaigns motivated by relatively stark national interest will labor under domestic constraints similar to those for operations conceived of purely for humanitarian aims. In the lead-up to the Persian Gulf War in 1990, the Bush administration struggled to define the purpose of the war in terms the public could accept. The original geostrategic justification, framed largely in terms of energy security, failed to arouse much popular enthusiasm. The next explanation, that Iraq's aggression affronted international law, was framed in moral terms; it too fell short of inspiring the nation to great sacrifices. Only when the Bush administration managed to depict Saddam Husayn as

numbers of soldiers. Yet this distinction often blurs a far more complex reality: elites often are able to influence public opinion to a great degree, while at times public opinion restricts the very range of the elite debate. For a review, see David Skidmore and Valerie Hudson, eds., *The Limits of State Autonomy: Societal Groups and Foreign Policy Formulation* (Boulder, CO: Westview Press, 1993); and Joe Hagan and Jerel Rosati, eds., *Foreign Policy Restructuring: How Governments Respond to Global Change,* (Columbia, SC: University of South Carolina Press, 1994).

4 Jeremy Shapiro and Matthew Waxman, "Domestic Constraints on the Use of Air Power," in *Strategic Appraisal: Aerospace Power in the 21st Century*, Zalmay Khalilzad and Jeremy Shapiro, eds. (Santa Monica, CA: RAND, 2001).

evil and genocidal *and* portray his possession of WMD as a threat to U.S. national interests was the public finally engaged and supportive.[5]

Actions that seem motivated solely by moral purposes will inevitably be presented to the public with a veneer of national interest that must be reflected in the campaign. For example, during the Haiti intervention in 1994, an operation often plausibly asserted to have little national interest component,[6] the Clinton administration maintained that U.S. interests demanded the support of democracy and the protection of human rights in the Caribbean.[7]

This sort of manipulation of U.S. interests and justifications by political leaders has important implications for the design of U.S. coercive strategies. For one, the means used and the measures of effectiveness established typically follow from the ends publicly announced by the political leadership. If the ostensible purpose of a military operation is to save lives, military planning may be constrained to choices of instruments and mechanisms that do not entail substantial adversary civilian suffering. If the purpose is to end ethnic cleansing, measures of effectiveness that count tanks destroyed will fail to sustain public support.

The U.S. public will also want to see any military campaigns as conforming to international legal norms and its own collective sense of morality, in terms of both the decision to launch military operations and the way operations are conducted. In this regard, international law serves as an imperfect reflection of contemporary morality and an impeachable arbiter of the morality of any action. Actions that appear to violate international law acquire an extra burden to justify themselves in moral terms. The U.S. public is generally more supportive of operations that involve a U.S. contribution to the collective self-defense of a friend or ally than of operations involving internal interventions.[8] This

5 On this issue, see John Mueller, *Policy and Opinion in the Gulf War* (Chicago: University of Chicago Press, 1994).

6 For an example, see Michael Mandelbaum, "Foreign Policy as Social Work," *Foreign Affairs,* Vol. 75, no. 1 (January/February 1996), p. 16.

7 See William J. Clinton, "Remarks by the President in Television Address to the Nation," September 14, 1994, http://www.pub.whitehouse.gov/uri-res/I2R?urn:pdi://oma.eop.gov.us/1994/9/15/6.text.1 (accessed on March 14, 2000).

8 On this point, see Bruce W. Jentleson, "The Pretty Prudent Public: Post–Cold War American Public Opinion on the Use of Military Force," *International Studies Quarterly*, no. 36 (1992), pp. 49–74; and Bruce W. Jentleson and Rebecca Britton, "Still Pretty Prudent: Post–Cold War

differentiation may stem partly from beliefs in the messiness of civil wars, but it also probably stems from the relative ease with which stopping external aggression maps onto widespread notions of certain state actions being right or wrong.

For similar reasons, the support of the U.S. public and U.S. policy makers for military force typically rises if military force is seen as an option of last resort—that is, if that nonforceful options have been given a chance.[9] Again, part of this tendency may be attributable to pragmatic rather than ethical concerns. For instance, it is natural for the public and policy makers alike to be drawn to options short of force that may obviate difficult choices about placing U.S. service members, diplomatic relations, and other interests at risk. One implication is that decision makers may choose coercive strategies that are optimal in terms of domestic politics but suboptimal in terms of sheer potency of threat.

A public preference for multilateralism is reflected in the common U.S. practice of conducting coercive operations alongside allies or coalition partners. This is the subject of the next chapter, so we do not discuss here how coalition building bolsters or undermines coercive threats. It must be noted, however, that like the other political policy preferences discussed in this chapter, the U.S. preference for multilateral action may severely limit options in a crisis as policy makers strive to forge strategies within the tight bounds of many intersecting (or at times not intersecting) policy preferences.

U.S. CASUALTY SENSITIVITY

U.S. military operations today are typically planned and conducted with high sensitivity to potential U.S. casualties. Policy makers and military planners generally fear that U.S. casualties will, or at least might, erode support for sustained operations. Fears about U.S. casualties form critical inputs to decisions about whether to intervene militarily in

American Public Opinion on the Use of Military Force," *Journal of Conflict Resolution*, Vol. 42, no. 4 (August 1998), pp. 395–417.

9 U.S. public support for going to war with Iraq rose after sanctions were given time to work and after the UN Security Council voted to set a deadline for Iraq to withdraw. Andrew Kohut and Robert C. Toth, "Arms and the People," *Foreign Affairs,* Vol. 73, no. 6 (November/December 1994), pp. 48–49.

a crisis at all; once U.S. forces are used, operations are often designed to provide high levels of protection for U.S. forces, and military decision making is heavily risk averse.

Until the Gulf War, commentators cast American casualty sensitivity as part of the "Vietnam syndrome"—a lingering legacy of a particular intervention gone awry at terrible human cost. Contrary to the predictions of those who saw Desert Storm as putting the Vietnam experience to rest, the relatively low U.S. death total in Desert Storm only raised public expectations of bloodless foreign policy and fed perceptions among policy makers that the public had softened in this regard. The further erosion of already fragile U.S. public support that followed the October 1993 deaths of 18 U.S. servicemen in Mogadishu evinced the strong pull that U.S. casualties can exert on policy. The extended deployment of U.S. ground forces to enforce the Dayton peace accords in the former Yugoslavia only confirms this tendency: unlike the troops of other NATO partners, U.S. troops patrol in convoys and avoid actions likely to provoke hostile responses from local factions.[10]

In part because of perceived casualty sensitivity, U.S. foreign policy also exhibits a tendency to choose military instruments that do not require putting U.S. personnel in harm's way any more than necessary. A long-standing tenet of the "American way of war" has been a reliance on materiel over manpower, high-technology over low-tech mass.[11] The heavy reliance on the vast U.S. technological superiority, featuring in particular modern stealth and precision-guidance systems, has contributed to what Eliot Cohen has dubbed "the mystique of U.S. air power."[12] Such high-technology instruments not only provide sufficient target discrimination to satisfy the public's demand for minimizing civilian suffering; they also allow U.S. forces to bring massive firepower to bear without placing significant numbers of (or, in the case of cruise missiles, without placing any) U.S. personnel in danger.[13] The use of cruise missiles to attack suspected terrorist targets in Afghanistan in

10 Edith M. Lederer, "Tuzla Off Limits to Off-Duty Troops," *Detroit News*, February 20, 1997, p. A12.

11 Russell F. Weigley, *The American Way of War: A History of United States Military Strategy and Policy* (New York: Macmillan, 1973).

12 Cohen, "The Mystique of U.S. Air Power."

13 The apparent downing of an F-16 by Bosnian Serb forces in 1995 and an F-117 by Serbian forces in 1999 attests that U.S. forces remain at least somewhat vulnerable even to older generations of anti-aircraft defenses.

August 1998 and their threatened use against Iraqi forces in November 1998 reflect this tendency, which can prevail even at the expense of predictably degraded strategic effectiveness.[14]

American and NATO officials widely hailed the use of air strikes during the 1999 Kosovo crisis as a success, as Serbian President Milosevic accepted allied demands to pull back his military forces and negotiated an international contingent on the ground to monitor compliance. These results obscure, however, what the debate behind the potential use of force, particularly the reluctance by U.S. officials to advocate operations that would put U.S. troops at risk, portends for future coercive strategies and how adversaries may counter them. As NATO threatened air strikes, Clinton administration officials failed to reach consensus on what types of military forces the United States would commit, with Secretary of Defense William Cohen openly expressing his recommendation that the United States not insert ground forces. This reluctance, at the same time the United States appeared enthusiastic about air attacks, corroborates recent evidence from the Iraqi weapons inspection crises and the U.S. attacks on suspected terrorist sites that the United States will employ only low-risk, high-technology instruments unless other means are absolutely necessary.

To be sure, casualty sensitivity, or perceptions of it, is partially a product of the current international security environment. A number of empirical studies have shown that the effects of U.S. casualties on public support depend heavily on a number of contextual factors and other variables. For example, support is likely to erode with casualties when vital interests are not at stake, when the public views victory as unlikely, or when the policy elite do not support the policy.[15] But many U.S. coercive operations *will* involve crises on the periphery—or at least not always at the core—of U.S. strategic interests. And they *will* involve

14 Paul Mann, "Strategists Question U.S. Steadfastness," *Aviation Week and Space Technology*, August 31, 1998, p. 32.

15 For such conclusions and evidence drawn from other studies, see Eric V. Larson, *Casualties and Consensus* (Santa Monica, CA: RAND, 1996). Larson's study shows that in a number of past cases, support for a military operation declined as a function of the log of the casualties, although sensitivity to casualties depended on the perceived benefits of and prospects for success. See also Mueller, *Policy and Opinion in the Gulf War*, which reports empirical findings from previous conflicts to support the theory that U.S. casualties, especially under certain circumstances, erode public support for continued operations (pp. 76–77).

crises where clear-cut victory is hard to define, let alone achieve (an issue elaborated in Chapter 7). As a result, they will likely be conducted in the face of some dissension among the U.S. public and policy elite.

SENSITIVITY TO ADVERSARY CIVILIAN SUFFERING

U.S. military operations are also planned with concern for minimizing adversary civilian deaths, property damage, and other forms of so-called collateral damage, even though policy makers' and public sensitivity to collateral damage, like their sensitivity to U.S. casualties, depends on a number of contextual factors and other variables. During the Vietnam conflict, public disaffection was fueled by perceptions that U.S. and South Vietnamese forces were conducting indiscriminate operations—perceptions that appeared validated by coverage of My Lai and other actual or alleged atrocities—combined with the inability of the United States to demonstrate that it was close to victory.[16] Concern regarding collateral damage is not a hard and fast rule. There was little adverse public reaction to the hundreds of Somali civilian deaths resulting from firefights with U.S. and UN forces, nor has there been an outcry since the Gulf War about Iraqi civilian deaths resulting from air strikes or economic sanctions, even though a majority of the U.S. public at the height of the Gulf War believed that the people of Iraq were innocent of any blame for Saddam Husayn's policies.[17] Nevertheless, significant segments of the U.S. population demonstrate major concern

16 As Guenter Lewy explains, "The impact of the antiwar movement was enhanced by the widely publicized charges of American atrocities and lawlessness. The inability of Washington officials to demonstrate that the Vietnam War was not in fact an indiscriminate bloodbath and did not actually kill more civilians than combatants was a significant factor in the erosion of support for the war" (Guenter Lewy, *America in Vietnam* [New York: Oxford University Press, 1978], p. 434).

17 A *Los Angeles Times* poll (February 15–17, 1991) showed that 60 percent of respondents thought that the people of Iraq were innocent of any blame, while only 32 percent thought that the people of Iraq must share blame for Saddam Husayn's policies (Mueller, *Policy and Opinion in the Gulf War*, p. 316). Likewise, accidental NATO attacks on a Serbian passenger train and Kosovar refugee convoys in the early weeks of Operation Allied Force did not undermine U.S. public support for air strikes. A *USA Today* poll (April 16, 1999) taken shortly after these events showed 61 percent support (approximately equal to the previous week's support), though such incidents began to take a toll as the conflict continued.

for minimizing risk to adversary civilians, and even if other segments are unlikely to withdraw support as collateral damage occurs, general support is likely to be less stable, and hence potentially more vulnerable to unpredictable dips, if military planners and operators do not take steps to minimize such risk. Moreover, as with U.S. casualties, collateral damage is likely to undermine public support when combined with the perception that U.S. victory is unlikely.[18] The bottom line is that policy makers are wary of authorizing actions posing high risks of significant collateral damage, especially when U.S. vital interests are not immediately threatened.

Political constraints emanating from concern over collateral damage have for the past several decades severely limited planning options during conflicts. During much of the Vietnam conflict, and in every military operation since, political and diplomatic pressures—especially those related to civilian damage and injury—have translated into restrictions on which targets could be struck, as well as when and how.

This is not to say that U.S. forces always operate in perfect accordance with the law of armed conflict. Interpretations of legal obligations and accounts of factual circumstances vary. Moreover, some political pressures push against rather than with the humanitarian goals of the legal regime; while concern about collateral damage may caution tremendous restraint in conducting air operations, concern about force protection, military effectiveness, and even financial expense may cause planners to undervalue civilian costs to operations, arguably beyond legal bounds.[19] Also, curiously, the U.S. public and policy makers appear

18 A survey by the Pew Research Center in May 1999 suggested that public support for NATO air attacks on Yugoslavia decreased because of unintended civilian casualties combined with public concern that the attacks were ineffective (Richard Morin, "Poll Shows Most Americans Want Negotiated Settlement," *Washington Post*, May 18, 1999, p. A18).

19 For a critical account of U.S. targeting policy and practice in the Gulf War, see Middle East Watch, *Needless Deaths in the Gulf War*. For charges of indiscriminate NATO bombing practices in Operation Allied Force, see Jan Battles, "Robinson Hits at Clinical Bombing," *Sunday Times* (London), May 16, 1999, p. 18; Simon Jenkins, "NATO's Moral Morass," *The Times* (London), April 28, 1999; Mark Lawson, "Flattening a Few Broadcasters," *Guardian* (London), April 24, 1999, p. 18; and Fintan O'Toole, "NATO's Actions, Not Just Its Cause, Must Be Moral," *Irish Times*, April 24, 1999, p. 11. It should be noted that such critiques often ignore that alternative, ground options might entail much greater risk to local civilian persons and property.

to show considerably less sensitivity toward adversary civilian suffering that accompanies resource deprivations caused by infrastructure attacks or economic sanctions. Perhaps it is because instant imagery of bomb victims can be powerfully emotive that collateral damage resulting from, say, errant military attacks appears to affect public perceptions more strongly. In their critique of U.S. sanctions policy, John and Karl Mueller speculate that "[s]ome of the inattention [to loss of Iraqi lives] may . . . be due to the fact that, in contrast to deaths caused by terrorist bombs, those inflicted by sanctions are dispersed rather than concentrated, and statistical rather than dramatic."[20]

Targeting restrictions and rules of engagement are the most visible and perhaps important mechanisms through which collateral damage concerns affect operations.[21] In the Vietnam War, the rules of engagement dated December 30, 1971, governing strike aircraft operations specified that "[a]ir attacks directed against known or suspected VC/NVA [enemy] targets in urban areas must preclude unnecessary danger to civilians and destruction of civilian property, and by their nature require greater restrictions than the rules of engagement for less populated areas."[22] These restrictive policies stood in contrast to U.S. bombing practices during the Korean War, where by the end of the conflict U.S. air forces were attempting to compel a favorable settlement through massive bombardment of industrial centers. No doubt, the bombing of North Vietnam also was intended to press Hanoi by destroying the standard of living for urban populations. Urban targets during the later conflict, however, were much more strictly circumscribed.

The difference between the U.S. targeting policies in the two conflicts is certainly attributable in part to the nature of the conflicts and the justification for U.S. involvement. The North Korean invasion in 1950 provided clear grounds for U.S./UN intervention, while the Vietnamese communists' propaganda machine harnessed pervasive media coverage

20 Mueller and Mueller, "Sanctions of Mass Destruction," p. 47.

21 The Defense Department defines *rules of engagement* as directives that delineate the circumstances and limitations under which military forces will initiate and/or continue combat engagement with enemy forces (*Department of Defense Dictionary of Military and Associated Terms*, Joint Chiefs of Staff Publication 1-02 [Washington, DC: Department of Defense, 1994]).

22 Reprinted in W. Michael Reisman and Chris T. Antoniou, *The Laws of War* (New York: Vintage Books, 1994), p. 121.

to exploit doubtful world opinion concerning the legitimacy of U.S. efforts.[23] The Vietnam War marked a turning point in the conduct of U.S. military operations, and the means and methods by which the U.S. armed forces have pursued military objectives since then have come under intense scrutiny at home and abroad.

With strategic options that are likely to directly cause massive civilian casualties largely off the table unless U.S. vital interests are immediately threatened, restrictive rules of engagement at the tactical level are increasingly the locus of a contentious policy and legal debate. A key planning challenge has been to select from among the politically, and legally, acceptable options while still achieving satisfactory levels of military effectiveness within financial and resource limitations.[24] As higher and higher levels of military effectiveness are demanded, the aperture of practicable options becomes smaller and smaller.[25]

During the Gulf War, planners imposed strict rules of engagement on coalition air forces, particularly with regard to engaging urban targets: "To the degree possible and consistent with allowable risk to aircraft and aircrews, aircraft and munitions were selected so that attacks on targets within populated areas would provide the greatest possible accuracy and the least risk to civilian objects and the civilian population."[26] To this end, aircrews attacking targets in populated areas were directed not to drop munitions if they lacked positive target identification.[27] Comparable emphasis on minimizing collateral damage had generated similar restrictions on aircrews during the April 1986 bombing of Libyan terrorist-related targets; the rules of engagement for U.S. pilots required redundant target identification checks, and several aircraft

23 Stephen T. Hosmer, *Constraints on U.S. Strategy in Third World Conflicts* (New York: Crane Russak and Co., 1987), pp. 60–61.

24 J. Ashley Roach (JAGC, U.S. Navy), "Rules of Engagement," *Naval War College Review*, Vol. 36, no. 1 (January/February 1983), pp. 46–55.

25 However, it must be noted that effectiveness and casualty concerns are not entirely independent. For example, the U.S. political leadership may be willing to tolerate higher risk levels of U.S. or enemy civilian casualties as long as they would assure higher levels of effectiveness. And, as explained above, low levels of military effectiveness may erode public tolerance for casualties.

26 U.S. Department of Defense, *Conduct of the Persian Gulf War*, final report to Congress (Washington, DC: Government Printing Office, 1992), p. 612.

27 Ibid.

therefore could not release their bombs.[28] Operation Deliberate Force rules of engagement for U.S. forces over Bosnia stated that "target planning and weapons delivery will include considerations to minimize collateral damage."[29] Ninety-eight percent of all munitions dropped by U.S. aircraft were precision-guided munitions (PGM).[30] The precision and restrictions on targeting probably reduced collateral damage significantly, but they also reduced the overall level of force applied, decreasing the costs inflicted and threatened.

Rules of engagement and targeting restrictions are sometimes subject to major revisions during the course of crises or conflicts. Sometimes they are modified to *expand* targeting options and operational flexibility. The Nixon administration's frustration with unproductive air attacks on North Vietnam led it to remove many of the Johnson administration's limitations, particularly those that circumscribed urban areas. A similar loosening of restrictions took place during Operation Allied Force, as NATO governments allowed military planners greater leeway to attack strategic targets after initial waves of attacks failed to move President Milosevic.[31] Once targeting restrictions loosened, it was easier for the United States in these cases to achieve escalation dominance, because it could more credibly threaten not just a continuation of military strikes but an expansion of their scope or intensity in the absence of settlement.

In many instances, however, and of particular concern to planners of coercive strategies, rules of engagement constrict during operations. While rules of engagement are often restrictive as U.S. operations commence, incidents or claims of excessive collateral damage sometimes generate pressure for even tighter constraints as operations continue. After the North Vietnamese accused the United States of flagrantly attacking civilian areas and causing massive suffering during December 1966 air strikes against railway targets near Hanoi, Washington responded by prohibiting attacks on all targets within 10 nautical miles of

28 W. Hays Parks, "Air War and the Law of War," *Air Force Law Review*, no. 32 (1990), p. 155.

29 Ronald M. Reed, "Chariots of Fire: Rules of Engagement in Operation Deliberate Force, in *Deliberate Force: A Case Study in Effective Campaign Planning*, Robert C. Owen, ed. (Maxwell Air Force Base, AL: Air University Press, 2000), p. 411.

30 Ibid.

31 Tim Butcher and Patrick Bishop, "NATO Admits Air Campaign Failed," *London Daily Telegraph*, July 22, 1999, p. 1.

Hanoi without specific presidential approval.[32] Indeed, of all the recent conflicts involving U.S. forces, the Gulf War involved the highest perceived interests; yet even here, domestic constraints still tightly bound operations. The potential for public support to erode in the face of civilian injury, a potential that is difficult to measure or anticipate accurately, is sometimes enough to drive political decision making.

For military planners trying to translate political constraints into limits on operational decision making, the problem is not just the degree of political restrictions but the unpredictability of support if constraints are violated. One mistake or errant missile can dramatically affect perceived support for an operation. In May 1999, for example, NATO warplanes refrained from attacking targets in Belgrade for several days after accidentally striking the Chinese embassy.[33] Accidents of war, always inevitable, can severely disrupt political support for operations. Planners thus face a tension between conducting effective but risky operations and choosing easily sustained but far more limited types of actions.

U.S. POLITICAL CONSTRAINTS AND ADVERSARY COUNTER-COERCION

Many commentators, especially academics, question the notion that the U.S. public will is fragile and prone to collapse in the face of mounting casualties, whether they be U.S. or foreign. According to Anthony Erdmann, "[R]eports of the demise of the American will have been greatly exaggerated."[34] In this view, the U.S. public is often quite willing to tolerate high levels of costs in terms of both U.S. and adversary civilian casualties.[35] "Students of American power," Walter Russell Mead reminds us, "cannot ignore one of the chief elements of American

32 Hosmer, *Constraints on U.S. Strategy in Third World Conflicts*, p. 61; *The Pentagon Papers: The Defense Department's History of U.S. Decisionmaking in Vietnam* (Gravel edition), Vol. IV (Boston: Beacon Press, 1971), p. 135.

33 Similarly, after a U.S. warplane mistakenly hit a refugee convoy, the previous month's procedures had been modified to require that U.S. aircrews radio for authorization before striking military convoys (Elaine Harden and John M. Broder, "Clinton's War Aims: Win the War, Keep the U.S. Voters Content," *New York Times*, May 22, 1999, p. A1).

34 Andrew P. Erdmann, "The U.S. Presumption of Quick, Costless Wars," *Orbis*, Vol. 43, no. 3 (Summer 1999), p. 374.

35 Kohut and Toth, "Arms and the People," pp. 47–51.

success. The United States over its history has consistently summoned the will and the means to compel its enemies to yield to its demands."[36]

Aside from the undeniable fact that notions of public sensitivity to casualties and suffering affect military policy making in major ways, the features of coercive crises, as opposed to those of other types of crises, render the debate about whether these notions are scientifically valid or not moot or at least less consequential than one might think. Adversaries will design counter-coercive strategies based on their perceptions, accurate or not, of U.S. resolve and U.S. vulnerabilities. Moreover, misperceptions about wavering U.S. resolve may cause adversaries to hold out in the hope that the United States will withdraw its threats in the face of counterthreats. Even if inaccurate, such assessments can doom coercive strategies. It is therefore critical to view U.S. domestic political constraints through the adversary's eyes.

Adversary optimism is a result of the typical features of U.S. coercion as well as the open and contentious nature of the American political process. For instance, adversaries often view casualty sensitivity as a key component of the United States' most vulnerable pressure point: its political will to sustain operations. Ho Chi Minh famously warned the United States: "You can kill ten of my men for every one I kill of yours. But even at those odds, you will lose and I will win."[37] The implication, of course, was that the United States could not maintain a policy in the face of mounting U.S. casualties, even if the adversary was suffering vastly more and U.S. policy makers could plausibly claim to be winning. This assessment probably seemed, to some potential adversaries, validated by the U.S. withdrawal from Vietnam. Saddam Husayn echoed Ho's sentiments prior to the Gulf War, postulating that the United States would be unable to stomach the losses he could inflict in a ground conflict. According to one account:

> Saddam strongly believed that the United States' Achilles' heel was its extreme sensitivity to casualties, and he was determined to exploit this weakness to the full. As he told the American Ambassador to Baghdad, April Glaspie, shortly before the invasion of Kuwait: Yours is a society which cannot accept 10,000 dead in one battle.[38]

36 Walter Russell Mead, "The Jacksonian Tradition," *The National Interest*, no. 58 (Winter 1999), p. 6.

37 Stanley Karnow, *Vietnam: A History* (New York: Penguin, 1997), p. 184.

38 Freedman and Karsh, *The Gulf Conflict*, p. 276.

In retrospect, Saddam may have underestimated U.S. resolve—U.S. planners prepared for upwards of 10,000 casualties in the lead-up to Desert Storm—though the coalition rout left his estimates untested. But clearly the U.S. concern for U.S. casualties remains, especially in the eyes of adversaries, perhaps *the* weak point in an otherwise overpowering military capability.

Saddam's miscalculation illustrates one way in which perceptions of U.S. casualty sensitivity impede coercion: by undermining the credibility of U.S. threats to intervene or escalate. Another way is by encouraging counterstrategies that aim to inflict U.S. casualties and that may create false hopes of quick U.S. withdrawal in adversary decision making.

Adversaries are likely to adopt counterintervention strategies that impose high risks of U.S. casualties. Somali warlord Mohamed Farah Aideed reportedly made this warning to Robert Oakley, the U.S. special envoy to Somalia during the U.S. intervention there: "We have studied Vietnam and Lebanon and know how to get rid of Americans, by killing them so that public opinion will put an end to things."[39] Prior to the Operation Allied Force air campaign, Milosevic appears to have shared previous estimations that U.S. political will would erode as U.S. casualties mounted. As he noted in an interview, NATO is "not willing to sacrifice lives to achieve our surrender. But we are willing to die to defend our rights as an independent sovereign nation."[40] Rhetorically embellished as this statement might have been, Milosevic probably perceived NATO's capacity to sustain pressure on Serbia in the face of casualties to be fragile. Accordingly, Serbia adopted a defensive strategy designed to induce U.S. and allied casualties and, if necessary, to exploit any collateral damage to disrupt alliance cohesion.[41] Milosevic's expectations that U.S. resolve would dissipate upon seeing that his regime planned to hold its ground help explain why he resisted NATO demands for several months in the face of overwhelming military might arrayed against him. The realization that he might lack the ability to inflict casualties on NATO air forces, and possibly on ground forces in

39 As quoted in Barry M. Blechman and Tamara Cofman Wittes, "Defining Moment: The Threat and Use of Force in American Foreign Policy," *Political Science Quarterly*, Vol. 114, no. 1 (Spring 1999), p. 5.

40 United Press International, text of interview with Slobodan Milosevic, April 30, 1999.

41 Posen, "The War for Kosovo," p. 51.

the event of a land assault, probably contributed significantly to his ultimate concessions.[42]

Because of the U.S. penchant for utilizing high-technology instruments involving low personnel danger, adversary options for attacking U.S. forces directly are often limited. In such cases, adversaries are likely to exploit the U.S. concern with actions that place noncombat U.S. or allied personnel at risk. The Bosnian Serbs made use of lightly armed UN peacekeepers and aid workers as hostages to stave off NATO air strikes during the Yugoslav crisis. Their ability to counter-coerce the Western powers became readily apparent in April 1993 when NATO began enforcing the no-fly zone. Although the Serbs issued no specific threats, the UN suspended aid flights the day before the first NATO air patrols for fear of reprisals.[43] On a number of occasions, the Serbs responded to NATO air strikes against military installations by detaining peacekeeping personnel on the ground. In all of these cases, the Serbs threatened the weakest points of the allied effort—the humanitarian assistance and ground personnel—to up the ante and deter immediate follow-up strikes. The use of hostages further indicates that many adversaries are willing to exploit U.S. adherence to legal norms while flagrantly violating those norms themselves. Even without matching the Western powers militarily, the Serbs were able to manipulate the allies' cost-benefit equation with relative ease.

Although the taking of hostages has proven an effective deterrent to U.S. and allied strikes, adversaries may hesitate to execute—as opposed to injure or kill in combat—U.S. or allied personnel for fear of a backlash, thereby negating potentially effective counter-coercive strategies. Adversaries considering this strategy face a dilemma: threatening the lives of American or allied personnel may cause coalition planners to rethink military action, but carrying out such threats may prompt the reverse. Images of UN peacekeepers chained to Serb military vehicles in the face of NATO threats in the summer of 1995, while effective as a deterrent to strikes, further demonized the Serbs in Western eyes. Any deaths that had resulted would likely have generated intense calls for aggressive retribution by NATO, just as earlier deaths of U.S. service members in Somalia and Lebanon had done. Indeed, in both cases the

42 Byman and Waxman, "Kosovo and the Great Air Power Debate," pp. 31–32.

43 Marcus Tanner, "Aid Flights Halt on Eve of No-Fly Patrol," *Independent* (London), April 12, 1993.

United States swiftly overcame its aversion to inflicting casualties on adversary civilian populations when its service members were threatened. The firefight that killed 18 U.S. soldiers in Mogadishu also killed perhaps 1,000 Somalis, and the United States responded to the attacks in Lebanon by shelling Shi'a villages.

Reliance on high-technology military instruments that involve relatively low risk to U.S. personnel carries an additional disadvantage for coercion. Adversaries may be tempted to wait out initial waves of U.S. air or missile attacks, believing that the United States is not committed. The very reliance on high technology validates images of U.S. resolve as fragile. This view is likely to be further reinforced by public debates within the United States about backup plans if initial strikes fail to bring about positive results, with domestic opponents of U.S. military action depicting that scenario as a Vietnam-like quagmire.

Adversary efforts to capitalize on U.S. policy makers' sensitivity to U.S. casualties often take place alongside efforts to capitalize on their similar sensitivity to enemy civilian casualties. Lacking the U.S. degree of commitment to certain international norms or facing strategic, political, and diplomatic pressures very different from those of the United States, adversaries are likely to exploit asymmetrical commitments to reducing civilian suffering. Knowing that U.S. planners and operators will be obliged to verify their target objectives, adversaries can disperse dual-use sites, camouflage military assets, and otherwise hinder U.S. information gathering. Knowing that U.S. planners and operators will avoid incidental civilian losses, adversaries can employ so-called human-shield tactics, commingling military and civilian assets and persons. And knowing that U.S. planners and operators will avoid attacks likely to cause excessive civilian damage, adversaries can manipulate the media to portray exaggerated destruction following attacks.

In adopting these techniques, adversaries hope that the potential for U.S. casualties or political backlash resulting from anticipated collateral damage will deter U.S. intervention. In the event that the United States does intervene, these techniques aim to confront U.S. planners with a dilemma: refrain from attacking certain targets (or attack them only under extremely tight operational restrictions) and risk degraded military effectiveness, or attack them effectively and risk collateral damage or perhaps higher levels of U.S. casualties.

Adversaries' willingness and ability to exploit the extreme U.S. sensitivity to these sorts of accusations often have debilitating effects on coercive strategies. U.S. sensitivity *invites* adversary practices designed to put at risk the very civilians the United States seeks to leave unharmed. The typical U.S. responses to these practices then *reward* them in that the United States places further constraints on its own threats of force. For instance, the United States often responds to charges that it attacked civilian targets—even if the attack was largely the result of the adversary's efforts to collocate civilian and military assets or persons—by restricting its own rules of engagement or placing additional limits on targeting. North Vietnamese allegations of U.S. attacks on Red River Valley dikes caused the Johnson administration to publicly denounce any intention to conduct such strikes. This response ratified the immunity North Vietnamese officials desired for military assets placed near the dikes, and it vindicated the strategy of target commingling and propaganda.

An identical pattern of encouraging and then rewarding strategies based on civilian suffering occurred during the Gulf War. Iraqi leadership placed civilians in the Al Firdos bunker, believed by U.S. intelligence to be a command and control facility. On the night of February 13, 1991, U.S. F-117 strikes destroyed the bunker, killing dozens of civilians, a tragedy that the Iraqis attempted to exploit in the media. The U.S. political leadership took no further chances: attacks on Baghdad were suspended for several days. Thereafter, the Bush administration (which had previously been committed to avoiding the micromanagement of target selection that plagued the Johnson administration's efforts in Vietnam) required that Baghdad targets be cleared beforehand with the Chairman of the Joint Chiefs.[44] This last example of collateral-damage risk aversion is particularly significant because, contrary to the fears of some political and military leaders, the U.S. public's opinion of the air war was actually unmoved by the incident.[45] And

44 Gordon and Trainor, *The Generals' War,* pp. 326–327.

45 A *USA Today* poll on February 15, 1991, reported that, when asked if the shelter bombing changed their support of the war, only 14 percent of respondents answered affirmatively, while 38 percent expressed no change in their support and 41 percent said they were more supportive of the war. Mueller also cites public opinion data showing that a majority of the public, both before and after the bunker incident, thought that the United States was making enough effort to avoid collateral damage (Mueller, *Policy and Opinion in the Gulf War,* pp. 317–319). See also Daniel Byman, Matthew Waxman, and Eric Larson, *Air Power as a Coercive Instrument* (Santa Monica, CA: RAND, 1999). U.S. public

each of these incidents reveals that U.S. decision makers respond to adversary counterstrategies almost as predictably as they create the conditions for such strategies in the first place.

THE ASYMMETRY OF CONSTRAINTS

An adversary's ability to exploit constraints on U.S. operations depends on a number of factors, including its own bases of support, its strategy, and its propaganda capabilities. Some dictatorial regimes, for example, may not depend on popular support. If their people suffer, they have less to fear politically than do democratic leaders, who would soon be voted out of office. Saddam Husayn for many years rejected the UN oil-for-food deal, which permitted limited Iraqi oil exports to purchase essential humanitarian supplies, even though it would have reduced privations among the Iraqi people—he saw popular suffering as a tool for ending Iraq's isolation.[46] The United States, ironically, has proven more sensitive in its actions to the suffering of the Iraqi people than has the Iraqi government.

Adversaries will typically be less constrained than the United States and its allies by international legal norms. In general, the United States benefits from status quo stability and international order while its adversaries are often interested in overturning that order; that is, "[S]ince law is generally a conservative force, it is more likely to be observed by those more content with their lot."[47] Apart from their possible differences from the United States in commitment to international norms and preservation of the international legal regime in general, some adversaries are likely to view the United States, with its vastly superior military technology, as a manipulator of the law of armed conflict for its own benefit. Strategic setting is critical to this analysis: almost any small-scale contingency for the United States is likely to be a major war for an adversary. Conflict with the United States may implicate an adversary's most vital interests and may strain its willingness to remain

opinion is often unpredictable, and the public's aversion to civilian suffering under certain circumstances may by overestimated. However, the U.S. political leadership still tends to expect negative public reactions to civilian suffering and thus behaves in a risk-averse manner.

46 Baram, *Building Toward Crisis*, pp. 65–66.

47 Louis Henkin, *How Nations Behave: Law and Foreign Policy* (New York: Praeger, 1968), p. 49.

bound by international legal rules that at a given time may favor U.S. military dominance, much like the United States might be inclined to cast off legal duties if its own most vital interests were immediately threatened.

Finally, because of asymmetries in media scrutiny and in sensitivity to that scrutiny, many adversary leaderships have greater flexibility than their U.S. counterparts do in taking actions likely to put civilians at risk. Dictatorial regimes typically maintain tight control over media. While manipulating the content of information flowing to its own population, such a regime can also influence the timing and, indirectly, the substance of information disseminated abroad by selectively permitting journalistic inspection.[48] The North Vietnamese were either notoriously obstructive or invitingly supportive of Western television, depending on the situation. Sudan, for years having virtually blacked itself out in the international media, welcomed television crews when the August 1998 cruise missile strike destroyed a pharmaceutical facility in Khartoum. Milosevic displayed a pattern of cracking down on independent media each time crises with the international community flared.[49] During NATO's Operation Allied Force, he shut down independent newspapers and radio stations inside Serbia, used state-run television to stoke nationalist reactions, electronically jammed some U.S. and NATO broadcasts intended for the Serbian populace, and prohibited the Western press from much of Kosovo (while granting it permission to film bombed sites).

Propaganda efforts of this kind have historically affected U.S. policy making, especially when the United States could not effectively counter charges of indiscriminate targeting. During the Rolling Thunder campaign, the North Vietnamese government used U.S. air strikes as propaganda, often with great success in undercutting U.S. coercive pressure. North Vietnamese authorities repeatedly asserted that U.S. air attacks were directed at Red River Valley dikes and were having devastating ef-

48 Of course, U.S. and allied governments may themselves make efforts to "sanitize" coverage of operations, but their degree of censorship is far less than that in most authoritarian regimes. The spread of information technology may reduce the ability of governments to dominate the news in the future.

49 Chris Bird, "Kosovo Crisis: Yugoslav Media Fear Crackdown amid War Fever," *Guardian*, October 8, 1998, p. 15; and Jane Perlez, "Serbia Shuts 2 More Papers, Saying They Created Panic," *New York Times*, October 15, 1998, p. A6.

fects on the local civilian population. These efforts played on U.S. decision makers' fears that such allegations would destroy public and foreign support; concern over this issue caused the Johnson administration to emphasize that these dikes were off limits to campaign planners. These targeting restrictions then gave the North Vietnamese freedom to place anti-aircraft and other military assets at the sites, operationally countering the air campaign.[50]

To be sure, adversary efforts to profit by civilian casualties or U.S. losses often fail and may even backfire if the U.S. and international publics view the adversary leadership as at fault. But even when adversary efforts to exploit collateral damage do not result in a tightening of self-imposed U.S. constraints, they publicly put U.S. policy makers on the defensive and may harden the resolve of adversaries that expect the U.S. will to erode.

CONCLUSION

The U.S. government and military have only limited influence over deeply rooted features of the U.S. polity. Some of the self-imposed U.S. constraints discussed in this chapter result from short- or long-term policy choices, but others reflect deeply entrenched cultural norms and values that have long guided U.S. foreign policy. While recent political and social developments such as the end of the Cold War and real-time media coverage have exacerbated certain political sensitivities, they did not create them. U.S. leaders could spell out interests more precisely, operate more unilaterally, restrict media coverage, and otherwise try to minimize the resulting constraints on military options, but eliminating those constraints—or even reducing them substantially—will prove impossible. A more constructive approach is to recognize the viability of corresponding adversary counter-coercive strategies, take them into account when deciding to use coercive threats, and design coercive campaigns to mitigate the adversary's use of counterstrategies.

50 W. Hays Parks, "Rolling Thunder and the Law of War," *Air University Review*, Vol. 33, no. 2 (January-February 1982), pp. 11–13. The North Vietnamese similarly accused the United States of flagrantly attacking civilian areas and causing massive suffering during December 1966 air strikes against railway targets near Hanoi (Hosmer, *Constraints on U.S. Strategy in Third World Conflicts*, p. 61; and *The Pentagon Papers*, p. 135).

This approach means recognizing that the United States often finds itself caught in increasingly problematic feedback cycles. For example, adversary efforts to exploit collateral damage (both real and fabricated) resulting from U.S. attacks may prompt the United States to restrict its own future efforts, both undermining the potency of its follow-on threats and encouraging further exploitation of suffering. The following chapter describes a similar phenomenon with respect to U.S. preferences for multilateral military actions: adversary responses that cause rifts in coalitions may prompt the United States to alter its approach in an effort to repair the rupture, thus emboldening the adversary to direct further efforts at coalition splitting.

Political strategies obviously must aim at building stronger domestic and international backing for coercive operations. Because of the dynamic nature of coercive contests, public support, adversary resolve, and levels of available force will vary as crises unfold due to the moves and countermoves of each side. As a result, successful propagation of coercive strategies will require building sufficiently high and robust domestic and international support so that sudden drops in that support do not induce U.S. policy makers to respond with the very restrictions on coercive strikes that the adversaries seek. It will also require projecting an image of resolve to adversaries, because even excessive optimism by an adversary that its counter-coercive strategy will succeed can cause U.S. coercion to fail or, at least, can raise the costs of U.S. success substantially.

6

Coercion and coalitions

The United States seldom coerces alone. It usually uses force as part of a multinational coalition, sharing the dangers and burdens of operations with NATO allies, friends in the region, and other partners. Coalitions place decision makers in a dilemma. On the one hand, coalition building enhances the potency and credibility of coercive threats by shoring up the coercer's domestic political support, combining the military and economic resources of various coalition members, and helping to isolate the adversary. On the other hand, coalition building may erode the coercer's potency and credibility as decision makers try to accommodate the sometimes conflicting priorities of various coalition members with respect to the use of force. To the extent that coalition maintenance is critical to overall U.S. strategic interests or is seen as such by the adversary, coalition busting becomes a tempting countermove for adversaries.

Consider the U.S. and UN experience in Somalia. What began as a humanitarian operation to care for starving Somalis slowly expanded in scope as local Somali warlords refused to allow UN and humanitarian groups to feed the hungry. On December 3, 1992, the UN Security Council passed Resolution 794 authorizing "all necessary means to establish as soon as possible a secure environment for humanitarian relief operations in Somalia." The United Task Force, which employed minimal force, was replaced in May 1993 by the UN Operation in Somalia (UNOSOM II), which had a more ambitious mandate that included accommodating reconciliation and power sharing as well as supporting the overall relief effort. In addition to working through the UN, U.S. forces also worked with Pakistan, Morocco, Italy, and other allies—a total of 28 states were involved in various stages of the operation.

The presence of so many countries demonstrated the near-universal support for feeding the starving Somalis and ending the strife there. But the price for this support was high. Coalition members did not agree on the operational objectives or the instruments to be used. After forces of warlord Mohammad Farah Aideed ambushed Pakistani peacekeepers, the United States tried to capture or kill him through a series of raids and strikes. The Italian contingent, important in Somalia given Italy's colonial legacy in the region, opposed this heavy-handed approach, favoring instead a less forceful role for the UN in support of negotiations and humanitarian relief. Following gunship strikes on Aideed's headquarters, Italy publicly protested the U.S.-led actions and threatened to withdraw its 2,400 troops. Ireland, the Vatican, the Organization of African Unity, and several nongovernmental organizations (NGOs) involved in the relief effort also questioned the U.S. response. As Italy and other members condemned the anti-Aideed stance, UN leadership asked Italy to remove the commander of its peacekeeping contingent, General Bruno Loi, charging him with refusal to obey orders from the overall UN military commander in Somalia because Loi and other members of the Italian contingent had negotiated unilaterally with supporters of Aideed while the UN tried to isolate him.[1]

Aideed exploited these rifts through small-scale attacks on UN personnel, thereby further feeding Italian opposition. Uncomfortable with the apparent disconnect between the humanitarian purpose of the mission and the overall escalation of violence between peacekeepers and local factions, the UN Security Council revised UNOSOM II's mandate and aborted further UN intervention in interclan conflicts. Soon after, President Clinton called for withdrawal of U.S. forces. Coercive strikes are supposed to alter an adversary's cost-benefit calculus by demonstrating the credible threat of future, increasingly painful costs. In this case, however, the U.S. strikes had precisely the opposite result: they had caused coalition fragmentation, thereby undermining the threat of damage yet to come.

This chapter, like Chapter 5, aims to relate political dynamics *within* the coercer—this time focusing on issues involved in building and sustaining consensus among coalition member states—to strategic dynam-

1 Donatella Lorch, "Disunity Hampering UN Somalia Effort," *New York Times*, July 12, 1993, p. A8.

ics *between* the coercer and the adversary. In addition to having to match mechanisms with instruments appropriately in the abstract, U.S. coercive strategy making must balance diplomatic and other foreign policy priorities with the exigencies of military crises.

After examining why U.S. policy makers typically elect to operate through multinational coalitions and what some advantages of coalition building are for coercion, this chapter explores the limits that coalitions place on the threat or use of force. This analysis is then used to explain how coalition maintenance may undermine escalation dominance and provide adversaries with effective countermoves predicated on widening rifts among coalition partners. The United States will need to enlist partners and establish coalition decision-making structures judiciously if it is to threaten military force effectively while furthering its broader interests vis-à-vis its allies.

WHY COALITIONS?

With few exceptions, all coercive military operations of U.S. forces since the end of World War II have been carried out under the auspices of international organizations or ad hoc collections of interested states. This tendency is likely to continue in the coming decades. For designing coercive strategies, coalition building offers numerous material and political advantages.

By *coalition* we mean a collection of actors cooperating to achieve a common objective. Coalitions include standing bodies (such as NATO) acting as a unit, as well as ad hoc collections of states and other international bodies working together toward a particular goal.[2] Although coalitions differ widely in shape and size, their key attribute with respect to coercive operations is the members' pooling of military, economic, or diplomatic efforts against a common adversary.

Coalitions can bring additional assets to the table. In World War II, Russia provided the majority of the fighting forces, tying down and defeating the bulk of the German Army while the United States and

2 Jack Levy, "Alliance Formation and War Behavior," *Journal of Conflict Resolution*, Vol. 25, no. 3 (September 1981), p. 587; Glenn H. Snyder, *Alliance Politics* (Ithaca: Cornell University Press, 1997), p. 4; and Stephen M. Walt, *The Origins of Alliances* (Ithaca: Cornell University Press, 1987), p. 12.

Britain conducted operations on the Western Front.[3] In Korea and Vietnam, South Korea and South Vietnam contributed far more troops than did the United States—and suffered far more casualties—in efforts to defeat communist regimes.

Although the increasing disparities in skill and equipment between the United States and many allies have diminished the military utility of allied contributions in recent years, coalition partners may bring key assets to the table that prove useful for coercive operations, including additional bases, local access, and diplomatic support.[4] When coalitions are united, coercers are better able to sustain military operations, to defeat enemy forces, and to gather intelligence.[5] Basing and overflight privileges provided by coalition partners may be critical in allowing the United States and its allies to use air power effectively. Deploying and using ground forces requires supply routes, ports and airfields, and other forms of support that are often available only from regional allies. The more states that support the coercion effort, the more likely that the necessary military resources can be provided.

Broad international support allowed for the massive buildup of U.S. ground and air power in 1990–1991, enabling the coalition to decisively overwhelm Iraqi forces during the Gulf War. The erosion of this support by 1998 severely diminished the ability of the United States and its allies to coerce. During the February 1998 inspection crisis, the United States had access to fewer than 40 land-based aircraft for strikes on Iraq, as the 200 or so aircraft deployed in Turkey, Bahrain, and Saudi Arabia were not available due to concerns of the host nations. Deployment of carrier-based aircraft to the region helped make up the lost combat potential, though the aggregate firepower that could be brought

3 Richard Overy's account of the Normandy invasion makes clear how dicey an operation it was, and how much harder it would have been had the Wehrmacht been able to concentrate its forces in France (Overy, *Why the Allies Won*, pp. 134–179).

4 Robert W. Riscassi, "Principles for Coalition Warfare," *Joint Force Quarterly*, no. 1 (Summer 1993), pp. 58–71; and Inis L. Claude, Jr., "The United States and Changing Approaches to National Security and World Order," *Naval War College Review*, Vol. XLVIII, no. 3 (Summer 1995), pp. 49–50.

5 Stephen M. Walt, "Why Alliances Endure or Collapse," *Survival,* Vol. 39, no. 1 (Spring 1997), pp. 157–158. Walt argues that "the primary purpose of most alliances is to combine the member's capabilities in some way" (p. 157).

to bear was substantially reduced, and some specialized capabilities (e.g., stealth fighters and the most sophisticated airborne early warning craft) only operated from land bases. As a result, the United States struck fewer targets and took more risks when it conducted operations. Even more important, coalition rifts probably heartened Saddam Husayn, giving him hope of achieving a political victory.[6]

To put it another way, coalition building may expand the range of effective coercive instruments available to the United States in a given crisis. As noted in Chapter 4, some instruments only create coercive pressure when operated by a coalition, and their effectiveness varies with the breadth and strength of the coalition. Unilateral economic sanctions have proven to be quite ineffective, but once the major economic powers join together, the pain of sanctions can grow acute as the adversary's markets or sources of investment and aid decrease. The same is true of political isolation, which requires wide international consensus to create pressure and preclude the adversary from finding alternative sources of diplomatic support.

Aside from yielding direct military contributions or other support essential to certain coercive instruments, coalition building may produce political benefits at home and abroad that bolster the effectiveness of coercive threats.[7] In this regard, the issues in this chapter are entwined with those of the previous one: domestic politics help drive coalition building, but because they do, coalition busting provides a possible way for adversaries to threaten to erode U.S. domestic support for coercive strategies.

Enlisting the backing and assistance of international partners often solidifies domestic public opinion in favor of forceful crisis intervention. International support lends legitimacy to the political leadership's claims that the operation has a moral purpose. During Operation Allied Force, for example, Clinton administration officials defending the Kosovo campaign repeatedly emphasized that U.S. operations had the support of all the NATO allies and often claimed the support of the entire world community.[8] In addition, the backing of the UN and other

6 See Daniel Byman and Matthew C. Waxman, *Confronting Iraq,* pp. 37–70.
7 Shapiro and Waxman, "Domestic Constraints on the Use of Air Power."
8 A typical example comes from President Clinton himself: "What I have tried to say to the American people is, [the Kosovo campaign] is not some crusade America went off on its own. We've got all of our NATO allies, 19 countries, all believing that is something that needs to be contained and

international organizations strengthens claims that U.S. operations accord with international norms. UN mandates provided the primary justification for the U.S. war against Iraq in 1991 and the operation in Haiti in 1994.[9]

Allied participation also counters criticism that U.S. forces bear a disproportionate share of the burden of solving the world's problems. The U.S. public debate has long been sensitive to the implication that the United States spends more than its allies and risks more of its military personnel. Allied contributions to operations, both financial and military, ease this concern.[10]

Finally, and perhaps most subtly, the presence of allies implicates an entirely different set of interests than those that originally motivated the operation. The presence of international partners can expand the domestic coalition that supports the operation to include the partisans of the ally or alliances involved. For example, by intervening in Kosovo under the auspices of NATO, the U.S. government could reasonably claim that the credibility of NATO was at stake in the operation, thereby helping to win the assent of opinion leaders who saw preserving NATO as an important foreign policy goal even though they questioned the importance of saving Kosovo.

Besides state partners, the United States also seeks to secure international support from nonstate actors. Increasingly, this has come to mean gaining the backing of various international organizations and NGOs that provide relief supplies, monitor human rights violations, offer medical care, or otherwise address humanitarian concerns. These organizations have proven adept at mobilizing international and domes-

reversed" (William J. Clinton, "Remarks by the President to Majority 2000," April 16, 1999, Fairlane Club, Dearborn, Michigan).

9 The absence of that mandate in the 1999 operation in Kosovo presented an important obstacle to securing the support of other nations, and therefore U.S. public support, and helps explain the almost feverish need U.S. policy makers felt to emphasize that the operation was taking place under NATO auspices. On the legality of the NATO operation in Kosovo in the absence of a UN mandate, see Robert Tomes, "Operation Allied Force and the Legal Basis for Humanitarian Interventions," *Parameters*, Vol. XXX, no. 1 (Spring 2000), pp. 38–50.

10 See Andrew Bennett, Joseph Lepgold, and Danny Unger, "Burden-Sharing in the Persian Gulf War," *International Organization,* Vol. 48, no. 1 (Winter 1994), pp. 39–75; and Charles A. Kupchan, "NATO and the Persian Gulf: Examining Intra-Alliance Behavior," *International Organization,* Vol. 42, no. 2 (Spring 1988), pp. 317–346.

tic opinion on issues ranging from the ban on landmines to the international criminal court.[11] Securing the support of these organizations is often difficult in the case of military action, because such organizations generally abhor forceful methods and are critical of U.S. military operations. However, especially in the case of humanitarian intervention, such organizations not only can play an important legitimating function, but also may offer significant local knowledge and capabilities that can aid U.S. humanitarian operations, an issue discussed in more detail in Chapter 7. The U.S government and military have therefore begun to recognize that securing the support of these organizations, though often difficult, is increasingly important for sustaining public support.[12]

LIMITS IMPOSED BY COALITIONS

The material and political benefits of coalition building, while sometimes critical to coercive strategy making, are often offset by implementation problems and new vulnerabilities. Coalition members typically have diverse goals and different preferences, leading the coalition as a whole to adopt positions that often reflect the lowest common denominator rather than more assertive positions. In addition, the shared control and divergent goals inherent to most coalitions often make decision making cumbersome and responses weak, damaging the credibility of threats. The differing goals of coalition members further damage the coalition's credibility and may increase the difficulty of sustaining operations. Escalation in particular becomes more difficult due to the burdensome rules of engagement that coalitions often employ. Moreover, although coalition building may help solidify domestic political support for coercive strategies, as discussed in the previous chapters, it also opens up new adversary counterstrategies to which the United States often finds itself vulnerable.

11 See P. J. Simmons, "Leaning to Live with NGOs," *Foreign Policy,* no. 112 (Fall 1998), pp. 82–96.

12 Daniel L. Byman, Ian Lesser, Bruce Pirnie, Cheryl Benard, and Matthew Waxman, *Strengthening the Partnership: Military Cooperation with Relief Agencies* (Santa Monica, CA: RAND, 2000); and Kevin M. Kennedy, "The Relationship Between the Military and Humanitarian Organizations in Operation Restore Hope," in *Lessons from Somalia,* Walter Clarke and Jeffrey Herbst, eds. (Boulder, CO: Westview Press, 1997), pp. 99–117.

Lack of common agenda

The inevitable lack of harmony among members' interests complicates coalition operations. Different grand strategies, distinct threat perceptions, third-party relations, and a host of other influences cause members' policy preferences to diverge, despite initial commitment to a common goal. According to Alexander George and William Simons:

> Coercive diplomacy is likely to be more difficult to carry out when it is employed by a coalition of states rather than by a single government. Although a coalition brings international pressure to bear on the target of diplomacy and can devote greater resources to the task, the unity and sense of purpose of a coalition may be fragile.[13]

This prediction has been borne out by recent crises and international responses. In the aftermath of the Gulf War, economic motivations reduced French support for a confrontation as France sought to renew trade and financial relations with Iraq. In Somalia, Italian resistance to military assaults reflected a preference for reconciliation with, rather than marginalization of, Aideed's faction. In Bosnia, coalition members constantly squabbled over the type and degree of force and its targets.

Even when coalition members share a common ultimate goal with respect to the adversary, their interests are unlikely to be perfectly aligned. The Clausewitzian notion that military operations reflect political purposes suggests that true coalition effectiveness with regard to the application of force requires harmony of ends. But each state brings to the table its own strategic and political interests. In addition, each state's military is guided by its own set of doctrines and preferences for certain military instruments. During the course of coercive operations, individual members' interests may further diverge as a result of certain contingencies or different vulnerabilities. For instance, if a particular contingent suffers disproportionate casualties, a member may seek a change in policy to limit further harm, contrary to the preferences of other coalition members.

The international response to the Yugoslav conflict in the early 1990s illustrates how coalition objectives may begin to diverge, even if members ostensibly share a common objective with regard to the adversary. A variety of factors combined to limit the potency of threats available to the coalition, despite an abundance of assets at its disposal.

13 George and Simons, *The Limits of Coercive Diplomacy*, p. 273.

U.S. and European operational perspectives split because only the European partners had troops on the ground as part of UNPROFOR, the UN mission. While the United States generally favored a more robust coercive air strategy, Britain and France resisted, fearing that air strikes would provoke the Serbs into retaliatory responses against vulnerable coalition ground personnel. The flouting of the no-fly zone over Bosnia ultimately produced Resolution 816, which authorized more active measures by NATO to control flights, and NATO began Operation Deny Flight. However, divergent demands of major coalition members resulted in a compromise agreement stipulating severe restrictions on NATO's use of force: NATO aircraft could not strike preemptively at airfields or pursue violating aircraft into Serbian airspace. The most forceful NATO response as part of Operation Deny Flight occurred in November 1994, when Serb forces launched air strikes from the Ubdina air base in Croatia to support ground operations in Bihac. In designing a response, however, NATO planners bowed to UN demands for restraint and avoided hitting Serb planes at the airfield. Thus, for most of its existence, the no-fly zone was honored only in the breach. It was not until the summer of 1995, just prior to Operation Deliberate Force, that coalition members' objectives and preferences converged sufficiently to allow for intensive air strikes.

Similar problems plagued post-1991 attempts to coerce Iraq. In January 1993, the United States shot down several Iraqi aircraft and launched air strikes against military targets in response to Iraqi incursions and deployment of anti-aircraft missiles in protected zones. Turkey, which provided key air bases supporting no-fly zone enforcement, worried that an extended conflict could contribute to its own crisis involving separatist Kurds. Arab states, fearing public backlash in response to U.S. military action against a regional power, urged Washington to call off further strikes. The resulting widespread opposition to U.S. military action among coalition partners gave rise to speculation that Saddam Husayn had deliberately incited U.S. reprisals to win Arab support for the lifting of sanctions. Vocal criticism from Gulf War partners may have emboldened Saddam to test the coalition's resolve in 1996, 1997, 1998, and 1999 and convinced him that provocation might be an effective strategy for breaking international efforts to isolate him.[14]

14 Byman and Waxman, *Confronting Iraq*, pp. 48–70.

The erosion of coalition support for coercive air strikes to rein in Iraq was further exposed during the crisis precipitated by Iraq's expulsion of weapons inspectors in late 1997. With the exception of Kuwait, no Arab nation endorsed U.S. military threats in early 1998.[15] Military operations also were more difficult because regional allies did not want the United States flying strike sorties out of their bases. The United States found itself having to choose between employing coercive force in this instance and maintaining coalition support in general. Whereas coalition cohesion itself represented a key asset and may have enhanced coercive threats during Desert Storm/Desert Shield, the divergence of member interests several years later revealed a tradeoff between coalition unity and coercive potency.

Even if coalition members seek the same adversary behavior, they may have different negative objectives—that is, results they seek to avoid—that limit the means by which the coalition can influence the adversary. Arab support for military action against Iraq in early 1998 waned, despite a common desire to contain Iraqi WMD production, because Arab states could not support coercive measures likely to incite domestic opposition. British and French worries of provoking Serb reprisals against their UNPROFOR contingents substantially diluted their nations' support for air strikes, even though they may have supported coercive strategies in principle.[16] In the latter case, European concern for troop vulnerabilities negated one of air power's key attributes: its ability to strike at an adversary without exposing U.S. forces to the dangers inherent to ground operations. U.S. decision making had to account for potential risks to other members' interests in fashioning a coercive strategy.

These challenges for coercion are exacerbated by the fact that coalitions rarely speak with a single voice—each member may also communicate threats or signal messages to the adversary, perhaps in conflicting ways. As noted, coercion is more likely to fail when the adversary doubts the coercer's intentions. Conflicting signals emanating from various coalition members not only can contribute to such doubts, but also may encourage the adversary to comply with some members' demands but not others.

15 Douglas Jehl, "Only One Arab Nation Endorses U.S. Threat of Attack on Iraq," *New York Times*, February 9, 1998, p. A6.

16 Christoph Bertram, "Multilateral Diplomacy and Conflict Resolution," *Survival*, Vol. 37, no. 4 (Winter 1995–1996), p. 74.

A possible solution is for the coalition to issue a single, common threat. This solution, however, creates a lowest common denominator effect: to garner the necessary consensus, the coalition will gravitate toward the most-restrained members' preferences. Take, for example, the January 1994 NATO summit on the Balkans. To paper over differences among the allies, its declaration contained only vague threats of force and singled out only two of the safe areas—Srebrenica and Tuzla—for explicit protection.[17] The result was continued Serb bombardment of other safe areas, such as Sarajevo, culminating the following month with a marketplace explosion that killed 68 people. This lowest common denominator effect emboldens rather than discourages an adversary. For U.S. policy makers, this means that diplomatic efforts to raise that denominator before and during a crisis are crucial to success.

Finally, coalition members may also prefer different points along the same linear spectrum. Consider several such points along a spectrum for the Iraq-Kuwait crisis in February 1991:

(1) Iraq remains intransigent

(2) Iraq agrees to withdraw with minimal concessions

(3) Iraq agrees to withdraw with significant concessions

(4) Iraq agrees to withdraw unconditionally

U.S. efforts to disarm Iraq were nearly derailed because the Soviet Union, while sharing the common desire to see Iraq withdraw, momentarily appeared willing to accept (2) rather than support military action to achieve (3) or (4). A Moscow-sponsored initiative was eventually rejected by the United States and other coalition members, though not without the initiative's threatening to draw away some members' support for military action.[18] Strictly speaking, the Soviet Union was not even a member of the military coalition that arrayed against Iraq. But it wielded influence over coalition decision making similar to that of a

17 Dick A. Leurdijk, *The United Nations and NATO in Former Yugoslavia* (The Hague, Netherlands: Netherlands Atlantic Commission, 1994), pp. 50–51.

18 David Hoffman and Ann Devroy, "Too Many Strings Attached, U.S. Finds," *Washington Post*, February 22, 1991, p. A1.

true coalition member by virtue of its permanent UN Security Council seat and its diplomatic sway over other coalition members.

Shared control

Because both positive interests and negative interests are rarely in perfect harmony, coalition members generally all seek a say in decision making to ensure that their objectives are protected. Even if it takes the lead in forging a coalition, the United States must yield a certain degree of control over the conduct of coercive operations as the price of members' commitment to the coalition. Shared control can offset the difficulties caused by divergent interests, but it creates problems of its own. It reduces the coercer's flexibility, damages credibility, and makes escalation dominance more difficult to attain.

The control retained by member states can take a variety of forms, though usually it will involve a combination of two major types: decision-making input and predecisional agreements. The first type, direct decision-making input, refers to the ability of individual members to shape case-by-case coalition decisions as they arise. In UN operations, the highest military command positions are often filled by representatives of several member nations, ensuring multinational input. Multinational political bodies often retain some control or veto power over strategic- or operational-level military decision making. The result may be a dual- or multiple-key command procedure whereby the chain of command is split to ensure that all military decisions are approved by various leadership bodies.

In Bosnia, the United States and its allies made burdensome command arrangements to ensure that force was threatened and applied only up to a level that the coalition as a whole could support. To ensure that air strikes (both close air support for endangered UNPROFOR troops and air strikes against forces violating UN-protective resolutions) would reflect unanimous coalition support, a dual-key command and control structure governed requests (see Figure 6.1).

Both chains of command shown in the figure had to approve air strikes before they could be launched. Because operational control of NATO's tactical air assets had been delegated down to the director of the Combined Air Operations Center, little coordination within the NATO chain was necessary to approve air strikes. The UN chain, how-

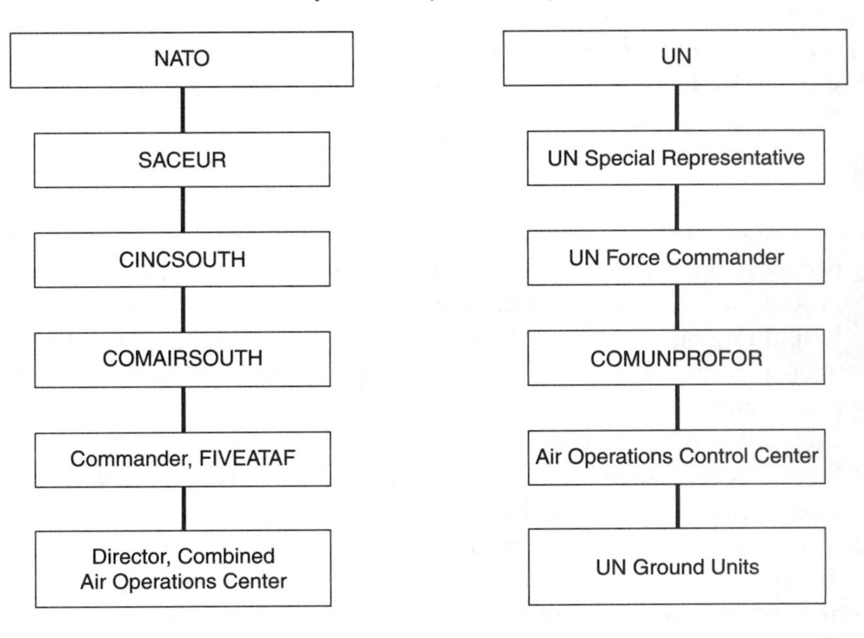

Figure 6.1. Command and Control Structure in Bosnia

ever, was burdensome leading to frequent delays. As Air Marshal Tony Mason remarked:

> [A]mong the characteristics of air power are rapid responsiveness and high speed. It would be difficult to imagine a command and control structure more unwieldy, obstructive and operationally irrelevant to the needs of close air support than those procedures approved by the NATO council.[19]

Although the UN and NATO eventually streamlined their authorization procedures—UN commanders agreed to delegate approval authority to lower levels, such as the UN Force Commander—these problems plagued coalition air operations throughout the conflict.[20] By the time air strikes were authorized, Serb forces had often already achieved their

19 Tony Mason, *Air Power: A Centennial Appraisal* (London: Brasseys, 1994), p. 177.

20 Peter Hunt, "Coalition Warfare: Considerations for the Air Component Commander," master's thesis, School of Advanced Airpower Studies (Air University Press, June 1996), pp. 56–57.

immediate objectives, or the moment to provide endangered UN personnel with close air support had passed.

The second type of retained national control, predecisional agreements, refers to arrangements negotiated in advance of contingencies to limit the actions of coalition forces. Like direct decision-making input, these measures help ensure that the coalition will not act contrary to individual members' interests. In this case, however, there is no need to deliberate on a contingency-by-contingency basis, because the agreements limit coalition options to those that, *ex ante*, are amenable to all members given foreseeable scenarios. These agreements can increase the speed with which force is applied but can decrease that force's flexibility.

At the strategic level, predecisional agreements include legal compacts, such as UN mandates, that might limit the use of force to certain levels or to certain situations (e.g., authorizing coalition reprisals only in response to attacks on designated safe areas). At the tactical level, rules of engagement can restrict the freedom of coalition forces to take certain actions. Negotiating rules of engagement provides a means by which countries providing forces can shape the conduct of coercive operations. Both legal mandates and rules of engagement help alleviate coalition members' anxieties about unwanted escalation. The tradeoff, of course, is that they cap the potential level of force and yield escalatory initiative to the adversary, who thus can more effectively dictate the level of force to be used.

Given that ambiguity is an inherent part of both politics and war, compacts and rules of engagement often limit the effectiveness of coercion. Situations that are not covered by existing rules of engagement can be a recipe either for paralysis or for dissension if one member acts without the authorization of others. In addition, the constant bickering over interpretation of the rules of engagement may send conflicting signals to the adversary.

Most coalition operations involve both direct input and predecisional agreements, both of which can severely restrict coercive operations. Members' demands for decision-making input often conflict with unity of command—a key tenet of U.S. military doctrine and that of many of its allies. Predecisional agreements, while useful for guaranteeing member support, restrict the potency and flexibility of coercive instruments. States are unlikely to turn national forces entirely over to foreign command. At the same time, the costs of reaching consensus on individual contingencies as they arise are prohibitively high, providing the impetus to negotiate mutually amenable agreements on the use of force in advance.

Rules of engagement are designed to prevent the use of excessive force while minimizing unnecessary passivity—a balance that coalition dynamics often upset. Rules of engagement seek to authorize sufficient force so that commanders can respond to threats without appearing weak and thus inviting further attack. They also seek to prevent commanders from using excessive force, escalating beyond political objectives. There is, of course, a tradeoff between these competing concerns, and rules of engagement are generally formulated to balance the two as well as possible.[21] The coalition context exacerbates the tension between these worries. Each coalition partner brings its own concerns regarding possible contingencies; even if the partners share the same ultimate objective for a common adversary, individual members may have differing negative objectives. This often produces a greater collective concern with undesired escalation than many individual members acting alone might sense. As a result, the possible set of effective rules of engagement may narrow to the point where there is no intersection between sets of rules that assure adequate military options in response to contingencies and sets of rules that preclude excessive escalation.

The difficulties of balancing escalation with control in coalition contexts surfaced during the Bosnia crisis in the UN-issued rules of engagement governing UNPROFOR ground operations. These orders required, among other things,

- Specific approval for offensive operations
- Minimum force necessary
- No retaliation and use of weapons only as a last resort
- Ceasing fire when an opponent ceases fire

Note that these rules allowed the adversary to avoid unintended escalation and to test the threshold of UNPROFOR military response. The Serbs could take the initiative and fire only when conditions were advantageous, halting whenever they faced a superior force. The rigid limits on force in this case stemmed partly from the particular demands

21 Scott D. Sagan, "Rules of Engagement," *Security Studies*, Vol. 1, no. 1 (Autumn 1991), p. 88.

of peacekeeping operations (an issue discussed in more detail in the following chapter) but also from the need to secure consensus among coalition members.[22] The same problems plagued rules of engagement governing close air support for endangered UNPROFOR personnel. Those rules required that hostile forces still be engaged when NATO aircraft arrived. On a number of occasions, this rule allowed Serb forces to harass peacekeeping forces and then pull back before NATO aircraft could respond.

Coalitions and escalation dominance

The various reasons cited for the U.S. preference for operating within coalitions may at times enhance the U.S. ability to threaten and inflict costs and therefore may contribute to escalation dominance. Two strong states are more threatening, in the abstract, than one. But while a large coalition may bring more aggregate firepower to the table than a small one or the United States alone can, the difficulties of maintaining coalition unity can actually erode much of that potential leverage.

Coalition rules of engagement are generally inflexible: once the parameters are set, they are difficult to expand when contingencies arise. At the strategic level, coalition members demand input into any major changes made in rules of engagement. UN Security Council mandates are subject to permanent-member vetoes, meaning that such members can prevent additional authorizations of force even if they supported initial, lower-level authorizations. Although the U.S. political and military leadership can recalibrate rules of engagement during the course of a crisis or conflict as circumstances change, coordinating coalition rules of engagement is a far more laborious process. This inflexibility undermines the credible threat of escalation.

Similar limits on escalation appear in coalition command and control schemes. One danger is that in an effort to alleviate coalition members' concerns, the organization as a whole will adopt command and control arrangements that negate the effectiveness of air power or other instruments as potent escalatory options, as was the case in the dual-key arrangement employed by NATO and the UN in the former Yugoslavia

22 Bruce Berkowitz, "Rules of Engagement for UN Peacekeeping Forces in Bosnia," *Orbis*, Vol. 38, no. 4 (Fall 1994), pp. 635–646.

during Deny Flight operations. The dual-key approach can be applied to other uses of force as well, limiting their flexibility and robustness.

Coalition concerns also affect the target choices of campaign planners, who must anticipate the political worries of partners and protect allies from an adversary's escalation. During Desert Storm, for example, the United States limited attacks on Baghdad in part due to the real and anticipated complaints of other major powers, such as the Soviet Union and other UN Security Council members.[23] As important as this restraint was the need to use massive sorties for the "Scud hunt." The United States feared that a failure to show Israel that the coalition was expending considerable resources on finding and destroying Iraqi Scuds would lead Israel to enter the war itself. Fearing that Israeli intervention would drive Arab partners to withdraw support, planners directed some 1,500 sorties against Scud targets, roughly 3.6 percent of the total number of sorties flown.[24] This last example is an interesting one in that given the political landscape of the crisis, the United States found itself acceding to demands of a regional ally in order to keep that ally *out of* the conflict. The point, however, remains the same: the need to divert resources to operations designed to protect or placate coalition partners may trade off with options for escalation.

Finally, a coercer that chooses to operate through a coalition will often find itself faced with a choice between maintaining coalition support and resorting to new, higher levels of force. In the Korean War, U.S. planners felt strong allied pressure to avoid destroying certain targets or resorting to atomic weapons use, which Britain feared might prompt Soviet reprisals.[25] Likewise, the United States could likely not have loosened the rules of engagement for forces in Somalia following the Mogadishu firefight in the summer of 1993 without permanently

23 William M. Arkin, "Baghdad: The Urban Sanctuary in Desert Storm?" *Air Power Journal,* Vol. 10, no. 1 (Spring 1997), p. 12.

24 Keaney and Cohen, *Gulf War Air Power Survey*, pp. 83–84.

25 Futrell, *The United States Air Force in Korea,* p. 453; and McGeorge Bundy, *Danger and Survival* (New York: Random House, 1988), pp. 242–243. A 1953 U.S. State Department report analyzing atomic options concluded that the United States "would be faced with choosing directly between Allied and neutral support and the pursuit of the proposed course of action" (U.S. Department of State, Policy Planning Staff, *Foreign Relations of the United States 1952–1954*, political annex prepared June 4, 1953, Vol. XV, Part 1 [Washington, DC: Government Printing Office, 1984], p. 1140).

alienating certain key coalition members. Even the ultimately successful U.S. strikes against Serb targets in 1995 engendered criticism from U.S. NATO allies, which decried unauthorized escalation.[26] Perhaps ironically, then, coalition disagreements over how to respond to Iraq's refusal to admit U.S. weapons inspectors in November 1997 seemed to put *upward* pressure on the potential level of coercive force. While most Arab nations publicly condemned the U.S. stance of military threats, their governments intimated that they could not support limited, punitive strikes but would welcome robust strikes that incapacitated Saddam Husayn's regime.[27] But this exception proves the more general rule that coalition maintenance often trades off with policy options—indeed, if international support is sufficiently important to decision makers, it may drive them—in designing coercive strategies.

Diminished credibility

In theory, coalition building can enhance credibility by increasing aggregate potential force behind a threat and by reducing the likelihood that the coercer will back down for fear of diplomatic backlash. Somewhat counterintuitively, however, coalition threats are often less credible than those of states acting alone because adversaries recognize that members' interests diverge and see the lumbering coalition decision-making process as proof of limited commitment.

Fluctuating levels of coalition unity and national support among coalition members for military action resulted in a recurrent pattern of Serb violations of NATO ultimata during the Yugoslav conflict. In July 1993, Serb forces were on the brink of capturing Mount Igman, the last high ground surrounding Sarajevo held by the Bosnian Muslims. On August 2, the NATO allies threatened Serb forces with air strikes unless they ceased interference with humanitarian relief to the city. Although Serb forces pulled back in the face of NATO threats, strangulation of the city resumed and culminated in the February 1994 marketplace massacre, which renewed coalition support for forceful action. Again, Serb forces pulled back in the face of a coalition ultimatum, though this time with the help of a Russian-brokered bargain. Later that year, em-

26 Holbrooke, *To End a War*, p. 143.
27 John Lancaster, "Egypt Urges Diplomacy, Not Force, in U.S.-Iraq Dispute," *Washington Post*, November 14, 1997, p. A35.

phasis shifted to Gorazde, where Serb forces mounted an assault on the town despite the threat of air strikes. Although NATO close air support was called in ostensibly to protect UNPROFOR troops, a rift emerged between NATO and the UN because the UN refused to "turn its key" for further air strikes even though the Serbs had not completely complied with allied demands.[28] The eroding credibility of UN-NATO threats precipitated a crisis in the summer of 1995. Serb forces overran the safe area of Srebrenica in July 1995, despite the presence of a Dutch peacekeeping contingent and pin-prick air strikes. Complicated decision-making procedures contributed to delays in providing adequate air support to Dutch units. The Zepa safe area fell shortly after. NATO threats made the Serbs hesitate, but the lack of NATO credibility in responding quickly to Serbian aggression led the Serbs to press on with their attacks.

When coercion is conducted through a coalition, success or failure is likely to be a function of coalition unity. A more unified coalition will be better able to withstand the application of higher levels of force and will also be likely to issue more-credible threats, to use force more decisively, and to better withstand adversary countermeasures. But coercion is not a static process that occurs only at a single instant. Coercion occurs over time. The United States and its partners used the threat of air strikes against the Bosnian Serbs over the course of several years. During that time, coalition unity itself varied, with important implications for coercion. Following the February 1994 Sarajevo shelling attack, NATO members achieved sufficient unity to issue a credible threat of air strikes, leading to the withdrawal of Serb artillery. This outcome contrasts sharply with the previous month's events, when differences of opinion among NATO partners surfaced at the January NATO summit, leading to intensified Serb strangulation of the city.[29] A variance in coalition unity is likely to encourage an adversary's belief that it can outlast the coercer.

Just as coalition unity can alter the efficacy of coercive threats, coercive threats and strikes can dramatically affect coalition unity. The use of coercive instruments over time can expose divergent preferences,

28 Leurdijk, *The United Nations and NATO in Former Yugoslavia*, pp. 41–66.

29 Douglas Jehl, "In NATO Talks, Bosnia Sets off a Sharp Debate," *New York Times*, January 11, 1994, p. A1; and Leurdijk, *The United Nations and NATO in Former Yugoslavia*, pp. 50–51.

both positive and negative, and the distinct vulnerabilities of coalition members. The result often resembles a feedback cycle: a round of air strikes that has positive effects on adversary behavior may rally coalition support, making the threat of future rounds of strikes more credible, which then further alters adversary behavior in a positive direction. In contrast, a round of strikes that causes negative results (for instance, one that prompts reprisals) may cause coalition rifts, further emboldening the adversary, and so on.

COALITIONS AND ADVERSARY COUNTER-COERCION

Adversaries try to shatter coalitions. Because the United States exhibits a strong desire to conduct coercive operations as part of a coalition rather than unilaterally, coalition unity itself becomes a vulnerable center of gravity that adversaries attempt to exploit. Exploiting coalition fissures offers adversaries an enticing counter-coercive strategy, one that can serve as an alternative or adjunct to combating threats of force directly.

Adversary efforts to undermine coalition unity can deleteriously affect coercive strategies in several ways. First, to the extent that the coalition itself amplifies the coercive threat by aggregating military assets, rupturing coalition relations can cause the withdrawal of members' contributions, which are particularly important when access and basing are limited. Second, adversaries can undercut the domestic support that comes from the additional legitimacy that international backing brings. Third, internal coalition disagreements can force those members most willing to escalate to lower their own ceilings of practicable force in order to repair coalition unity.

The potentially disruptive effects that coalition fissures can have on coercion mean that even relatively minor actions by an adversary can have enormous strategic implications. Low-level violence in Somalia by Aideed's faction following air assaults on his compounds caused a major crisis within the coalition. Iraqi Scud attacks against Israel in the Gulf War were, from a purely military standpoint, of minimal effectiveness. Had they succeeded in drawing Israel into the war or induced Israel to launch its own defensive air strikes, however, Arab support for the war might have collapsed, threatening overall U.S. regional strategy.

Besides simply waiting out waves of air attacks in the expectation that allied support would wane in the face of mounting costs and casualties, Milosevic tried to undermine the anti-Serb coalition by encouraging Russian support for a cease-fire on Serbia's terms and welcoming a German peace delegation to Belgrade.[30] Diplomatic rifts among NATO partners and public disagreement over strategy probably contributed to his defiance by fostering his beliefs that NATO unity would collapse. Greece and Italy opposed an extended bombing campaign and pushed for limits on the damage inflicted, France resisted plans for a naval blockade, and Germany opposed any consideration of ground options.[31]

Toward the end of the campaign, Milosevic's hopes of disrupting NATO unity seemed to evaporate as the allies' shift in momentum toward possible ground assault signaled greater cohesion. It also became clear that Russia would not split with the rest of Europe and come to Serbia's aid.[32] NATO had parried perhaps Serbia's strongest countermoves. In addition, the air campaign actually intensified as time went on, further diminishing hopes that NATO's own disagreements would collapse the coercion effort.

That the air campaign took far longer than U.S. and allied policy makers expected illustrates that even an adversary's miscalculation about the unity of a coalition arrayed against it may cause a coercive strategy to fail. Coercion relies on manipulating adversary perceptions of future costs, so just a belief that those costs will subside as a coalition fragments can induce an adversary to hold out.

CONCLUSION

As previously noted with respect to domestic politics, the key constraints on a coercer's military options are often self-imposed. Coercion is not simply a product of relations between a coercer and an adversary, it is also a product of the dynamics within the coercer. The effects of coalition building on coercion confront policy makers with a balancing calculation. The United States may, for a variety of reasons, need to build and maintain coalitions in conducting military operations. At some point, however, the marginal benefit of further coalition building

30 Posen, "The War for Kosovo," pp. 66–69.

31 Michael R. Gordon and Eric Schmitt, "Thwarted, NATO Agrees to Bomb Belgrade Sites," *New York Times*, March 31, 1999, p. A1.

32 To be sure, Russia was not a coalition member. Indeed, its interests and objectives in the crisis sometimes appeared to be contrary to NATO's.

for a particular coercive strategy—whether in terms of size or degree of cooperation and unity—may level off and even turn negative.

This chapter offers a reminder that coercive strategy making takes place within the context of broader U.S. foreign policy. Even though coalition building and maintenance at times may undermine the potency and credibility of coercive threats, other foreign policy concerns, such as protection of bilateral cooperation with various coalition partners, may override those immediate concerns. On the one hand, coalition-imposed constraints may degrade coercive effectiveness in a particular crisis. On the other hand, they may serve to protect other strategic and political goals—goals that may be critical enablers of coercive strategies more generally.

The recognition that coercive strategies are just one element of broader U.S. foreign policy helps explain the United States' difficulty in achieving escalation dominance despite its preponderance of overall force. As numerous examples in this chapter illustrate, coalition partners recruited to shore up political support for a hard-line policy or to protect U.S. relations with third parties to a crisis often impose restrictions on forceful options. Adversaries, for whom a conflict with the United States may well be equivalent to risking their very survival, clearly recognize that the United States always has important regional interests at stake beyond those immediately at issue in a particular crisis.

Another tradeoff occurs in weighing allied capabilities and their political contribution. Ironically, the United States often recruits allies and coalition partners for political purposes, such as promoting an image of burden sharing. These partners, however, often contribute little militarily because their forces lack the necessary capabilities to satisfy political constraints emanating from casualty sensitivity and collateral damage concerns. They often cannot suppress enemy air defenses, and they lack precision munitions, sophisticated battle management assets, or other capabilities that allow the United States to suffer few casualties and cause minimal adversary civilian suffering.[33] Thus, if they were to participate in difficult strikes, they might cause more problems politically than they would solve operationally.

33 See David Gompert, Richard Kugler, and Martin Libicki, *Mind the Gap: Promoting a Transatlantic Revolution in Military Affairs* (Santa Monica, CA: RAND, 1999), for a review.

When the United States coerces as part of a coalition, it accepts a tradeoff between its nominal strength and its ability to wield it effectively. Allies may be necessary in order to employ various instruments or to gain domestic legitimacy, yet their presence often places severe limits on escalation. Finding the balance between political necessity and operational effectiveness is often difficult, but it is essential if the coercer is to properly muster its strength.

7

Humanitarian coercion and nonstate actors

The U.S. military has regularly supported relief operations following natural disasters, but since the end of the Cold War it has increasingly also intervened to assist the victims of man-made crises such as civil war and poor governance. During the Clinton administration, using force for humanitarian reasons was arguably the dominant form of intervention. And coercion is often a key element of humanitarian intervention.[1]

U.S. and allied military planners face severe limits on the use of force during humanitarian crises, making it hard to achieve escalation dominance. This challenge arises partly in response to the common attributes of humanitarian crises: low levels of strategic interests, tentative domestic support, and heavy reliance on coalitions, each coming with the

1 In essence, these operations fall into what the U.S. government has cumbersomely labeled "complex contingency operations." Presidential Decision Directive-56, which mapped out U.S. procedures for intervention in these crises under the Clinton administration, defined the term *complex contingency operations* by examples: "Peace operations such as the peace accord implementation operation conducted by NATO in Bosnia (1995–present) and the humanitarian intervention in North Iraq called Operation Provide Comfort (1991); and foreign humanitarian assistance operations, such as Operation Support Hope in Central Africa (1994) and Operation Sea Angel in Bangladesh (1991)." (White House, *The Clinton Administration's Policy on Managing Complex Contingency Operations*, Presidential Decision Directive-56 [May 1997].) As this list suggests, complex contingencies can be understood as much by what they are not as by what they are. The term does not include smaller operations such as domestic disaster relief, counterterrorism, hostage rescue, and noncombatant evacuation. Nor does it include international armed conflict at the other extreme.

attendant issues discussed in previous chapters. In humanitarian operations, however, the degree to which each of these factors impedes achievement of escalation dominance is often higher than it is for interventions driven by what is more traditionally defined as national interest. In addition, humanitarian intervention often has its own demands, such as the need to preserve impartiality and to avoid damage of all sorts, that create special limits on the use of force.

The type of adversaries commonly faced in humanitarian crises—nonstate actors—magnifies these challenges. In humanitarian interventions in Bosnia, Haiti, Somalia, Zaire (now Congo), and other countries, the United States has had to confront a range of nonstate actors such as warlords, guerrillas, and factions local to the crisis area. The United States and its allies regularly face nonstate adversaries or potential adversaries in nonhumanitarian contexts as well. Consider not only past experience with guerrilla insurgencies but also current threats from international terrorist networks and narcotics organizations. Confronting nonstate actors outside the humanitarian context is not the focus of this chapter. However, the lessons of humanitarian intervention offer some insights to challenges involved in coercing nonstate actors in other contexts as well, and lessons from past efforts to coerce terrorists or other nonstate groups for strategic reasons are often relevant to the challenges faced in humanitarian intervention.

After surveying common military tasks and the role of coercion in humanitarian intervention, this chapter analyzes constraints on U.S. and allied forces that impede achievement of escalation dominance in these contexts. It then examines how nonstate actors exploit asymmetries in capabilities and political constraints to counter-coerce the United States and its partners. This chapter aims to explain past failures of coercion in humanitarian contexts in an effort to gain a clearer understanding of how strategic context and the organizational structure of adversaries affect coercive strategies.

HUMANITARIAN INTERVENTION AND COERCION

Perhaps surprisingly, coercion is a critical tool in most humanitarian operations. As defined in the beginning of this book, coercion is the use of threatened force, and the limited use of actual force to back up the threat, to induce an adversary to change its behavior. Although humanitarian coercion sounds like an oxymoron, it is often critical to the overall mission. Helping to feed the hungry, to care for refugees, and to return people to their land of origin—all of these sound like unassailable goals. But for the militias, warlords, and governments that deliberately starve people and drive them from their home, these goals are themselves threatening. Often the hungry are members of an enemy population, the refugees want the land that the guerrillas now control, and so on. The belligerent groups must be coerced to allow aid workers to succor those in need and, more generally, to stop contributing to the suffering.

In the 1990s, the United States and its allies conducted a wide range of humanitarian operations that included a major coercion component. Examples include a failed attempt to reconstitute a viable central government in Somalia (Operation Restore Hope, Operation Continue Hope), return of a democratically elected government to Haiti (Operation Uphold Democracy), alleviation of human suffering in Rwanda and Zaire (Operation Support Hope), operations to end conflict and recreate a multiethnic government in Bosnia-Herzegovina (Operation Joint Endeavor, Operation Joint Guard), and an effort to stop ethnic terror in Kosovo (Operation Allied Force, Operation Shining Hope, and Operation Joint Guardian).

In all of these operations, the threat (and often the use) of force was necessary to achieve humanitarian objectives. In many cases, however, self-imposed constraints on the use of force prevented the United States and its allies from meeting all, or even most, of their objectives or from succeeding quickly.

THE DECISION TO INTERVENE

The decision to intervene, whether in humanitarian or in more conventional, national-interest-related disputes, is bound up in a complex web of domestic, international, bureaucratic, and other factors. Why a state intervenes, however, often provides the context for the application of force. It often shapes the goals in question, the limits on the use of force, and other essential ingredients of coercive strategy making.

In the post–Cold War world, intrastate conflicts, which sometimes have given rise to U.S. and allied humanitarian intervention, have occurred more often than interstate conflicts, although they became less prevalent in the late 1990s.[2] Intrastate conflict usually has deep underlying causes: oppressive, illegitimate, or incompetent governments; dramatic class differences and economic grievances; ideological and religious antagonisms; national, racial, and ethnic divisions; and gang-style rivalries to exploit sources of wealth.[3]

Dozens of crises might merit intervention if the criterion were the number of deaths, the number who die from preventable disease, the suffering of refugees, or other humanitarian measures. Of course, the U.S. decision to intervene is not driven entirely, or indeed primarily, by the demands of a particular crisis or the scope of the suffering. The U.S. intervened in Kosovo, for example, but stayed away from the more massive tragedy in the Sudan. For geopolitical reasons (among others), the United States is more likely to mount operations close to home, especially in the Caribbean and Central America, and close to its NATO allies, such as in the Balkans, rather than in more-distant regions. In addition, the United States remains firmly committed to Korean security and would likely respond strongly to a humanitarian crisis resulting from the implosion or fall of the North Korean regime. Due in part to the Somali debacle, the United States will probably hesitate to become deeply involved in sub-Saharan Africa, despite the region's turmoil and suffering. Yet even there, the prospect of a truly massive conflict—such as a possible repeat of the 1994 Rwanda genocide—might lead to U.S. intervention.

It is difficult to predict when the United States and others will decide to undertake humanitarian operations. Washington decides where it will intervene and how much effort it will devote to intervention on a case-by-case basis. Although the United States has an interest in the advancement of human rights, it does not act consistently on such a basis and therefore must choose on more particular grounds. For example, it may want to support its allies, protect U.S. citizens abroad, inhibit or reverse flows of refugees, or counter threats to its prosperity. Policy

2 Zalmay Khalilzad and Ian O. Lesser, eds., *Sources of Conflict in the 21st Century, Regional Futures and U.S. Strategy* (Santa Monica, CA: RAND, 1998); Peter Wallensteen, "Armed Conflict and Regional Conflict Complexes, 1989–97," *Journal of Peace Research,* Vol. 35, no. 5 (1998), pp. 621–634; and Ted Robert Gurr, "Ethnic Warfare on the Wane," *Foreign Affairs*, Vol. 79, no. 3 (May/June 2000), pp. 52–64.

3 Daniel Byman and Stephen Van Evera, "Why They Fight: Hypotheses on the Causes of Contemporary Deadly Conflict," *Security Studies,* Vol. 7, no. 3 (Spring 1998), pp. 1–50.

makers differ widely on definitions of these interests and on whether these interests are sufficiently jeopardized in particular cases to merit intervention.

Media coverage and grassroots efforts by NGOs can put great pressure on the U.S. government to act.[4] In Somalia, the Balkans, and other crisis areas, the highly publicized suffering prompted popular support for intervention. Media coverage, however, is uneven. Kosovo, for example, received tremendous attention, whereas bloodier conflicts, such as that in Sudan and the Ethiopian-Eritrean war, received almost none. Often, other news events relegate a humanitarian crisis to obscurity. In many crises, the initial suffering receives tremendous attention, but the media coverage wanes in subsequent months.

Refugee flows and associated allied concerns are another major driver of intervention. Particularly in Europe, U.S. allies push for action because they fear massive flows of refugees into their own countries and the spread of violence. The United States also responded to Turkey's concerns about Kurdish refugees after the Iraqi civil strife in 1991, in part prompting Operation Provide Comfort.

The Rwandan crisis, which began on April 6, 1994, illustrates the twists and turns that often characterize the decision to intervene. During the first three weeks, extremist Hutus hacked to death with machetes, shot to death, and burned alive almost one million people.[5] At the time, the United Nations Assistance Mission for Rwanda (UNAMIR) had about 2,100 personnel, too few to be decisive. The United States believed there was insufficient international or domestic support to mount a successful operation and urged the reduction of UNAMIR. The Security Council drew UNAMIR strength down to 270 personnel and gave them the mission of acting as monitors and intermediaries between the parties. The French subsequently launched the

4 Ken Menkhaus, "Complex Emergencies, Humanitarianism, and National Security," *National Security Studies Quarterly*, Vol. IV, no. 4 (Autumn 1998), p. 55.

5 United Nations, *The Blue Helmets, A Review of United Nations Peace-Keeping* (New York; United Nations Department of Public Information, 1996), pp. 346–348; Alison Des Forges, *Leave None to Tell the Story: Genocide in Rwanda* (New York: Human Rights Watch, 1999), http://www.hrw.org/reports/1991/rwanda; and Philip Gourevitch, *We Wish to Inform You That Tomorrow We Will Be Killed with Our Families: Stories from Rwanda* (New York: Farrar, Straus, and Giroux, 1998).

controversial Operation Turquoise in southwestern Rwanda but soon relinquished control to the Tutsi-led Rwandese Patriotic Front (RPF). During June and the first week of July, the RPF won decisive victories in Rwanda. Beginning on July 3, 1994, some three million panic-stricken Hutus, including most perpetrators of the genocide, fled to neighboring countries in what was one of the most sudden and massive refugee flows in history. Refugees who fled to the neighboring Congo (then Zaire) lacked water, food, and sanitary facilities. Under these conditions, they rapidly began dying of cholera—a tragedy captured for the world to see by the international media. On July 17, the Clinton administration decided to provide humanitarian assistance to these refugees as Operation Support Hope. Thus, the United States decided not to forcefully oppose Hutu genocide against Tutsis, but then mounted an operation to save Hutus, including an exiled regime responsible for genocide and plotting a return to power in Rwanda. These U.S. decisions may have been understandable responses to specific emergencies, but no one would have predicted them.[6]

A U.S. decision to stay out of a conflict or crisis is not necessarily final. When the Balkan wars began in 1991, the Bush administration refrained from intervening, believing that the United States lacked sufficient national interests in the crisis to justify the massive military effort that intervention would require. In following years, the Clinton administration appeared equally determined to stay out, even though its European allies were floundering. As the suffering mounted and the refugees continued to flee, pressure grew. In 1995, the Clinton administration decided to lead and contribute heavily to a humanitarian operation in Bosnia that was to last one year. The administration subsequently decided to prolong the operation indefinitely. As the previous two chapters discussed, the politics of intervention are critical determinants of successful coercion. The special politics of humanitarian crises thus bear heavily on humanitarian coercion.

6 For a persuasive argument that good outside intentions led to the genocide, see Alan Kuperman, "The Other Lesson of Rwanda: Mediators Sometimes Do More Damage Than Good," *SAIS Review,* Vol. 16, no. 1 (Winter/Spring 1996), pp. 221–240. For a review of the humanitarian relief effort following the genocide, see Taylor Seybolt, *Coordination in Rwanda: The Humanitarian Response to Genocide and Civil War* (Cambridge, MA: Conflict Management Group, February 1997).

COMMON TASKS DURING A HUMANITARIAN INTERVENTION

Humanitarian operations is a broad term that encompasses a wide range of tasks. Several of the most common tasks are described in this chapter to provide an understanding of the types of accompanying military operations the United States and its allies typically seek to conduct. As is clear from the descriptions, all the tasks usually involve a significant coercive element.

When the suffering is caused by human agency, providing humanitarian aid is not enough to end a crisis—relief supplies must also be protected. Belligerents often try to obstruct, divert, and even pillage humanitarian aid. They may want to deny aid to their enemies, reward their own supporters, or simply enrich themselves. In Somalia and Liberia, factional leaders plundered humanitarian aid, demanded a percentage for allowing aid to pass, and compelled aid organizations to hire their supporters as guards, in effect extorting bribes.[7] Bosnian Serbs often prevented UN agencies from reaching isolated Muslim communities or insisted on receiving comparable aid themselves, regardless of need.

Belligerents may try to disrupt the aid flow by attacking the aid providers or by intimidating them. Aid personnel represent a weak link: if warlords disrupt their activities, the whole operation may collapse. In Angola, Burundi, Chechnya, Rwanda, Sierra Leone, Sudan, and other countries, belligerents have attacked and murdered relief agency per-

7 The same drought that devastated Somalia also devastated neighboring Ethiopia and northern Kenya, but only Somalia suffered massive casualties because chaos made it impossible to deliver relief. A key military task in Somalia was to secure ports, airfields, and lines of communication to Somalia's interior in order to help the delivery of relief. (Jonathan Dworken, "Operation Restore Hope: Coordinating Relief Operations," *Joint Forces Quarterly,* no. 8 [Summer 1995], pp. 14–20; Jonathan Dworken, *Improving Marine Coordination with Relief Organizations in Humanitarian Assistance Operations* [Alexandria, VA: Center for Naval Analysis, 1996]; Andrew S. Natsios, "Humanitarian Relief Intervention in Somalia: The Economics of Chaos," in *Lessons from Somalia*, Walter Clarke and Jeffrey Herbst, eds. [Boulder, CO: Westview Press, 1997], p. 79; and Kennedy, "The Relationship Between the Military and Humanitarian Organizations in Operation Restore Hope," p. 100.)

sonnel.[8] Belligerents may target relief efforts because they oppose a peace operation that is simultaneously in progress.[9]

To secure humanitarian assistance, the military may also have to provide security for airports and seaports where supplies initially arrive; for internal distribution, including warehouses, convoy routes, and distribution points; and for relief agency personnel who provide humanitarian aid. These operations all involve coercing local warlords and militias to cease interference with relief supplies.[10]

In addition to protecting the flow of aid, the military may have to coerce nonstate actors to protect refugees and internally displaced persons (victims of war or disaster who flee their homes but do not cross international borders). Strife victims may be attacked, exploited, abused, and plundered, while refugee camps can become new sources of violence and instability. Warlords may recruit among refugees, and camps can even become military bases, using their humanitarian status to guarantee a safe haven. In Zaire, for example, the new Tutsi-led Rwandan government regularly battled Forces Armees Rwandaises (FAR) marauders based out of UN-run refugee camps. In Somalia, many food distribution centers were located in the area controlled by warlord Mohammed Farah Aideed. As a result, people from other areas moved to Aideed's area of control, strengthening his power.[11] Eventually, refugees and in-ternally displaced persons must either return

8 United Nations High Commissioner for Refugees, *The State of the World's Refugees* (New York: Oxford University Press, 1997), pp. 48 and 132.

9 In February 1994, for example, a Somali militia leader bombed the headquarters of World Vision in Baidoa because he opposed the UN-led peace operation, even though it was unrelated to World Vision's operations (Andrew S. Natsios, "The International Humanitarian Response System," *Parameters,* Vol. XXV, no. 1 [Spring 1995], p. 72).

10 Kennedy, "The Relationship Between the Military and Humanitarian Organizations in Operation Restore Hope," p. 100. Securing NGO personnel can be exceptionally difficult because NGOs usually have to disperse their workers in order to accomplish their missions. For example, NGOs had 585 offices, residences, feeding centers, clinics, and other facilities scattered throughout Mogadishu during Operation Restore Hope. They refused to consolidate their activities because they wanted to maintain close contact with the local population. (Dworken, "Operation Restore Hope," p. 17; and Natsios, "Humanitarian Relief Intervention in Somalia," p. 92.)

11 Natsios, "Humanitarian Relief Intervention in Somalia," p. 88.

home or find a new home elsewhere. Refugees will not return, however, if their security is threatened. In northern Iraq, Kurds refused to go home until they were sure that Baathist forces had left. In Bosnia, many refugees still refuse to return if their former home lies in a region dominated by another ethnic group.

Another coercion task in humanitarian operations is enforcing provisions of peace agreements to disarm, demobilize, and demilitarize forces of formerly belligerent parties. In Somalia, U.S. forces confiscated certain types of weapons, especially the so-called technicals (jeeps and trucks with heavy machine guns mounted on them) and began licensing all weapons. In Haiti, U.S. forces confiscated unauthorized weapons and conducted a program to purchase weapons from civilians. In Bosnia, NATO forces helped enforce arms limitations under the Dayton agreement. In Kosovo, they disarmed the Kosovo Liberation Army (KLA) under an agreement concluded with its leadership.

Force is often necessary to intimidate those who might otherwise disrupt order and the normal functioning of government. Military forces frequently have to provide security for electoral activity, including registration, political campaigning, and casting of ballots. In Haiti, U.S. forces provided security for Jean-Bertrand Aristide, the democratically elected president who had been living in exile since a military coup, and for government buildings in Port-au-Prince. Aristide's assassination, very possible in the prevailing environment, would have deprived democratic forces of a charismatic leader and possibly caused a spiral of violence. The major accomplishment of UN forces in Cambodia was a relatively peaceful general election conducted in May 1993. In June 1996, 3,000 NATO troops helped assure that municipal elections were conducted peacefully in Mostar, despite a bitter division between Croats and Muslims.

CONSTRAINTS ON HUMANITARIAN COERCION

The United States makes its fundamental decisions for humanitarian interventions—when and where to conduct operations, what goals to set, how many resources to invest, when to terminate operations—with domestic and allied audiences in mind, just as it does for all interventions. During humanitarian operations, however, the military faces constraints that would not usually be present to the same extent during war or in response to a simple natural disaster—constraints that greatly shape coercive strategy making and that may impede coercion. In most humanitarian operations, the United States and its allies have few if any vital or important geopolitical interests at stake.[12] Casualty sensitivity limits the types of missions available to decision makers and produces restrictive rules of engagement. In addition, the United States usually must conduct humanitarian operations in cooperation with allies and often must try to maintain at least nominal impartiality among warring parties—two more requirements that can hinder coercion.

Typically, the stakes involved in the intervention are low for the United States. In contrast to most interventions during the Cold War, which were seen (whether justifiably or not) as part of the overall containment of the Soviet Union, and to the intervention after Iraq's invasion of Kuwait, humanitarian intervention typically has little in the way of a direct national interest component. In Kosovo, one of the reasons why the United States weighed in was concern about its allies—though even the rationale that intervention became necessary to preserve NATO's credibility was itself partly derivative of prior NATO threats to intervene if human rights abuses continued—but the primary impetus was a sense of outrage over Serb actions. In Somalia, the humanitarian versus national interest balance was even more heavily tilted toward the humanitarian end.

Because direct, tangible interests are few in humanitarian operations, U.S. policy makers' casualty sensitivity identified in Chapter 5 typically is more intense than in other operations. The reluctance among policy makers to risk casualties is unsurprising considering that these operations seldom involve a vital interest, but it constrains military commanders and overall operations. Preventing any casualties often becomes for the military a higher priority than any positive objectives, humanitarian or otherwise. As the U.S. military discovered in Somalia, casualties can speed an intervention's abrupt termination or lead to curtailment of many of its activities.

Concern for casualties may also lead to restrictions on where troops can go, which areas receive aid, and the types of military activities con-

12 James Gow, *Triumph of the Lack of Will: International Diplomacy and the Yugoslav War* (New York: Columbia University Press, 1997), pp. 299–300.

ducted. Because of concerns about casualties in the ongoing fighting in Rwanda, U.S. commanders tightly circumscribed the areas to which soldiers could deploy. The more dangerous areas thus received only limited aid. In addition, both U.S. and allied policy makers usually hesitate to assign potentially dangerous tasks to the military, such as disarming or separating combatants, even if these are essential to achieving the overall goals of mitigating a conflict.[13]

Some limits on the use of force derive from the very nature of the mission. Selling the mission at home often involves painting a picture of suffering and describing the humanitarian intervention as being at the behest of the peoples in question and necessary to save lives. Squaring this benign image with the reality that some elements of the local population may oppose the mission—and must be coerced—is often difficult. Destroying a village to save it from famine is hard to justify, even if the buildings destroyed housed a warlord or militia interfering with the overall relief effort. On a purely intuitive level, it does not appear to make sense to threaten destruction as part of a mission that is nominally to restore people's lives.

In addition to constraints stemming from domestic sources, restrictions on when and how to use force are likely to be emplaced to build and maintain a coalition. Seldom, if ever, will the United States mount a humanitarian operation unilaterally. Allies often share U.S. humanitarian objectives because the media concerns that drive U.S. decision makers also affect other Western publics. In addition, allies' concerns about refugees are often a major reason why the United States decides to intervene. These allies may include host countries, regional actors, and, almost invariably, other major powers, including other permanent members of the UN Security Council. They may include regional actors whose support will be critical. Donor countries, principally the West European countries and Japan, that finance key activities such as refugee return, social programs, and reconstruction also play a vital role. Troop contributors, some of whom are minor powers with exten-

13 In Rwanda, the head of the United Nations High Commission for Refugees (UNHCR), Sadako Ogata, called for UN member states to use force to separate the "genocidaires" from the legitimate refugees, but no government was willing to take on the dangerous and difficult task. In the end, the UNHCR settled for paying Zairian army troops to keep order in the camps.

sive experience in peace operations, such as Austria, Canada, Finland, India, Norway, Pakistan, and Sweden, also are important partners.[14] As a result, the coalition issues discussed in Chapter 6 are almost invariably intensified.

A common result of casualty sensitivity and restrictions on the use of force more broadly is a gap between the tasks assigned and the means available to accomplish them. Restoring order, enforcing a peace agreement, protecting aid, and other key tasks often require confrontations with local warlords and frequent uses of force. The restrictions on operations, however, lead the military to avoid showdowns. If the intervening forces cannot risk casualties and can operate only in proscribed areas, warlords gain zones of safety in which to operate, to arm and train with impunity, and to otherwise disrupt operations.

To the extent that military force is authorized, humanitarian missions are often particularly difficult because of an inability to discriminate between military and civilian targets. Separating rival militias, disarming combatants, preventing militias from controlling refugee camps, and other such tasks all require knowing who is a warrior and who is a civilian. Poor intelligence, however, is a weakness particularly common during humanitarian intervention. Often the groups in question are poorly known to the West before a crisis occurs. Intelligence about Somali warlord Aideed was extremely limited, making it more difficult to track his whereabouts.[15] The nonstate nature of such adversaries often reduces the availability of even basic information: the United States does not have diplomats, businesspeople, or cultural figures visiting, and learning about, "Hezbollahland." Before the genocide in Rwanda, the United States had no in-country intelligence resources there. U.S. officials, like officials elsewhere in the world, initially misunderstood the complex events in the region and did not recognize the genocide as it was occurring.[16] Even after an intervention is under way,

14 Actors almost always include organs of the UN and its family of organizations, the World Bank Group, the International Monetary Fund, and regional security organizations such as ECOWAS, NATO, Organization of African Unity, Organization of American States, and Organization for Security and Cooperation in Europe.

15 Jeffrey R. Smith, "Tracking Aideed Hampered by Intelligence Failures," *Washington Post,* October 8, 1993, p. A19.

16 Alan Kuperman, "Rwanda in Retrospect," *Foreign Affairs*, Vol. 79, no. 1 (January/February 2000), pp. 94–118.

the United States often does not gather in-depth intelligence because it believes the mission will be brief.

Like most of the problems addressed in this section, the issue of target discrimination is not unique to humanitarian operations. However, this issue is likely to be exacerbated in contexts where the adversary lacks a professional military (which may be identifiable by official markings) and, particularly, where nonstate actors operate within highly militarized societies. For most humanitarian operations, target distinction is difficult or impossible. In Somalia, for example, the UN faced enemy personnel virtually indistinguishable from the heavily armed civilian populace.

As a result, the coercer often cannot escalate without risking the political support of its constituent publics. As discussed in Chapter 5, U.S. operational planners try to minimize the deaths of noncombatants and other forms of collateral damage in order to maintain domestic support.

At times, the United States and its allies intervene for humanitarian reasons with no pretense of impartiality, as they did in aiding the Kurds against attacks by Saddam's regime after the Gulf War and when NATO went to war in 1999 against Belgrade on behalf of the Kosovar Albanians. Often, however, impartiality, or the image of it, is critical to a humanitarian mission's success. An image of impartiality may be necessary to secure international cooperation. Members of the UN Security Council, for example, may sympathize politically with different sides in a conflict zone, so perceived even-handedness may be required to avoid dissension. An image of impartiality may also be necessary at the ground level, to help coopt hostile factions local to a crisis. As discussed below, even seemingly benign forms of aid may threaten the interests of some factions, and anything viewed as biased enforcement can only exacerbate tensions between those factions and intervening forces. Finally, intervention forces may be collaborating with or working alongside aid groups. Aid workers are vulnerable and have much to fear from having their own image of even-handedness compromised by association. Impartiality, however, often requires constraints on military force that impede the transmission of credible and potent threats.[17]

17 Impartiality is frequently confused with neutrality. *Neutrality* implies that military force is not permitted; *impartiality* implies that military force may be used against parties that violate agreements, assuming that the operation is coercive. *Impartiality* further implies that enforcement will be even-handed, that is, directed equally against all violators. In

In practice, even the illusion of impartiality is difficult to maintain, no matter how much restraint U.S. and allied military forces show. Simply by helping to enforce a peace and providing humanitarian assistance, intervening powers are aiding some parties to a conflict more than others.[18] Belligerents regard relief supplies as sources of power. Food, medicine, and other supplies are highly valuable in war-torn regions, and those who control them can expand and fortify their influence. Warlords want to secure supplies for themselves and deny them to their enemies, and belligerents may have no qualms about looting humanitarian relief agencies or extorting supplies as the price for allowing these agencies to operate. Sometimes, humanitarian aid can even increase suffering by supplying the forces of belligerents. During the Somali civil war, the provision of aid bolstered clan-based militias via looting and payment for protection. In Liberia, warlords deliberately impoverished and displaced local communities to attract aid for the victims.[19] During the Bosnian conflict, humanitarian aid helped all parties prolong the struggle.[20] Intervening forces can try to minimize their impact on the local balance of power, but warlords and other local parties will be acutely aware of any impact, no matter how benign the intent. Regardless of whether the United States and its allies try to avoid measures that can shift the local balance of power, the fundamental problem is one of perceptions.

Impartiality imposes restraints on escalation that hinder coercion. Most basically, the United States will find it hard to threaten or use increased levels of force against one side because that side will then claim it is being singled out. Also, U.S. and allied forces may not be willing to

Somalia, for example, the Special Representative of the Secretary General sought to apprehend Mohammed Farah Aideed because he was in violation of agreements concluded with the other parties. Through this action, the Special Representative did not cease to be impartial as long as he was equally willing to apprehend all violators. Of course, the targets of punitive action usually claim, as Aideed did, that the UN and its agents have unfairly singled them out.

18 Richard K. Betts, "The Delusion of Impartial Intervention," *Foreign Affairs*, Vol. 73, no. 6 (November/December 1994), pp. 20–33; and Taylor B. Seybolt, "The Myth of Neutrality," *Peace Review*, Vol. 8, no. 4 (1996), pp. 521–527.

19 United Nations High Commission for Refugees, *The State of the World's Refugees*, pp. 46–47.

20 Susan L. Woodward, *Balkans Tragedy: Chaos and Dissolution after the Cold War* (Washington, DC: Brookings Institution, 1995), pp. 363–367.

launch punitive actions without irrefutable evidence that the target of those actions perpetrated violations of peace agreements or other sets of rules. Adversaries may therefore find it easy to disrupt order, harass aid workers, or otherwise provoke conflict while the United States and its partners find it hard to respond forcefully and quickly.

Because of impartiality concerns, coalition anxieties, and fragile domestic support, the military usually has to operate within extremely restrictive rules of engagement during humanitarian operations. It is typically allowed all measures necessary for self-defense, but it may be severely restricted with regard to offensive actions, even in response to severe provocations. Belligerents and even civilian populations quickly grasp the importance of rules of engagement, divine their content, and attempt to exploit them. In Somalia, for example, clan-based militias knew that U.S. forces were restricted in applying deadly force when it could endanger innocent civilians. They tried to exploit these rules of engagement by firing from the protection of crowds, using their own civilians as human shields.[21] During the Bosnian conflict, all parties exploited UNPROFOR's overly elaborate and highly restrictive rules of engagement, especially as concerned close air support.[22]

The United States and its allies have learned from past problems, and rules of engagement in future operations are likely to be better designed and more flexible than in the past. In more recent Bosnia and Kosovo operations, NATO drew upon the UNPROFOR experience to put the former belligerents on notice that its own rules of engagement were robust enough to enable its forces to use whatever force was needed to protect themselves and keep the peace (though, to be sure, these two

21 The United States responded by using snipers to engage the Somali gunmen, but in some situations it relaxed the rules of engagement. During the fighting on October 3, 1993, for example, U.S. forces delivered heavy fires in sections of Mogadishu to protect special operations forces, which were surrounded by supporters of Aideed.

22 "When UNPROFOR arrived in Bosnia the locals mentally paused to assess what impact UN forces would have on their country. They expected that the UN would make a big difference. It had some impact but overall UNPROFOR appeared to be ineffective. So-called experienced peacekeepers applied their methods too rigidly. Therefore, after UNPROFOR's first arrival, the Bosnian conflict carried on much as before, with the United Nations' forces simply being regarded as an annoyance that was sometimes in the way." (Robert A. Stewart, *Broken Lives: A Personal View of the Bosnian Conflict* [New York: HarperCollins, 1993], p. 326.)

operations lie at the high-intensity end of the humanitarian intervention spectrum). The recently increased political recognition of the importance of rules of engagement will probably generate similarly robust rules in future interventions.

THE CHALLENGE OF NONSTATE ADVERSARIES

In addition to their distinct operational and political constraints, humanitarian operations also often involve a distinct type of adversary: nonstate actors. Of course, adversaries in humanitarian crises can include states, such as in the cases of Serbia and Iraq, but the United States and its partners have recently also confronted militias and other midsize substate groups in humanitarian crisis regions. Because the remainder of this book focuses on state actors and because state and nonstate actors often have different strengths and vulnerabilities, nonstate adversaries deserve particular attention here.

Nonstate actors may be highly motivated. For the United States, intervention in Somalia, Rwanda, the Balkans, and elsewhere was largely an act of goodwill, with only minor national interest considerations. For the local warlords who opposed U.S. intervention, however, power and even survival were at stake. Because of these stakes, nonstate adversaries are likely to sacrifice more, and suffer more, to achieve their goals.

The often-brutal internecine strife characterizing the environment in which such factions and their leaders operate attests to their intense motivations. Factional leaders were in constant peril in Afghanistan, Congo, Lebanon, Somalia, the former Yugoslavia, and other war zones. Assassination from rivals in their own faction and death in combat are near-constant concerns: these leaders seldom die of natural causes. At the same time, these leaders have much to fear in giving in to coercive threats and signaling weakness in the eyes of local competitors.

One of the most glaring difficulties for planners of coercive strategies aimed at nonstate adversaries, particularly those in humanitarian crisis areas, is that these adversaries often lack the types of assets that military planners are schooled in identifying and targeting. Nonstate actors seldom possess munitions factories, electric grids, power plants, or other elements of a modern military-industrial infrastructure. Because nonstate actors by definition do not control the state, efforts to target national infrastructure may hold less promise of moving adversary decision making than they might against a state.

Consider the case of Somalia. Aideed's military assets consisted of little more than several thousand militiamen and a few hundred "technicals," or vehicles equipped with machine guns, anti-aircraft guns, or recoilless rifles.[23] As an undeveloped country, Somalia lacked significant military or administrative targets valuable to Aideed. His military strategy relied on scattering his forces and mingling with noncombatants. UN planners were limited to targeting Aideed himself (along with his closest advisors), Somali National Alliance (SNA) headquarters, and an SNA-operated radio station. But Aideed had already weathered a brutal civil war and faced constant threats from Mohammad Ali Mahdi and other rival leaders. Given that Somali society was already in a state of chaos, there was little that could be held at risk by UN military forces.

At times, a militia may have assets that make it more comparable to a state's forces than to a typical guerrilla group, as was the case with the Bosnian conflict. Compared to many nonstate actors, the Bosnian Serb military was relatively sophisticated, thereby creating certain targeting options for allied planners. Operation Deliberate Force planners struck, among other things, infrastructure and communications networks seen as critical to Serb military effectiveness.[24] But in many cases, there are few elements, beyond the individual perpetrators of violence themselves, that intervention planners can hold at risk with military force. In considering a muscular response to the 1994 rampages in Rwanda, President Clinton confessed that, unlike in the former Yugoslavia case, air

23 Intelligence estimates put Aideed's forces at about 5,000 men, several hundred of whom were ardent supporters constituting his key forces. In addition to technicals, these forces possessed small arms and limited quantities of artillery and old, Soviet-model tanks. (Keith B. Richburg, "Aideed 'No Longer Part of the Process': UN Officials in Mogadishu Play Down Failure to Arrest Warlord," *Washington Post*, June 19, 1993, p. A14; and Jane Perlez, "U.S. Role Is Not to Disarm, Aide to Top Somali Insists," *New York Times*, December 6, 1992, p. A14.)

24 Rick Atkinson, "Air Assaults Set Stage for Broader Role," *Washington Post*, November 15, 1995, p. A1; and Craig Covault, "NATO Airstrikes Target Serbian Infrastructure," *Aviation Week and Space Technology*, September 11, 1995, p. 27. The costs inflicted by these strikes cannot be measured simply by looking at the targeted assets. Their main value lay in magnifying the threat to the Bosnian Serbs posed by the simultaneous Croat and Muslim ground offensives.

strikes were not an option: "Here you had neighbors going from house to house cutting people up with machetes. Who was there to bomb?"[25]

The lack of institutionalized state structures and other features of modern states and economies not only confounds planners trying to identify and hold at risk valuable adversary targets, but also may disrupt coercive strategies at the implementation stage of a crisis, after the adversary appears to have conceded. Successful coercion often concludes with an adversary leadership agreeing to back down. In most cases of state-versus-state coercion, the coercer can be confident that concessions negotiated with and promised by the adversary leadership will be carried out by its agents, such as military forces or other individuals and organizations under its charge. Nonstate actors of the type common to humanitarian crises, however, are less likely to control their constituents and agents and thus often cannot make or implement concessions. Because many nonstate actors lack formal or well-institutionalized control and decision-making structures, the lines of authority within nonstate actors can blur or break.[26] Altering the adversary leadership's cost-benefit calculus therefore may not generate desired changes in the behavior of subordinate agents. More broadly, even when coercion has its usual desired primary effects (persuading the adversary leadership to change course), those effects may not translate into the desired result: compliance.

The Serbia–Bosnian Serb entity operated much like a state at the outset of the Yugoslav conflict but gradually became less centralized, causing complications for allied planners during the Bosnian conflict. The initial allocation of military resources set up a series of dependency relationships among the various levels in the overall organization. As the conflict intensified, however, this hierarchical structure appeared to suffer from disrupted chains of command. Radovan Karadzic, head of the Bosnian Serb political leadership in Pale, and his self-styled government continually strove to circumvent the control of Serbian President

25 Elizabeth Shogren, "Rwandans Told World Shares Guilt for Genocide," *Los Angeles Times,* March 26, 1998 (electronic version).

26 Matthew C. Waxman, "Emerging Intelligence Challenges," *International Journal of Intelligence and Counterintelligence*, Vol. 10, no. 3 (Fall 1997), pp. 317–331.

Slobodan Milosevic, even though the Bosnian Serb war effort remained largely dependent on its benefactor in Belgrade. Similarly, the Bosnian Serb military leadership, particularly Senior Commander General Ratko Mladic, frequently defied the Bosnian Serb political leadership. Finally, General Mladic often seemed to lack control over individual Bosnian Serb military officers and militia units.

The Serb leadership was therefore able on several occasions to avert the launching of NATO strikes by claiming lack of control over certain military units. Following air strikes or the threat of them, the Serb leadership could comply satisfactorily with NATO and UN demands while certain Serb agents remained noncompliant. In a sense, so-called renegade units remained insulated from NATO strikes because NATO's coercive strategy aimed almost exclusively at altering the Serb leadership's cost-benefit calculation. At the same time, the "dislocation of authority" insulated those at the top from the threat of follow-on, escalatory strikes. While the Serb leadership would comply with Western demands, its agents would ignore them.[27]

Operation Deliberate Force further illustrates how the resulting multiheaded structure degraded the effectiveness of coercive threats. By September 4, 1995, air strikes appear to have had their intended *direct* effects: the Bosnian Serb political leadership issued a written commitment to pull back heavy weapons from around Sarajevo. For the next several weeks, however, General Mladic refused to withdraw his forces. The siege of Sarajevo continued, and the Western powers felt forced to escalate the intensity of their air campaign. NATO strikes successfully altered decision making at the political leadership level, but the adversary's organizational structure, or lack thereof, impeded transmission and execution of decisions. Even as the costs of maintaining the siege mounted in the eyes of the political leadership, the effects did not trickle down as coercion theory traditionally assumes. Mladic eventually complied, though not before raising the costs to all parties.

27 This problem is described in Holbrooke, *To End a War,* p. 157. Holbrooke believes that in this case the problems of dislocated authority were deliberately exaggerated by the Serbs: "Still, the same issue that had undermined so many previous cease-fires remained: making sure the orders agreed to at one level were carried out at another. The Serbs had become expert at pretending that they could not control their field commanders."

NONSTATE ACTORS AND COUNTER-COERCION

Nonstate adversaries, like the other types of adversaries discussed in this book, are not likely to sit idly by in the face of threats. They will employ counterstrategies to neutralize threats or to create explicit or tacit threats directed at the coercer. Lacking the ability to challenge the United States and its allies militarily on a grand scale, hostile groups generally focus their efforts on breaking the coercing powers' will to continue, disrupting their alliance, or shattering the domestic political support behind the intervention.

The means available to hostile, nonstate adversaries in this regard are limited, but the political fragility of coercive humanitarian operations from the U.S. point of view can make these limited means quite effective. The weapons available to nonstate actors are typically small arms and mortars, which can cause tremendous devastation in civil wars and against lightly armed foes but are of relatively little utility against well-armored forces and high-flying aircraft. Nonstate actors that do possess limited armored or air forces are seldom a match for any powerful state military—and they are well aware of their limits. Chechen President Dzhokhar Dudayev, a former major general in the Russian Air Force, even mocked the Russian military leaders after the destruction of the Chechen "air force" at the outset of the conflict in 1994, stating: "I congratulate you and the Russian VVS [the *Voenno-vozdushniye sily*, or Russian Air Force] on another victory in achieving air superiority over the Chechen Republic. Will see you on the ground."[28] Yet in certain contexts, even relatively low-technology weaponry has proven to be a powerful counter-coercive tool.

In terms of the concepts presented in Chapter 2, nonstate adversaries' strategies can be thought of as sort of "denial plus unrest": deny the intervening powers their preferred path to victory (coercing potential foes that seek to contribute to the humanitarian crisis) and erode the public support behind the intervention. Given the nature of these hostile actors and their lack of other means, it is not surprising that their strategy in this regard resembles the type of guerrilla warfare commonly employed by revolutionary groups. Such strategies rely on simply surviving in a way that is highly visible and disruptive to the stronger powers' policies. Over time, the continued survival of an adversary, punctuated emphatically with occasional episodes of violence, can call into question

28 As quoted in Lambeth, "Russia's Air War in Chechnya," p. 370.

whether the coercer is succeeding, thereby eroding domestic support for continuing the intervention.

The process of eroding public support for U.S. and allied intervention can be sped up considerably in some cases—especially when that support is already unstable—by even relatively low levels of casualties. This issue is detailed in Chapter 5, but it warrants repeating here because the conditions for a successful counter-coercive strategy aimed at U.S. casualty sensitivity—such as lack of vital national interests and lack of policy elite consensus—are particularly likely to exist in the humanitarian context.

Despite their lack of state institutions and resources, nonstate adversaries have sometimes proven adept at manipulating public opinion in the United States and elsewhere, and this skill has aided them in threatening to undermine political support for coercive intervention. The growth of the Internet, international organizations, NGOs, and the international media has ensured that warlords and militias have access to the international community.

Along with being able to manipulate foreign public opinion, nonstate actors may be adept at shaping local public opinion and using intervention to strengthen their own hands in the face of threats. Aideed, for example, was able to garner increased public support by depicting UNOSOM II as yet another foreign effort to dominate the Somali people and by exploiting civilian casualties resulting from engagements with UN forces.[29] This support occurred despite the fact that Somalia lacked high-technology communications for disseminating propaganda. (As noted earlier, several UNOSOM attacks were actually directed at an Aideed-controlled radio broadcasting station, which he used to spread propaganda.)

As also discussed in Chapter 5, some adversaries are likely to exploit restrictive U.S. and allied rules of engagement or even try to provoke reactions from intervention forces that are likely to endanger local civilians. Capitalizing on civilian tragedies may be particularly tempting in the humanitarian intervention context, because it potentially puts U.S. policy makers in the position of explaining how a seemingly benign operation spiraled out of control or why intervention forces are injuring the very people they were sent to assist. The difficulty of distinguishing

29 James O. Tubbs, "Beyond Gunboat Diplomacy: Forceful Applications of Airpower in Peace Enforcement Operations," master's thesis, School of Advanced Airpower Studies (1997), p. 35.

noncombatants from combatants makes it easier for adversaries to claim that the United States blithely disregards the lives of civilians.

Human-shield tactics to prevent reprisals are not uncommon, although the use of human shields to capitalize on coercers' rules of engagement or political constraints regarding incidental civilian casualties is, again, not unique to nonstate actors. Saddam Husayn has used his authoritarian state apparatus with great success to put civilians in harm's way when faced with the threat of air strikes.[30] But nonstate actors are often particularly agile at exploiting human shields and blurring combatant-noncombatant distinctions. In Somalia, the various factions had long organized militia forces that employed large numbers of part-time fighters who did not wear uniforms or otherwise distinguish themselves as fighters. As Colonel F. M. Lorenz (USMC), the senior legal advisor for Operation Restore Hope, explains:

> Somalis are a nomadic people organized into an extensive clan structure that has existed since the middle ages. The tactics used by the opposing factions were not new. . . . Both [Somali factions] used women and children as active participants. Since women and children were willing participants in the conflict, there was no apparent violation of international law.[31]

The tactics proved easily transferable to conflict with the UN, hindering U.S. and UN efforts to distinguish between combatants and noncombatants and compounding intracoalition rows. On one occasion, during a September 1993 ambush of UN forces by Somali militiamen using women and children as shields, U.S. Cobra helicopters shot into the crowd. Italy and other coalition members protested vehemently that the U.S. response was excessive, to which Major David Stockwell, the UN military spokesman, replied: "In an ambush there are no sidelines for spectators."[32]

Especially when coercive threats are employed concurrently with humanitarian operations, nonstate adversaries can exploit restrictive rules of engagement to initiate provocations without likelihood of

30 Barbara Crossette, "Civilians Will Be in Harm's Way If Baghdad Is Hit," *New York Times*, January 28, 1998, p. A6.

31 F. M. Lorenz, "Law and Anarchy in Somalia," *Parameters*, Vol. 23, no. 4 (Winter 1993–1994), p. 36.

32 Leslie Crawford, "Unrepentant Peacekeepers Will Fire on Somali Human Shields," *Financial Times*, September 11, 1993, p. 4.

drawing escalatory reactions (or with the knowledge that escalatory reactions carry their own dire political risks for the coercing powers). Requirements such as using minimum force and ceasing fire when hostile forces disengage allow the adversary to attack with little fear of a harsh response.[33] Such practices play on a fundamental disconnect between the humanitarian mission and the justification of coercion. Although coercion is often necessary to ensure the effective provision of relief, it is often hard to explain the apparent contradiction of using force against part of a population to, say, feed the remainder. In response to sporadic violence or local media criticism, the U.S. public may believe that U.S. forces are not wanted and thus question the mission, even if it is benefiting the majority of the local population.

Finally, nonstate actors have proven relatively flexible at countering coercive threats by escalating in unpredictable and unconventional ways. In fact, nonstate groups may see little to lose and much to gain in engaging in stratagems that states might shy away from. Serb forces obviously did not possess the military capabilities to retaliate in kind against NATO air strikes. However, the ability of the Serbs to counter-coerce the Western powers became readily apparent in April 1993, when NATO began enforcing the no-fly zone. Although no specific threats were offered by the Serbs, UN aid flights were suspended the day before the first NATO air patrols for fear of reprisals against UN personnel on the ground.[34] On several subsequent occasions, the Serbs responded to NATO air strikes against military installations by detaining lightly armed peacekeepers on the ground. As the chief U.S. negotiator during the conflict, Richard Holbrooke, recounts:

> In response, the Bosnian Serbs raised the stakes dramatically: they seized more than 350 UN peacekeepers and, calling them "human shields" against further attacks, handcuffed them to trees and telephone poles. The world's press was invited to film these men standing miserably in the broiling sun. Images of French soldiers waving white flags of surrender were broadcast around the world, to the horror of the new French President, Jacques Chirac. The television pictures were appalling. That the world's greatest powers would be brought to their knees by such thugs seemed to me inconceivable.[35]

33 Berkowitz, "Rules of Engagement for UN Peacekeeping Forces in Bosnia."

34 Tanner, "Aid Flights Halt on Eve of No-Fly Patrol."

35 Holbrooke, *To End a War,* pp. 63–64.

In all of these cases, the Serbs threatened the weakest points of the overall UN effort—the humanitarian assistance and ground personnel handicapped by restrictive rules of engagement—to up the ante and deter immediate follow-up strikes. Threats to peacekeepers and to aid flights have tremendous political significance, far greater than their direct military significance. Hence, the Serbs, even without matching the Western powers militarily, were able to manipulate the cost-benefit equation of the UN and NATO with relative ease.

As these various examples reveal, the humanitarian objective of coercive interventions typically puts new or tighter constraints on U.S. and allied military forces, usually without reciprocally binding adversaries. Adversaries in these contexts may resort to terrorism, as have many weak nonstate actors in the past. During the 1970s and 1980s, the PLO used terrorism to advance its cause, thereby undercutting Israel's drive to gain escalation dominance through superior conventional might. Similarly, Chechen forces seeking to undermine Russian efforts to subdue the breakaway republic took hostages to sap Russian morale. Indeed, the fragility of any political consensus behind humanitarian intervention may invite such tactics.

As with coercive operations in general, humanitarian operations often see perceptions play a greater role than do true capabilities and intentions in determining the outcome. The adversary's survival alone can convince the coercing power's elites and domestic populace that the strategy is failing. Dramatic attacks that can be counterproductive in operational terms can yield tremendous political, and hence coercive, benefits. Perhaps the best example is the Viet Cong's 1968 Tet Offensive, a massive and coordinated attack against U.S. and South Vietnamese public assets. Tet proved disastrous for the Viet Cong, devastating their ranks as their lightly armed forces were beaten back by their better-armed and better-coordinated foes. Politically, however, Tet was a masterstroke. Images of the fighting convinced the U.S. public that the U.S. strategy in Vietnam was failing, intensifying U.S. sentiment against the war In the words of North Vietnamese General Giap, "[U]ntil Tet [the United States] thought they could win the war, but now they knew they could not."[36]

36 As quoted in Robert D. Schulzinger, *A Time for War: The United States and Vietnam, 1941–1975* (New York: Oxford University Press, 1997), p. 263.

CONCLUSION

Effective coercion must be understood in the context of the escalation constraints imposed on the United States and its allies and the life-or-death struggle that characterizes the adversary's point of view. In humanitarian compared to other types of interventions, resource limits, rules of engagement, alliance cohesion concerns, and the fragility of domestic support all make it harder to credibly threaten the adversary with higher levels of military force. Moreover, the adversary is often willing to endure tremendous sacrifices and to take considerable risks because it fears that concessions will jeopardize its survival. As a result, the political difficulties in achieving escalation dominance tend to outweigh the operational ones.

Even when the adversary is a weak nonstate actor, its motivations are likely to be strong, particularly when compared to those of the coercing power. The perceived benefits of resisting coercive threats are likely to be considerable. In civil war or ethnic conflict, the two sides will have already resolved to accept extremely high costs in pursuit of their goals. In the case of religious or ideological movements, nonstate organizations may be driven by intense desires to achieve more-transcendent objectives. And in humanitarian crises, violence may stem from perceived necessities of survival. In these situations, the United States and its allies are likely to face adversaries willing to suffer because their survival is at stake.

Although humanitarian crises often pit the United States and its allies against nonstate adversaries in a low-stakes-versus-high-stakes coercive contest, the United States may find itself increasingly facing other types of nonstate adversaries in different circumstances. International terrorist organizations, most notably, share important attributes with the types of militia groups and other hostile actors common to coercive humanitarian operations: lack of a decision-making hierarchy, indistinguishability of civilians from combatants, lack of territorial control, and so on. As Joseph Lepgold has observed:

> While illegal drugs can be interdicted and the factories that make them can be destroyed, drug operations are so profitable to begin with and so easy to conceal that victimized states have a hard time making a dent in them. Dealing with terrorism may be even more of a challenge. Political extremists who are willing to die for a cause can be nearly impossible to stop, and even those not on suicide missions can be difficult to defeat by

> active or passive forms of denial, raids to disrupt infrastructure, and brute force.
>
> Terrorism and drug trafficking are extreme cases of asymmetric motivation: the potential targets of coercion find the activities so attractive that it is very hard to deny or punish them enough to make them stop.[37]

The often high and immediate stakes of future conflicts of this type, particularly those involving direct terrorist threats to U.S. personnel and citizens, will alleviate many political pressures that constrain U.S. coercive strategy making in purely humanitarian operations. But coercion during humanitarian missions is perhaps the best example of how the disparity between relative strengths and relative interests affects overall success or failure. In almost any conceivable intervention, the United States and its allies will have far more capabilities than the local opponents do, but they will often lack the will and credibility to use force effectively. Highly motivated adversaries are likely to exploit any limits, perhaps enabling them if not to triumph, then at least to deny the United States and its allies full or quick success.

37 Joseph Lepgold, "Hypotheses on Vulnerability: Are Terrorists and Drug Traffickers Coerceable?" in *Strategic Coercion,* Lawrence Freedman, ed. (Oxford: Oxford University Press, 1998), p. 149.

8

Weapons of mass destruction and U.S. coercion

The military challenges facing the United States today go far beyond those associated with operations against an adversary's conventional forces or other traditional tasks. Chapter 7 discussed the types of challenges the United States faces during "low-stakes" humanitarian interventions. This chapter examines the challenges of high-stakes interventions involving the threat of weapons of mass destruction (WMD).

The immediate aftermath of the Cold War may someday be seen as representing the height of U.S. coercive power. One source of this pessimistic view is that many regional adversaries are acquiring, or may soon acquire, nuclear, chemical, and biological weapons. Such WMD may give adversaries a means for countering the vast U.S. conventional superiority and offsetting U.S. regional influence. No longer would debates about U.S. coercive military operations focus on whether the United States is capable of bombing a stubborn enemy into submission; instead they would shift to focusing on how the United States should counter the danger of sustaining massive damage itself.[1]

1 For a review of deterrence thinking in the post–Cold War world, see Stephen A. Cambone and Patrick J. Garrity, "The Future of U.S. Nuclear Policy," *Survival*, Vol. 36, no. 4 (Winter 1994–1995), pp. 73–95; Kenneth Watman and Dean Wilkening, *U.S. Regional Deterrence Strategies* (Santa Monica, CA: RAND, 1995); Dean Wilkening and Kenneth Watman, *Nuclear Deterrence in a Regional Context* (Santa Monica, CA: RAND, 1995); Charles T. Allan, "Extended Conventional Deterrence: In from the Cold and Out of the Nuclear Fire?" *The Washington Quarterly*, Vol. 17, no. 3 (Summer 1994), pp. 203–233; Robert D. Blackwill, ed., *New Nuclear Nations: Consequences for U.S. Policy* (New York: Council on Foreign

This chapter focuses on how an adversary might use the possession of WMD to intimidate the United States as a counterstrategy to prevent the United States from successfully coercing it. To this end, this chapter examines the WMD challenge in the post–Cold War world, including the nature of likely adversaries and the types of arsenals they may possess. It then isolates several of the most salient factors related to coercing foes that possess WMD, noting how the presence of WMD affects key elements of escalation dominance, including credibility and international and domestic support. Finally, it asks the related—but analytically quite distinct—question of how actual use of WMD would affect the dynamics of coercive contests.

We have little direct experience (thankfully) to draw on for this analysis. Of the world's nuclear powers, two—Russia and China—are too strong and powerful to fall into the regional adversary category. The other five—Britain, France, India, Pakistan, and Israel—are either staunch U.S. allies or countries where any differences in strategic inter-

Relations, 1993); Thomas W. Dowler and Joseph S. Howard III, "Countering the Threat of the Well Armed Tyrant: A Modest Proposal for Small Nuclear Weapons," *Strategic Review,* no. 19 (Fall 1991), pp. 34–40; Richard K. Betts, "The New Threat of Weapons of Mass Destruction," *Foreign Affairs*, Vol. 77, no. 1 (January/February 1998), pp. 26–67; and Robert G. Joseph, "Deterring Regional Proliferators," *Washington Quarterly*, Vol. 20, no. 3 (Summer 1997), pp. 167–175. Most authors simply press for greater emphasis on arms control and deterrence and warn of dire consequences should deterrence fail. See, for example, John Arquilla, "Bound to Fail: Regional Deterrence After the Cold War," *Comparative Strategy*, Vol. 14, no. 2 (Spring 1995), p. 133. An excellent exception to this generalization is Barry R. Posen, "U.S. Security Policy in a Nuclear-Armed World (Or: What if Iraq Had Had Nuclear Weapons?)," *Security Studies*, Vol. 6, no. 3 (Spring 1997), pp. 1–31; George Quester offers an interesting assessment of nuclear deterrence in the post–Cold War world in George H. Quester, "The Continuing Debate on Minimal Deterrence," in *The Absolute Weapon Revisited*, T.V. Paul, Richard J. Harknett, and James J. Wirtz, eds. (Ann Arbor, MI: University of Michigan Press, 1998), pp. 167–188. Paul Davis provides a good overview of the issues involved in defending weak U.S. allies against aggression in Paul K. Davis, "Protecting Weak and Medium-Strength States: Issues of Deterrence, Stability, and Decision Making," in *Post Cold-War Conflict Deterrence* (Washington, DC: Naval Studies Board, National Research Council, 1997), pp. 153–181.

ests are limited.[2] Although the list of potential foes with chemical or biological weapons is far longer, the United States has used force against a WMD-armed adversary only once in recent times—when it confronted a Saddam Husayn armed with chemical and (underestimated by the coalition) biological weapons during the 1990–1991 Gulf War. Although conclusions drawn from the Iraqi experience are valuable, information on Iraq's perceptions and decision making during this period is meager. Because the historical record for this specific phenomenon is thin, this chapter is largely theoretical in nature. It draws on coercion theory for insights and notes the general characteristics of the regimes that the United States is likely to face. Based on this analysis, it assesses a range of often-proposed solutions to the problem, noting their merits and limits. Rather than seeking to lay out a blueprint for coercing WMD-armed adversaries, it seeks to build an analytic framework for evaluating options.

Although we address a number of specific issues surrounding types of WMD arsenals and particular coercive strategies, the key point of this chapter is a broader one: an adversary that possesses WMD does more than gain the ability to impose massive costs on the United States in a crisis—it changes the entire face of the crisis. Many of the changes will push in different directions. WMD allow an adversary, facing conventional threats from the United States, to threaten massive costs. But the threat of massive costs increases the stakes for the United States and thus makes it more willing to sustain costs. WMD threats may increase the vulnerability of U.S. allies, thereby undermining coalition unity in a crisis. But that vulnerability may also unify a coalition if allied members share a common perception of vital interests at risk. Understanding these tensions is critical to designing responses and future coercive strategies.

UNDERSTANDING THE DANGER

It is tempting to view the challenges of coercing a WMD-armed regional adversary within a Cold War paradigm. The challenge of WMD today differs in important respects from that faced during the Cold War, with important implications for coercive strategy making. Poten-

2 U.S. differences with Pakistan are increasing, however, raising the chances of future problems.

tial regional adversaries often seek WMD for reasons that do not resemble those of the Soviet Union, and their motives for possible use vary considerably. Because coercive contests turn heavily on the perceptions of parties—particularly perceptions about future costs and benefits and an opponent's willingness to bear them—these motivations are critical to analysis of the problem. Moreover, analysts and decision makers must recognize that the very term *weapons of mass destruction* is too broad for analytic purposes. Nuclear, chemical, and biological weapons differ from each other in important ways that will affect the dynamics of coercive contests. WMD types vary in the damage they inflict, the manner in which they are best used, and how they can be countered. An analysis of how to coerce adversaries armed with some combination of them must account for how an adversary's particular arsenal mix might dictate U.S. reactions during crises.

Regional adversary motivations and characteristics

WMD are slowly spreading to the developing world, making it increasingly likely that the United States and its allies will confront a WMD-armed foe in the coming years. Table 8.1 illustrates the presence of WMD in the developing world. Not surprisingly, many experts believe that even as the probability of an all-out nuclear exchange has shrunk, the likelihood of WMD use in general has grown.[3] Appropriately, the United States has elevated the WMD problem to near the top of its concerns, with President Clinton declaring in 1998 that WMD proliferation "constitutes an unusual and extraordinary threat to the national security, foreign policy, and economy of the United States."[4] President George W. Bush's administration has made the issue a top concern, as suggested by, among other things, its commitment to missile defense programs.

The regional powers listed in Table 8.1 pursue WMD for a variety of reasons. Like the superpowers during the Cold War, regional adversaries seek WMD to deter their neighbors and to augment already strong conventional forces. In this regard, the end of the Cold War

3 Betts, "The New Threat of Mass Destruction," p. 27.

4 As quoted in Gerald Steinberg, "U.S. Responses to the Proliferation of Weapons of Mass Destruction in the Middle East," *Middle East Review of International Affairs*, Vol. 2, no. 3 (September 1998), electronic version.

Table 8.1. Regional States' WMD Status

	Possesses or Seeks		
Country	Nuclear Weapons	Biological Weapons	Chemical Weapons
Algeria			√
Cuba			√
Egypt		√	√
Ethiopia			√
India	√	√	√
Indonesia			√
Iran	√	√	√
Iraq	√	√	√
Israel	√	√	√
Laos		√	√
Libya		√	√
Myanmar			√
North Korea	√	√	√
Pakistan	√		√
South Korea			√
Sudan			√
Syria		√	√
Taiwan		√	√
Thailand			√
Vietnam		√	√

Sources: Monterey Institute, "Chemical and Biological Weapons Resource Page" (accessed in February 1999); Robert W. Chandler, *Tomorrow's War, Today's Decisions* (McLean, VA: AMCODA Press, 1996), pp. 8–9.

stimulated the demand for WMD. Moscow's Cold War security guarantee to clients such as Libya, Syria, and Iraq—however tenuous and uncertain—provided at least some form of deterrence.[5] Israel, to take another deterrence case, used veiled threats of a nuclear response to check Iraqi chemical threats during the Gulf War and in previous crises. But, in contrast to the two Cold War superpowers, today's regional adversaries may not focus as heavily on deterrence as the core function of WMD. Some analysts expect Iran and Libya to use WMD primarily as a coercive instrument to intimidate their neighbors and gain regional

5 Ian O. Lesser and Ashley J. Tellis, *Strategic Exposure: Proliferation Around the Mediterranean* (Santa Monica, CA: RAND, 1996), p. 5.

preeminence.[6] North Korea has produced a vast chemical weapons arsenal as an adjunct to its conventional military power, enabling it to pose a serious threat to South Korea despite being outclassed conventionally. These motivations themselves make it likely that the United States will be drawn into crises at one level or another.

The devastating potential of WMD makes them attractive to regional powers as coercive instruments for several reasons. The realistic possibility of WMD use poses a tremendous threat that no adversary can afford to ignore. Inflicting massive punishment on a country is difficult by conventional means, but a WMD attack could wreak untold damage in a matter of hours. WMD are also status symbols. They demonstrate to the world, and to a regime's power base, that the leadership is strong and commands respect. Iraq, for example, has sought a chemical and nuclear arsenal to validate its claim as leader of the Arab nation. Such weapons would provide a visible counter to Israel's nuclear arsenal and demonstrate Iraq's strength.[7] Finally, adversaries may seek WMD to guarantee a regime's hold on power. An adversary might use WMD against an internal threat, such as a popular insurgent movement, or against the forces of an invading army that seeks to topple the government. In such cases, WMD become weapons of last resort: to be used when the regime is threatened or the state's most vital interests are at stake.[8]

Woven into many of these motivations is the idea that WMD can serve as a direct counter to vast conventional superiority, such as that of the United States relative to regional powers. As General K. Sandurji, a former chief of staff of the Indian Army, noted after the U.S. military victory over Iraq: "[T]he lesson of Desert Storm is don't mess with the

6 Lewis A. Dunn, "New Nuclear Threats to U.S. Security," in *New Nuclear Nations: Consequences for U.S. Policy*, Robert D. Blackwill and Albert Carnesale, eds. (New York: Council on Foreign Relations Press, 1993), p. 37.

7 Mike Eisenstadt, *The Sword of the Arabs: Iraq's Strategic Weapons* (Washington, DC: The Washington Institute for Near East Policy, 1990), p. 3; and Wilkening and Watman, *Nuclear Deterrence in a Regional Context*, p. 32.

8 Wilkening and Watman, *Nuclear Deterrence in a Regional Context*, pp. 35–38. For a theoretical treatment of state motivations, see Scott D. Sagan, "Why Do States Build Nuclear Weapons?" *International Security*, Vol. 21, no. 3 (Winter 1996–1997), pp. 54–86.

United States without nuclear weapons."[9] The spread of WMD certainly makes military missions more dangerous for the United States. WMD delivered by missiles, terrorists, or special operations forces can kill thousands of U.S. troops even when the adversary is completely outclassed on the ground, in the sea, and in the air. The threat of WMD can also interfere with U.S. access to a critical region, preventing the United States from bringing in reinforcements or supplying already deployed troops. Even when such dangers are not enough to defeat the United States, they may be enough to make the cost of victory too high.[10]

A number of regime and leadership attributes potentially increase the risks that regional adversaries will resort to WMD use. The leaders of such countries as Libya, Iraq, and Iran may not fit the pattern of stable deterrence, as they at times have proven willing to take considerable gambles and have different objectives and pressure points than Western and Soviet leaders had during the Cold War.[11] In general, leaders of many developing world regimes are more willing than Western leaders to embrace risks in their foreign policies—or at least they have a distinct perspective on what is risky and what is not. They have often come to power through daring and must frequently demonstrate their boldness to their followers. Perhaps more important, some dictatorial foes have demonstrated an insensitivity to casualties among their own citizens (to say nothing of the populations of their adversaries) and thus might risk a WMD exchange that would devastate their populace.[12] These leaders face few institutional and bureaucratic constraints on their actions, reducing obstacles to WMD use.

Regional adversaries' propensity to use WMD may also be affected by their domestic political institutions. Developing world militaries in general suffer from poor civil-military relations and cumbersome command and control procedures. Thus, a small clique in the military or government could conceivably use WMD without the full backing of

9 As quoted in Chandler, *Tomorrow's War, Today's Decisions*, p. 149.

10 Posen, "U.S. Security Policy in a Nuclear-Armed World," p. 5.

11 Michele A. Flournoy, "Implications for U.S. Military Strategy," in *New Nuclear Nations: Consequences for U.S. Policy*, Robert D. Blackwill and Albert Carnesale, eds. (New York: Council on Foreign Relations Press, 1993), pp. 143–145.

12 Ahmed Hashim, "The State, Society, and the Evolution of Warfare in the Middle East: The Rise of Strategic Deterrence," *Washington Quarterly*, Vol. 18, no. 4 (Autumn 1995), p. 69.

the rest of a regime. In Iran, for example, the Islamic Revolutionary Guard controls the country's WMD assets and has at times acted independently of the elected Iranian leadership.[13] Moreover, some adversaries might legitimately fear a U.S. first strike aimed at taking out their small arsenal or disrupting their command and control. To head off this possibility, they might adopt measures such as a "launch on warning" doctrine, which calls for missiles to be launched when warning of an attack is received, or they might allow local commands autonomy in the use of weapons.[14] UN inspectors discovered that Iraqi leaders had predelegated authority for chemical and biological weapons to be launched if nuclear weapons were used against Baghdad during the Gulf War.[15] Such measures make an accidental or unauthorized use of WMD more likely.[16]

The nature of regional WMD arsenals

Although the term *weapons of mass destruction* is used to refer collectively to nuclear, chemical, and biological weapons, each of these types of weapons has its own attributes that yield particular implications for coercing regional powers. Several important distinctions rele-

13 Michael Eisenstadt, "The Military Dimension," in *Iran Under Khatami*, Patrick Clawson, Michael Eisenstadt, Eliyahu Kanovsky, and David Menashri, eds. (Washington, DC: The Washington Institute for Near East Policy, 1998), pp. 72–74.

14 Peter D. Feaver, "Command and Control in Emerging Nuclear Nations," *International Security*, Vol. 17, no. 3 (Winter 1992–1993), pp. 165–168.

15 David Kay, "Iraq's Weapons of Mass Destruction: A Continuing Challenge," testimony before the Committee on International Relations, House of Representatives, March 28, 1996 (Washington, DC: U.S. Government Printing Office, 1996), pp. 58–59.

16 The U.S. record in the Cold War should give us pause. The United States had several "false alarms" with regard to a Soviet missile launch. Nuclear weapons at times fell off American aircraft, and in one case seven of the eight "safeties" that kept the bomb from detonating failed. (See Sagan, *The Limits of Safety*.) The Soviet Union accidentally released a biological agent at Sverdlosk, killing hundreds and perhaps thousands (M. Meselson, Jeanne Guillemin, Martin Hugh-Jones, Alexander Langmuir, Ilona Popova, Alexis Shelokov, and Olga Yampolskaya, "The Sverdlovsk Anthrax Outbreak of 1979," *Science*, no. 266 [November 18, 1994], pp. 1202–1208).

vant to coercion must be drawn in terms of arsenal size, damage infliction, likelihood of battlefield use, and critical support infrastructures.

Nuclear weapons are actually easy to build or acquire, at least relative to the most sophisticated conventional weapons.[17] It is therefore likely that some regional adversary will acquire one in the near future. Although only eight or nine states have obtained nuclear weapons, roughly 30 states have the capability to do so.[18] Possession of nuclear weapons would give a regional adversary the ability to threaten massive costs in areas that its conventional military forces or other coercive tools could not normally affect. An Iraq or a North Korea without a nuclear weapon can inflict only minimal damage outside its immediate region. With a nuclear device and even crude delivery means, it can threaten states around the world.

17 Acquiring any WMD is difficult for a nonstate group, such as terrorist organizations, but may be becoming easier. In general, WMD are difficult for such groups to produce and disseminate. However, in his sober analysis, Walter Laqueur notes: "It is entirely possible that the terrorist of the future—tomorrow, perhaps—will avail him or herself of one of these weapons" (Walter Laqueur, *The New Terrorism: Fanaticism and Arms of Mass Destruction* [New York: Oxford University Press, 1999], p. 254). Laqueur argues that WMD, including nuclear weapons, are easier to acquire than in the past. Already, the Japanese cult Aum Shinrikyo used sarin in a March 20, 1995, attack in Tokyo, killing 12 and injuring 5,000. Aum has also attempted to use a variety of biological weapons, including neurotoxins and the bacteria responsible for anthrax. Other groups have tried to acquire biological weapons, and a cult in the United States poisoned food with salmonella bacteria. (Laqueur, *The New Terrorism*, pp. 254–262.) For specifics on Aum, see Sheryl WuDunn, Judith Miller, and William J. Broad, "How Japan Terror Alerted World," *New York Times*, May 26, 1998, p. 10; and David E. Kaplan and Andrew Marshell, *Cult at the End of the World: The Terrifying Story of the Aum Doomsday Cult* (New York: Crown Publishers, 1996). It is also possible that a state actor might provide a nonstate actor with WMD. Such a possibility is highly unlikely, however, because even though developing world militaries sometimes suffer from poor civil-military relations (as noted earlier in this chapter), powers that possess WMD typically try to guard its deployment and use, ensuring that special units and hand-picked managers control it. Passing it to a nonstate actor, no matter how close, would go against this tendency.

18 Sagan, "The Commitment Trap," p. 113. Kenneth M. Waltz argues that roughly 40 states have this capacity in *The Spread of Nuclear Weapons: More May Be Better*, Adelphi paper no. 171 (London: International Institute of Strategic Studies, 1981), p. 29.

Regional nuclear arsenals are likely to be small in size and low in yield, in contrast to regional chemical or biological arsenals or to the superpower arsenals that existed at the height of the Cold War. The nuclear designs pursued by North Korea and Iraq, while immensely lethal, are smaller than the thermonuclear devices that typify the U.S. and Russian arsenals. Regional arsenals probably will consist of weapons of 10- to 20-kiloton yields (comparable to early U.S. nuclear weapons). The number of weapons is likely to be modest, as a larger program will be difficult to pursue through covert means and without outside support. Some adversaries may only be able to acquire weapons-grade plutonium or other essentials through clandestine purchase. Thus, nuclear arsenals of regional adversaries will probably be fewer than 50—and often as few as one or two—in the first decades of their programs.[19]

Chemical and biological programs, by contrast, are likely to be massive. Producing large numbers of chemical and biological agents is cheap and easy compared with producing nuclear devices. Between 1991 and 1994, UN inspectors supervised the destruction of nearly 700 tons of Iraqi chemical warfare agents, as well as thousands of tons of precursor chemicals. To deliver these agents, Iraq had tens of thousands of munitions. Although details on Iraq's biological weapons program are limited, Baghdad is also known to have produced tens of thousands of liters of botulinum, aflatoxin, and anthrax and to have tested other agents. UN inspectors reported that Iraq may have produced up to 10 billion doses of such biological arms.[20]

Various WMD also differ considerably in the damage they can inflict. In general, it is difficult to kill large numbers of people with relatively small quantities of chemical weapons, which makes them comparable to high explosives—except in terms of psychological value. During the Iran-Iraq War, for example, both sides used chemical weapons, trying to kill each other's soldiers. Although these weapons

19 This small size is due to the need to acquire expertise before using larger plants and because of the high cost of these programs (Wilkening and Watman, *Nuclear Deterrence in a Regional Context*, pp. 23–24).

20 Anthony H. Cordesman, *The Military Balance in the Gulf, Volume II: Iran and Iraq* (Washington, DC: Center for Strategic and International Studies, January 1998), pp. 110–112. For a review of the findings of UN inspection teams, see Stockholm International Peace Research Institute, "Iraq: The UNSCOM Experience," SIPRI Fact Sheet (Stockholm: SIPRI), October 1998, pp. 3–4.

were at times devastating in their terrorizing effects, their physical effects were hardly comparable to the probable effects of a nuclear device or disease epidemic, which could kill tens of thousands of people or more if properly used.[21]

In part because they differ so substantially in their destructive and lethal impact, various WMD differ in their utility for the battlefield. Chemical weapons are in general less lethal than biological or nuclear weapons in sheer quantum of potential destruction, but they are more appropriate for battlefield use even though their employment is difficult to master. Iraq, Iran, and Egypt have used them in recent decades. Biological weapons, in contrast, are extremely difficult to employ in battle. Their impact is often delayed, and if they are contagious they can infect the user's own troops, though they might be seen as useful for attacking civilian sites and rear echelons.[22] Nuclear weapons could be used on the battlefield and could be particularly useful for destroying large troop concentrations or supply depots, but the small number available to most regional powers would probably make those powers less likely to employ them on the battlefield than to hold them in reserve as a "strategic" weapon.[23] Moreover, the likely small size of adversary nuclear devices may even render them incapable of destroying a properly deployed U.S. Army division or halting all U.S. tactical air operations.[24]

Missiles for now remain the most likely means of delivery, but some adversaries will use a wider array of systems. Almost all the major rogue proliferators of WMD also possess short- and medium-range missiles, and several are working on, and are near completion of, long-range systems that can strike U.S. territory or that of U.S. allies outside the immediate theater of likely operations.[25] North Korea relies heavily on special operations forces as part of its military doctrine and could, for instance, use them to deliver WMD during a confrontation. Iran has often used terrorist proxies to attack opponents in the past and might provide these forces with WMD as a means of projecting power.

21 Betts, "The New Threat of Mass Destruction," p. 32.

22 Colonel David Franz's testimony before the United States Senate Joint Committee on Judiciary and Intelligence, March 4, 1998, http://www.senate.gov~judiciary/franz.htm (accessed on November 17, 1998).

23 John P. Rose, *The Evolution of U.S. Army Nuclear Doctrine, 1945–1980* (Boulder, CO: Westview Press, 1980), p. 73.

24 Wilkening and Watman, *Nuclear Deterrence in a Regional Context*, p. 25.

25 Dunn, "New Nuclear Threats to U.S. Security," p. 35.

Adversaries do not need intercontinental ballistic missiles (ICBMs) to threaten the U.S. homeland or U.S. allies far from the theater of conflict.[26]

WMD AND ESCALATION DOMINANCE

Having developed a profile of regional adversary motivations and the types of arsenals they might possess, we now turn to the central question posed in this chapter: How are efforts to coerce such an adversary likely to be affected by its possession of WMD? The scenario we explore initially is an adversary that has issued either an explicit or a veiled threat of possible WMD escalation but has not yet carried it out. To put it another way, we are investigating a scenario in which the United States attempts to coerce a regional foe to take some action—for instance, reverse its invasion of neighboring states or cease support for terrorist or insurgency groups—and the adversary responds with a threat of WMD use as part of its counter-coercive strategy. This section explores the probable effects of WMD on three factors that often determine the success or failure of coercion: the balance between casualty sensitivity and political will, escalation dominance, and coalition cohesion. (The subsequent section examines how assessments in this section might be altered by an adversary's limited actual use of WMD—a sort of "warning shot" scenario.)

The devastating potential of WMD, particularly nuclear and biological weapons, makes it almost impossible for the United States to achieve the same escalation dominance against a WMD-armed foe that it could achieve against a foe having only conventional forces. A small WMD capability can afford regional adversaries a powerful counterescalatory threat. In absolute terms, U.S. capabilities dwarf those of potential rivals. The United States, for instance, could devastate all of Iraq after a smallpox attack on a U.S. city. This ability to devastate Iraq would hardly constitute escalation dominance from a policy maker's viewpoint, however, because the tremendous loss of lives in one U.S. city (say, New York) would not neutralize Iraq's ability to impose unaccept-

26 Richard K. Betts, "What Will It Take to Deter the United States?" *Parameters,* Vol. 25, no. 4 (Winter 1995), and ibid., pp. 75–76.

able costs on the United States.[27] Thus, while U.S. escalation dominance is unquestioned in terms of sheer capabilities, the uncertain U.S. resolve in the face of WMD threats might undermine U.S. credibility in using that advantage. As also explained below, however, WMD threats inject additional, vital stakes for the United States into any crisis. Heightened stakes could bolster the credibility of U.S. threats, perhaps helping to offset at least some of the escalation advantages an adversary hopes to gain.

U.S. sensitivities and political constraints

WMD arsenals have the potential to kill and injure large numbers of U.S. and allied personnel and civilians. This alone might fatally undermine the chances of successful U.S. coercion. In essence, the United States could be deterred from issuing or carrying out coercive threats, fearing that an adversary would unleash its WMD arsenal in response. All else being equal, the effectiveness of U.S. coercive threats will decline as the risk of substantial casualties rises if the adversary perceives a corresponding drop in U.S. willingness to carry out threats.

Yet with WMD, all else is not equal. Just as WMD can impose massive costs on the United States in the form of casualties, their very presence also raises the level of interests at stake. As Alexander George and William Simons have concluded, a coercive strategy "is more likely to be successful if the side employing it is more highly motivated than its opponent by what is at stake in the crisis."[28] The threat of WMD strikes implicates core U.S. concerns and, when introduced, may even propel the United States toward intervention in a crisis it might otherwise have ignored by creating a readily comprehensible threat that the U.S. public or policy elite will rally to combat. A plausible argument could be made that if the United States backs down from a crisis involving WMD, it will provide an incentive for others to acquire WMD to use against the United States in future, perhaps even more momentous

27 Richard Betts makes the point that the threat to destroy parts of one or two U.S. cities is puny compared to the standard used during the Cold War, but that this threat may outweigh any U.S. interests in a regional conflict (Betts, "What Will It Take to Deter the United States?" pp. 70–79).

28 George and Simons, *The Limits of Coercive Diplomacy*, p. 281.

crises. This contention, however, represents one side of a no-win argument. If the United States does not back down, it will provide an incentive for others to acquire large WMD arsenals, as this may be the only way to effectively counter Washington's overwhelming power.

The effect that WMD will have on the balance between casualty sensitivity and political will is difficult to predict. WMD can lessen the perceived U.S. will to act, because the grave harm that they can inflict might be expected to deter forceful intervention, but this very danger may stiffen U.S. resolve far beyond that generated by other policy interests in a crisis. The rules of thumb on domestic support discussed in Chapter 6 apply most consistently in the low-stakes contests of the post–Cold War world, but future WMD contests, by definition, will not be low-stakes. Thus, cautious adversaries may actually have a strong incentive to avoid any chance of WMD-level escalation. They may, for example, avoid any military actions that might be seen as increasing WMD strike readiness or any provocative rhetoric that could be construed as a WMD threat precisely because they want to keep U.S. interests in a crisis moderate.

Add to this another analytic layer. Recent U.S. efforts to limit adversary civilian casualties have reinforced the perception abroad of U.S. political sensitivity in this regard. Regardless of its accuracy, this perception could undermine the credibility of U.S. counterthreats. More broadly, U.S. actions in humanitarian interventions or other low-stakes conflicts may condition adversaries to expect U.S. restraint, leading to the false belief that the United States will limit the injuries or horrors it inflicts on adversary civilians. Regardless of empirical validity, adversaries may continue to resist the United States in the mistaken belief that threatening to use WMD can promptly disintegrate U.S. public support and produce limits on the scope and scale of any U.S. coercion campaign. Whereas the presence of WMD may actually loosen political constraints on U.S. decision makers, the possibility that the adversary will not recognize this erodes some potentially advantageous coercive effects.

The U.S. advantage in WMD capabilities is partially offset by the fact that many, if not most, potential adversary governments may be less sensitive than the United States to the suffering of their people as a whole. On the list of WMD-armed foes in Table 8.1, only India, Israel, and Taiwan are democracies. In the remainder of the countries, the people have little influence in government, and some listed regimes have proven willing to sacrifice (or even kill) thousands of their own citizens to ensure their hold on power. At the same time, U.S. leaders may be viewed by adversaries as sensitive to enemy civilian suffering and perceptions of proportionality. Put simply, adversaries may often be willing to absorb more punishment than the United States is seen as willing to inflict.

Maintaining a coalition

Even the low probability that an adversary would resort to WMD use risks dividing a U.S.-led coalition, because allies will fear that they might be the target of an adversary's escalation, even if no such threat is issued explicitly. Given current ballistic missile ranges of possible WMD-armed foes (e.g., Iran, Iraq, Libya, and North Korea), regional allies such as Israel, the Gulf states, and Japan might fear that they will be attacked if the United States launches military attacks. An Iranian threat to use biological weapons against Oman might, for instance, dissuade the Omanis from allowing the United States to launch an offensive from their soil. Libya might respond to U.S. intervention by threatening Rome, Istanbul, or Cairo. Indeed, an adversary can also escalate by dragging in neutrals or noncoalition members, thus raising the political costs to the United States of waging the coercion campaign. Saddam Husayn's effort to bring Israel into the Gulf War through missile attacks, for example, represented an attempt to counter-coerce the U.S.-led coalition. In essence, Saddam was saying that the United States should stop the coercion if it did not want its Gulf allies to suffer domestic political costs and its Israeli ally to suffer actual costs in lives. As the missiles possessed by regional adversaries become more advanced, the number of allies that might be threatened will grow.

At the same time, however, an adversary's WMD threat can serve to unify coalitions. Even if coalition members have different priorities and objectives with regard to the issue in immediate dispute, they may all see failure to react to WMD threats as implicating vital interests. It is difficult to generalize about how far this tendency might offset the potentially disruptive effects of WMD threats on coalition unity, because all of these effects will depend heavily on many factors, including geographic proximity of members to the crisis, policy approaches to WMD challenges, regional diplomatic relations, and so on. For instance, a state bordering the WMD-armed adversary is likely to have an extremely high interest in stopping WMD use and keeping the foe weak; that same state, however, may perceive an acute vulnerability due to its proximity and susceptibility to retaliation. The critical point is that WMD significantly magnify some of the competing pressures that may pull coalition members apart or together in the face of a crisis.

On balance, the effects of an adversary's threat of WMD use on alliance cohesion, and thus on credible coercion, are unpredictable but likely to be negative. Coalition partners are likely to look to the United States to respond even as they try to avoid involvement so as to limit their own vulnerability.[29] Allies may correctly perceive that their own capabilities are limited compared to U.S. capabilities but that their vulnerabilities are equal to, or perhaps surpass, those of the United States. This perception is likely to grow as U.S. forces train for the WMD battlefield while allies do not. Recent U.S. efforts to improve U.S. forces' ability to resist a WMD attack would exacerbate the different threat perceptions felt by the United States and its potential allies, unless those efforts are directed at improving allied preparedness and protective coverage too. If the risks to allies are significantly higher than those to the United States, U.S. brinkmanship during a crisis might engender allied resentment and lead to a loss of allied support, thereby jeopardizing escalation dominance.

BEYOND THE BRINK: HOW WMD USE AFFECTS COERCION

So far we have tried to construct a profile of likely challenges in coercing WMD-armed opponents, but it is critical to recognize how radically several analytic assumptions might change if an opponent were to *use* WMD against the United States or its allies. Although we have no historical experience to draw on, there is no doubt that the entire nature of a crisis would likely shift the very instant WMD were used.

The strategic and political stakes for the United States in a crisis would heighten dramatically after an adversary's use of WMD. An ac-

29 This phenomenon is explored in Mancur Olson, Jr., and Richard Zeckhauser, "An Economic Theory of Alliances," *Review of Economics and Statistics,* Vol. 48, no. 3 (August 1966), pp. 266–279. See also Snyder, *Alliance Politics,* pp. 50–52; and Thomas J. Christensen and Jack Snyder, "Chain Gangs and Passed Bucks: Predicting Alliance Patterns in Multipolarity," *International Organization,* Vol. 44, no. 2 (Spring 1990), pp. 140–141.

tual WMD strike would create a terrifying and powerful spectacle of bloodshed, a type to which the U.S. public and policy makers are not accustomed. Indeed, such a contingency might come about *because* the adversary wished to demonstrate conclusively its willingness to escalate (or failed to recognize that an increase in U.S. resolve might follow). Demand for a strong response would be extremely high; large numbers of U.S. casualties could create a "Pearl Harbor effect" and lead to vocal and overwhelming public pressure to act, and act strongly. Actual use of WMD by an adversary would intensify public calls for a robust U.S. response, both to punish the foe and to ensure that its leadership would not again threaten the United States. Policy makers would also believe that U.S. prestige was on the line and that absent a vigorous and decisive response, incentives for other adversaries to acquire and use WMD would climb. Policy makers would almost certainly have more freedom to escalate if WMD were used but would have difficulty reducing tension in a crisis. Besides, measures to defuse a crisis would be criticized for neglecting past losses and for encouraging future use.

U.S. responses to adversary WMD escalation may vary significantly with the type and size of the adversary's arsenal. The damage from a chemical attack (or a nonlethal or poorly executed biological one) might fall below the threshold of a massive response.[30] If few U.S. soldiers or civilians died in the attack, U.S. policy makers might hesitate to use nuclear weapons, fearing that such a response would be seen by allies and the U.S. public as disproportionate. Indeed, even the (successful) U.S. warning to Saddam during the Gulf War, which implicitly threatened the use of nuclear weapons in response to an Iraqi chemical strike, suggests this is so. President Bush and his National Security Advisor later remarked that if Iraq had used chemical weapons, the United States still would have responded only with conventional force.[31] The chemical arsenals of some adversaries may be formidable, but chemical weapons are relatively poor instruments of escalation in that it is difficult to kill many people with them. Unless they are used on the battlefield, their effectiveness is relatively limited.

Nuclear weapons have more escalatory application for a foe, but they carry their own particular disadvantages. While they represent a powerful means of escalation, they are the WMD type most likely to

30 Sagan, "The Credibility Trap," p. 106.

31 See George Bush and Brent Scowcroft, *A World Transformed* (New York: Knopf, 1998).

produce a devastating U.S. counterstrike. A nuclear strike not only would be likely to inflict considerable casualties and thus increase U.S. resolve; it would also allow the United States to respond with nuclear weapons and claim it was adhering to the norm of proportionality. In short, the gloves might be off once the adversary used nuclear weapons.

Biological weapons may become more important. If adversary stocks are large—which they can be with relative ease because of the ready scalability of biological agent stockpiles—they can be used almost indefinitely. Indeed, they may grow as fast as they are used. Moreover, some biological weapons may be able to provoke tremendous horror and yet not do *enough* damage to trigger a devastating U.S. response. That is, they can help foes walk the line between intimidation and self-annihilation.

The United States lacks in-kind options for responding to some WMD attacks. It no longer has a chemical or biological weapons program of its own, and even though it has nuclear weapons, its arsenal and the individual components of that arsenal dwarf those likely to be possessed by any regional adversary. Thus, the United States may find itself without a response that falls within the realm of proportionality, aside from conventional retaliation. Using the U.S. nuclear arsenal to target enemy population centers in response to a foe's use of WMD would be difficult because the United States lacks the capability to modulate its response. Depending on the effects of an adversary's attack, even a small (by Cold War standards) nuclear strike on one of that adversary's cities might be seen as disproportionate at home and abroad because it punishes the innocent along with the guilty. To be sure, much of this disproportionality concern would abate once an adversary were first to cross the WMD threshold and violate its surrounding norms. But to U.S. planners and those abroad trying to predict reactions, the lack of modulation is problematic. If an adversary only uses chemical or biological weapons that inflict limited damage, for example, it will be hard for the United States to justify an all-out response.

IMPLICATIONS FOR COERCIVE CONTESTS

The presence of adversary WMD arsenals in coercive contests creates a distinct type of struggle. The United States will seek means to neutralize WMD threats and transform crises into something more akin to a conventional confrontation, though perhaps sometimes still highlighting publicly the dangers of WMD if necessary to solidify political support. Adversaries will seek to counter those means, in an effort to preserve their WMD option and avoid a wholly conventional-forces confrontation. They may at times publicly downplay the WMD threat to avoid provoking a strong response. In other words, WMD threats, like all coercive threats, set in motion a back-and-forth contest of move and countermove, where identifying an opponent's key pressure points is critical and where perceptions of effectiveness and credibility matter as much, if not more, than actual capabilities. If an adversary uses WMD threats as part of a counter-coercive strategy, how might the United States seek to neutralize that counterthreat?

As in conventional crises, U.S. efforts to limit U.S. vulnerability to WMD will be met by adversary responses to recreate it. Options for reducing U.S. vulnerabilities—such as missile defenses or attacks on adversary WMD arsenals—must be recognized as imperfect, though useful, solutions to the problem of adversary WMD arsenals. Strong U.S. defense or preemption options may help coerce adversaries, but at times they may lead some adversaries to respond in ways that may also prove dangerous or difficult for the United States to counter, thereby undermining broader U.S. foreign policy goals.

Threatening strikes to destroy the arsenal before it can be used—a counterforce option—is commonly discussed as a solution to fend off the threat posed by an adversary's WMD capability.[32] The idea of integrating counter-WMD attacks into coercive strategies holds intuitive appeal because it promises to eliminate the WMD option from an adversary's arsenal, thus transforming a WMD crisis into a conventional coercive contest. Counterforce, if effective, would prevent an adversary

32 In *Nuclear Deterrence in a Regional Context*, p. 60, Wilkening and Watman make this recommendation for selected instances of deterring regional nuclear powers. One means of doing so is a preemptive nuclear attack, but counterforce could also be done through conventional means. A model seems to be the June 7, 1981, Israeli attack on Iraq's Osiraq reactor, which set back Iraq's nuclear program for several years (Franklin R. Wolf, "Of Carrots and Sticks, or Air Power as a Nonproliferation Tool," master's thesis, School of Advanced Airpower Studies [1994], pp. 28–30). Donald G. Boudreau, "The Bombing of the Osirak Reactor: One Decade Later," *Strategic Analysis* (June 1991), pp. 287–301, presents an overview of the raid that is critical of the effects of the strike on proliferation and the regional security environment.

from escalating and from threatening allied and domestic support in response to U.S. pressure.

As the United States develops a counterforce option, however, adversaries will respond by reducing their vulnerability and finding new ways to press the United States. Most obviously, when possible they will try to hide their WMD assets. Adversaries are adept at masking and dispersing their arsenals and delivery systems, using a confusing web of decoys and secretive sites to reduce the coercer's knowledge of what to strike.[33] Since the Israeli strike on Osiraq in 1981, adversaries also are better protecting their arsenals from attack by air. Libya, for example, is building a huge underground chemical weapons facility at Tarhuna.[34] Even a nuclear strike on adversary WMD systems and facilities would have to blanket much of an adversary's country to destroy covert and unknown facilities with the requisite certainty, while a conventional attack would have even less chance of success. An expanded U.S. counterforce capability may be matched, or even exceeded, by an adversary's reaction.

More ominously, an adversary might respond to a U.S. counterforce posture by trying to make systems more survivable through measures such as dispersing them or giving local commanders control over them. This response not only increases the risk that counterforce will fail, but also raises ominous possibilities of backfire. Such measures would reduce adversary vulnerability to command and control strikes but would multiply the chances of accidental or unauthorized use—particular problems for less-sophisticated regional adversaries.[35] Perhaps most worrisome, a U.S. counterforce attempt might put adversaries in a use-'em-or-lose-'em box. They might feel compelled to strike early during a crisis, before the remainder of their valuable arsenal is destroyed. These weaknesses are not stressed to prove that counterforce options are poor

33 The U.S.-Iraq experience illustrates this challenge. Despite almost eight years of unprecedented inspections by the United Nations Special Commission (UNSCOM) on Iraq, the extent of Iraq's WMD programs is not known with certainty. Delivery means are equally difficult to target. During Desert Storm, the United States may have failed to destroy any Iraqi Scud missile launchers despite devoting some 1,500 sorties to this task. (Keaney and Cohen, *Gulf War Air Power Survey*, pp. 83–84.)

34 International Institute for Strategic Studies, *The Military Balance 1996–1997* (London: International Institute for Strategic Studies, 1996), p. 120.

35 Dunn, "New Nuclear Threats to U.S. Security," p. 40.

tools of coercion, but to illustrate how their utility from both a coercion and an overall U.S. foreign policy perspective must be assessed in terms of likely adversary countermoves prior to and during a crisis.

In part because of the inevitable limits to counterforce and other offensive solutions to the WMD problem, much of the current public debate about combating WMD threats focuses on defensive solutions. "Active defenses," most notably missile defense systems, aim to prevent an attack from even reaching a target. "Passive defenses" include measures that limit damage once a WMD attack has taken place, such as suits for operating in a chemical environment and stores of vaccines that enable rapid immunization against a biological attack.

It is natural to think about the purpose of defenses in terms of limiting damage. But in coercive contests, the most pronounced purpose of defenses may be to enhance the credibility of threats. As Herman Kahn notes in his discussion of nuclear escalation, "Credibility depends on being able to accept the other side's retaliatory blow. It depends on the harm *he* can do, not on the harm *we* can do. It depends as much on *air defense* and *civil defense* as *air offense*."[36] If defenses are perceived to be strong, adversaries may be less likely or able to escalate, and the United States and its allies may be more confident in a crisis.[37] Furthermore, even imperfect defense systems, such as a porous missile defense shield, arguably may cause an adversary to doubt whether its attack would be successful and to avoid WMD threats for fear of inviting a muscular U.S. response.

Adversaries are likely to adapt, however, as active and passive defenses become stronger. If the United States develops an effective missile defense system, for example, adversaries might turn to other means of delivery, perhaps even low-technology ones (the so-called "suitcase bomb" scenario). Adversaries might respond to U.S. vaccination programs with development or threatened development of new strains of vaccine-resistant biological agents. If U.S. defensive options emphasize homeland defense, adversaries may also shift the target of WMD, focusing less on the harder, U.S. targets and more on U.S. allies whose defenses are less robust. The point is not that defensive options will fail to

36 Kahn, *On Thermonuclear War*, p. 32.

37 If an adversary actually uses WMD, passive defenses have probably failed to change the coercion dynamic significantly. Passive defenses, of course, may still affect warfighting in that they reduce U.S. and allied casualties and improve operational effectiveness.

improve the credibility of U.S. threats, but that their effectiveness in doing so will depend on staying one step ahead of adversary countermoves. Their effectiveness will also depend heavily on adversary risk tolerance: what may deter one adversary may fail to deter another. And in a long-term sense, this back-and-forth struggle of move and countermove means that the coercive value of defenses must be assessed also in terms of the incentives and disincentives they create for an adversary to develop WMD in the first place.

The differing strategies that the United States and likely adversaries will employ in this struggle for escalation dominance stem from vast disparities not only in their respective capabilities but in their respective pressure points. The most dramatic difference in this regard lies in sensitivity to casualties among one's own forces and population. It is plausible to argue that adversaries will act like the United States and be extremely cautious with WMD, fearing that too aggressive a stance will backfire, leading to WMD use against their own population. During the Cold War, such an approach by both sides worked well in keeping the peace: the fear of suffering massive civilian casualties made both Moscow and Washington careful about even the remote possibility of a nuclear exchange. Chapter 5 examined how U.S. policy makers often harbor sensitivities to both U.S. and adversary casualties that limit policy options in crises, and this chapter has acknowledged that some of these sensitivities may dissipate once an adversary threatens WMD and U.S. stakes in a crisis magnify accordingly. It therefore bears repeating that strategic setting is critical to this analysis. But, as also emphasized in Chapter 5, an adversary's tolerance for its own casualties may be higher than that of the United States. The regimes in North Korea, Syria, and Iraq have in the past shown little concern about their civilian populations, killing or allowing to suffer tens or even hundreds of thousands of their people in order to ensure the regime's control. These regimes might sacrifice large segments of the population in exchange for furthering their ambitions—particularly if the sacrifice also serves to shield the leadership. The costs the United States and its allies threaten may not be compelling to an adversary regime that sees its most vital interests at stake in a crisis. Although the United States may be more willing to impose massive human costs on an adversary once WMD enter the equation, adversaries may prove willing to bear those costs, negating some of the potency of U.S. retaliatory threats.

Planning for any of these scenarios is difficult because the coercer and coercee threats and responses will be dictated at least as much by immediate perceptions as by actual capabilities. Adversaries will seek to project an image that they might actually use WMD but only if provoked. Washington, for its part, will seek to convince adversary leaders that the United States and its allies will respond effectively. This requires demonstrating U.S. resolve, highlighting the effectiveness of defenses, and otherwise convincing a foe that the WMD game is not worth the candle.

Escalatory moves by both sides will be dictated by perceived rather than actual capabilities and vulnerabilities.[38] If adversaries believe the United States will be cowed by WMD, they are more likely to brandish this threat. Similarly, if the United States believes it is not vulnerable to a WMD strike because it has effective defenses, it will be less hesitant to escalate, even if those defenses are in fact flawed.

One particular perceptual issue that U.S. decision makers will have to confront in a WMD crisis is that adversary views about how U.S. decision makers behave is likely to have been shaped in part by recent low-stakes, conventional crises rather than high-stakes, WMD crises. An adversary might expect that a U.S. strategy aimed at killing great numbers of adversary civilians would be dismissed out of hand by most U.S. decision makers, to say nothing of regional allies. Recent U.S. interventions that have not implicated vital U.S. interests may have nurtured this expectation. Military operations in Bosnia and Kosovo and perhaps most notably in Iraq in December 1998 (Operation Desert Fox, where, as noted above, U.S. forces avoided striking some suspected chemical-weapon-related facilities for fear of releasing dangerous fumes injurious to the local population) have fed perceptions that the United States will not risk enemy civilian casualties, at least not through bombardment. This political unwillingness to impose civilian suffering might change if a WMD threat were to implicate core U.S. interests and result in the demonization of an adversary nation (U.S. air operations in World War II and the Korean War come to mind in this regard). And the United States has, through the use of sanctions and infrastructure attacks,

38 Indeed, prudence may force the United States to act as if adversary capabilities are greater than the available data suggest. Because even a small amount of a biological agent or a single nuclear device could cause massive damage, Washington will step carefully if an adversary can credibly claim it possesses such a capability.

caused civilian deprivations in the Balkans and Iraq. But the United States has probably undercut the credibility of its willingness to hold adversary populations at risk through its repeated interventions in limited-stakes missions around the world. Though the collateral damage sensitivity that has accompanied recent U.S. military operations may disappear in a WMD crisis, an adversary may misjudge U.S. willingness to punish innocents.

One last point to be made with regard to U.S. defensive options is that defensive capabilities should not be evaluated solely in terms of their effectiveness in protecting the public, military personnel, or allies. They also affect an adversary's perceptions. Specifically, if defenses are believed to be effective, they reduce the anticipated efficacy of threatening WMD use and bolster the credibility of U.S. threats to escalate in a crisis. Conversely, widespread knowledge that a WMD attack on the United States will lead to only limited damage for the adversary may prompt adversaries to stay their hands.[39]

CONCLUSION

Adversaries might not be willing to bear the immense costs of reciprocal WMD attacks in a future conflict with the United States—but they also might. This latter possibility makes it difficult for the United States to design and implement coercive strategies that secure a dominant escalatory position. The asymmetry in stakes and sensitivities also might create scenarios where an adversary's most sensitive pressure point is also the point which, if pressed, could provoke the most dramatic and dangerous response. For instance, as noted above, regimes often acquire WMD to ensure their survival. Pushing a regime against a wall may increase its incentive to use WMD or to escalate from limited uses of chemical weapons to the use of biological or even nuclear weapons. As Barry Posen notes, "A cornered rat with a nuclear weapon is a pretty dangerous animal. Leave the rat a bolt-hole."[40]

Because U.S. political constraints on military action will usually be tighter than an adversary's, and U.S. interests may be less than an adversary's even in a WMD crisis, Washington is likely to tread cautiously. When attempting to design a coercive strategy against a WMD-

39 Wilkening and Watman, *Nuclear Deterrence in a Regional Context*, p. 54.

40 Posen, "U.S. Security Policy in a Nuclear-Armed World," p. 22.

armed opponent, the danger of backfire is, almost by definition, far greater than it would be in a conventional scenario. But the benefits of WMD to an adversary should not be overstated. The United States and its allies must recognize that regional foes, too, often have a strong interest in avoiding WMD issues during a confrontation with the United States. That is, despite their potential advantages, WMD represent something of a quandary for U.S. adversaries. While the United States is quite risk averse, a core reason why it is vulnerable to counter-coercion is that most regional crises do not implicate stakes vital to U.S. interests. The introduction of WMD into a crisis (and especially the actual use of WMD) can overturn the usual assumptions about how the United States will use force and may propel the United States toward intervention it would otherwise avoid. WMD-armed foes obviously have a potential counter-coercive tool, but they may not want to wield it, simply because brandishing WMD may free U.S. and allied policy makers of some of the restraints that typically bind their actions.

Part Three

The Future of U.S. Coercion

The future of U.S. coercion

This book began by posing a riddle: Why do strong countries such as the United States repeatedly fail to intimidate much weaker foes? Although a complete answer remains outside our ken, the theoretical and empirical analysis contained in this book is an attempt to provide some insight. The overarching argument is that success in coercive contests seldom turns on superior firepower. If this were the case, the United States would never lose such struggles, as its military forces outclass those of any conceivable rival. Yet the United States has often seemed to have the most difficulty coercing its least powerful foes, if power is measured in number of tanks, army size, and other conventional indicators. Iraq, which possessed the world's fourth largest and battle-tested army, was easily routed in the Gulf War. In Somalia, Aideed's rag-tag militia forced the United States to back down, even though it "lost" the battle of Mogadishu, suffering perhaps a 50-to-1 casualty ratio.

Of the many problems that U.S. coercive strategy suffers, the greatest lie in the political rather than the military realm. Perceived casualty sensitivity, limited coalition cohesion, and a reluctance to commit high levels of military force—all of these weaken U.S. credibility in the eyes of adversary leaderships and constrain U.S. moves and countermoves. These restraints on the United States, and the adversary's ability to exploit them, often undermine U.S. strength, preventing the United States from using its military superiority to full advantage. Understanding these political dynamics will be critical if the United States is to coerce effectively in the future and wield its military might as an efficient foreign policy tool.

CHALLENGES TO STRATEGY MAKING

The United States faces several challenges as it attempts to coerce in the coming years. Several of these challenges seem inherently difficult to overcome completely, as U.S. efforts to meet them may make them harder to solve.

The biggest challenge is that the United States will have few opportunities to play to its own strengths. For example, the United States has demonstrated that it can deploy air power to devastating effect, particularly in open terrain against heavy, concentrated forces. Yet it is the nature of coercion that as a capability waxes, the opportunities to use it wane. Adversaries are not likely to initiate a challenge if the risk entails confronting the United States where it is strongest. Thus, for example, if the challenge involves activities that air power can foil, such as massing military forces to conquer open territory, adversaries are less likely to provoke a crisis in the first place. Only the desperate and the foolish pick a fight they know they will lose. If they do initiate a confrontation, they are likely to do so in a manner that avoids or offsets U.S. strengths.

The good news, in a way, is that recent, apparent U.S. failures to coerce mask a great deal of unobservable but nonetheless successful coercion—often in the form of deterrence of provocations in general or of particular military actions during the course of disputes. The threat of great-power war or invasion of key U.S. allies, while it exists, appears unlikely in the near term. Where the United States has trouble is not at the core but at the margins, where U.S. interests are questionable or untested. In other words, some of the greatest influence of U.S. instruments will be felt in what has *not* happened, a key measure of effectiveness but impossible to quantify. As a result, proponents of some coercive instruments, such as air strike capabilities and the threat of ground invasion and occupation, may find it difficult to argue for these instruments' relevance despite their having played a significant role in changing an adversary's behavior from what it otherwise would be.

A second, related challenge concerns the means by which an adversary will threaten the United States. An increase in conventional U.S. power may lead adversaries to switch to confrontations on both the lower and the upper end of the force spectrum, neither of which plays to U.S. strengths. Rather than engage in a pitched battle employing tanks, airplanes, and organized ground forces, adversaries may resort to terrorism against civilians, holding the troops of U.S. allies hostage, harassing aid workers, or otherwise trying to force the United States to make concessions or abandon a coercion effort by applying pressure outside the military realm. These tactics require only modest resources and little technological sophistication, but they offer considerable leverage, particularly if U.S. interests are low. Even though they involve less-powerful weapons than do conventional military operations, they may prove more effective because they exploit U.S. vulnerabilities. A risky but potentially higher-payoff strategy would be to threaten WMD—a ploy almost certain to provoke a response and to concentrate the attention of U.S. and allied policy makers in a way that a threat with conventional forces alone would not. As the U.S. military continues to increase its technological and operational sophistication or otherwise greatly augment its capabilities relative to those of potential foes, the incentives for adversaries to shift to lower-end or higher-end approaches may grow.

The tendency for adversaries to conduct themselves in ways that are not easily countered by the most-potent U.S. instruments contributes to the third challenge: the likelihood that adversary leaderships will be most practiced in protecting against the coercive mechanisms to which they seem most exposed. That is, although an adversary leadership may be highly susceptible to a particular type of coercive pressure, it is also likely to be skilled at defending against that pressure. Saddam Husayn, for instance, devotes the lion's share of his attention to preventing a coup or assassination from arising from his power base—the ranks of the Baath party, military, or security services. As a result, he is susceptible but not always vulnerable to the coercive mechanism of power base erosion. Regimes and leaders often (though not always) recognize their own weaknesses and avoid putting themselves in positions where these can be exploited by the coercer.

U.S. attempts to improve its capabilities to respond to these challenges also face limits. Historically, the United States has tried to respond to constraints on the use of force and to adversary counterstrategies with technological solutions. As Russell Weigley notes, "[T]o seek refuge in technology from the hard problems of strategy and policy [is] another dangerous American tendency, fostered by the pragmatic qualities of the American character."[1] In recent decades, technologies have been used both to minimize U.S. casualties and to counter accusations that the United States does not care about adversary civilian suffering. One answer to North Vietnam's attempt to exploit collateral damage was the U.S. introduction of more-advanced precision-guided munitions against targets likely to draw harmful propaganda, such as air defense

1 Weigley, *The American Way of War*, p. 416.

sites in populated areas. When striking terrorist camps in Afghanistan in 1998, the United States used cruise missiles, in part because they posed no threat to U.S. personnel, even though a manned-flight bombing mission could have inflicted greater damage on the terrorist training camps that the United States sought to destroy. Improved information-gathering technology will enable planners to put weapons technology to more efficient use and help reduce the likelihood of mistakes in identifying and striking targets from great distances. In addition to developing new technology, the United States has tried to improve the ability of all the military services to use this technology in order to minimize collateral damage and risks to U.S. personnel through changes in doctrine and training.

Technological advances, particularly in precision targeting and intelligence capabilities, are useful for overcoming certain political constraints on military operations, improving the potency of military threats, and neutralizing an adversary's countermoves. But viewing technological progress as a complete solution can magnify the very problems technology promises to alleviate. Overemphasis on technological answers can unreasonably raise expectations about the tragic but inevitable destructive impact of military force.[2] Indeed, the more the United States relies on high-technology solutions to address political anxieties about casualties and collateral damage, the more reason adversaries have to doubt U.S. credibility. They may conclude, for example—as did Mohammed Farah Aideed, Saddam Husayn, and others before them—that the U.S. emphasis on minimizing casualties means that the United States will back down in the face of combat deaths.

Just as adversaries will react to technological developments, political constraints themselves will shift as technology causes U.S. and interna-

2 Precision can have negative consequences even for casualty-sensitive nations. By vastly reducing the number of misses, precision leaves the United States open to greater criticism when a mistake happens. It is more difficult to explain away to an outraged foreign public an errant cruise missile than an errant "dumb bomb," since misses with the latter instrument are expected. Statements from Chinese officials suggest that this phenomenon fed beliefs within China that NATO's bombing of its Belgrade embassy in May 1999 was deliberate. (See Sheila Melvin, "Why Chinese Can Believe Worst About U.S. Bombing," *USA Today,* May 12, 1999, p. 15A; and Elisabeth Rosenthal, "Public Anger Against U.S. Still Simmers in Beijing," *New York Times*, May 17, 1999, p. A1.)

tional public opinion to expect more from U.S. military forces. Political constraints spring not from capabilities but from societal appraisals of what costs are worth paying and what constitutes just means. These appraisals are not independent of the technology used to conduct military operations. They are subject to shifts as technology evolves. For example, the existence of precision-guided munitions deliverable from great distances has fed public expectations that the United States can destroy the target with relatively low risk to U.S. personnel and few adversary civilian casualties. In future scenarios, when a high degree of discrimination between civilian and military targets may be impossible due to changes in terrain or adversary behavior, public expectations created by prior operations under more-advantageous circumstances may not adjust along with the situation.[3]

At base, the limitations of technology stem from the dynamic nature of both coercion and the political constraints that bind the players; neither adversaries nor domestic and allied audiences will stand still in the face of technological efforts to loosen the yoke of political constraints. Adversaries will react in ways calculated to capitalize on the political constraints demonstrated by the drive for new technologies. Domestic and international audiences will revise their requirements in light of the new possibilities revealed by increased technological proficiency.

These challenges suggest not only that a rote formula for successful coercion is unattainable, but that belief in its existence can spawn misguided policy. Of course, some technological advances will reduce the risks to civilians and property while simultaneously minimizing exposure of U.S. personnel, thus alleviating planning pressures that stem from the common tradeoff between these conflicting demands. In addition to the precision targeting and intelligence-gathering technologies mentioned above, strategic information warfare capabilities—that is, the ability to attack and degrade the adversary's information infrastructure—can provide planners with options that pose relatively little risk to U.S. forces as well as relatively little risk of immediate collateral damage. But overemphasis on technology may lead the U.S. public and policy makers alike to pay less attention to the political and diplomatic factors that are often the most important part of successful coercion. The dynamic nature of coercive contests and the changing nature of

3 Waxman, *International Law and the Politics of Urban Air Operations*, pp. 55–67.

technology and political constraints mean that future contests will differ from past ones. Although this book relies heavily on history to guide its conclusions, this reliance should be tempered by humility in the face of history's most constant lesson: all sides learn from the past and thus change their behavior in the future. Just as Washington learns what does and does not work best, so too do adversaries learn what strategies they must adopt if they are to succeed. Relying exclusively on observations of the past is an invitation to disaster, as adversaries will adapt their counterstrategies to avoid repeating past failures.

WHY POLICY MAKERS AND ANALYSTS DISAGREE

U.S. policy makers are likely to continue to rely heavily on air power and economic sanctions, even though analysts have repeatedly criticized the effectiveness of these instruments. Why this mismatch? Analysts generally define effectiveness solely in terms of convincing an adversary to back down, while policy makers focus on a much wider set of issues. Policy makers are likely to choose suboptimal strategies for a particular crisis because their actions must conform to broader foreign policy objectives and to domestic preferences (and they may want to bolster their political standing).

With this perspective in mind, the seemingly unwavering U.S. preference for air strikes and sanctions over other instruments is more comprehensible. Air strikes and sanctions share the virtues of not requiring overwhelming domestic and allied support. Air strikes generally involve at most a few casualties on the U.S. side and relatively few on the adversary's, making them ideal for maintaining public backing. Air power can also overcome coalition constraints, as its range and versatility allow it to be launched from a number of countries, enabling policy makers to mediate conflicting interests among different states. Sanctions too can often be imposed with little cost or risk to the coercer, particularly if the economy in question is small (e.g., Panama) or produces a good that can be acquired elsewhere (e.g., Iraqi oil). Sanctions require firm and broad international support if they are to have more than a symbolic effect, but policy makers use them regardless of the support level, thus scoring political points for responding to a crisis at relatively little cost or risk.

Ground forces, insurgencies, and the nuclear option are, of course, far more difficult for policy makers to use. Casualty sensitivity and the allied logistical support required for ground operations are considerable, particularly if the numbers involved are large. Insurgencies, even those that command domestic political backing, are often opposed by regional partners, making it hard to sustain support over the years usually required for their success. The use of nuclear weapons (or other forms of WMD) is not a realistic option for the United States today in the vast majority of foreign crises (though the U.S. nuclear arsenal certainly plays a major role in shaping the international environment, and its role in dissuading regional adversaries from considering certain moves in a crisis, including WMD use, is substantial). It is far more likely that the United States will use its overwhelming conventional might to inflict punishment, as this approach will be burdened with fewer restrictions stemming from domestic and international abhorrence.

Because of their political and diplomatic advantages over other alternatives, air power and sanctions will remain the featured instruments of choice for policy makers in many crises. As a result, analysts' criticisms of particular instruments or of broader coercive strategies are likely to have little impact on future policy. As David Baldwin argues:

> To justify a conclusion that 'sanctions are a notoriously poor tool of statecraft,' it is not enough to describe the disadvantages of sanctions; one must show that some other policy alternative is better. If the menu of choice includes only the options of sinking or swimming, the observation that swimming is a 'notoriously poor' way to get from one place to another is not very helpful. And if the principal alternative to economic sanctions is appearing to condone communism, racism, terrorism, or genocide, the observation that they are a 'notoriously poor tool of statecraft' may miss the point.[4]

Baldwin's criticism of the sanctions debate can be applied to the analysis of most coercive instruments. For analysts to have a greater impact, their criticism should recognize, and ideally address, the broader strategic and political concerns that policy makers face when choosing among particular strategies, as well as the limits of options available to policy makers.

As a corollary matter, analysts must also bear in mind U.S. pressure points, as well as those of adversaries, when they recommend polices—a point of which policy makers are only too aware. Analysts' calls for the United States to intervene more decisively, with more ambitious goals,

4 Baldwin, "The Sanctions Debate and the Logic of Choice," pp. 83–84.

or with different instruments often fail to take into account the political and diplomatic costs inherent to these agendas or instruments. Politicians, however, often recognize that domestic support is thin or the intervening coalition fragile and therefore choose instruments that will strengthen, or at least not severely weaken, domestic and international support. Policy makers often are, and should be, thinking several moves ahead. A shift to more-muscular instruments, even if more effective in terms of damage done to the adversary, may leave the United States more open to adversary counterstrategies that exploit the U.S. sensitivity to collateral damage and military casualties. Once again, the beneficial impact of a particular choice would not be observed—because it would be manifest in the adversary's choice *not* to make a particular countermove—but that does not diminish its overall value.

The disconnect between the assessments of policy makers and analysts mirrors a disconnect between policy makers and the U.S. military. The constraints that the United States imposes on military force, in the form of restrictive rules of engagement and other limits on escalation, are generated by the political process itself, even though the military sometimes opposes burdensome restrictions. And, indeed, the military is correct that tight restrictions on military discretion and stringent caps on escalatory options may doom coercive strategies from the start. From a policy maker's perspective, these self-imposed U.S. constraints reflect societal priorities and goals that may be in tension, including public demands about protecting U.S. service members, humanitarian proclivities, and other value choices. Restrictions on how force is used in a crisis zone may therefore be necessary to make the very use of force politically feasible. For military planners and political decision makers at all levels, a key challenge is to understand these tradeoffs, appropriately balance conflicting pressures, and design and promulgate restrictions that, although they may limit pure military effectiveness, make strategic effectiveness possible.

COERCION DYNAMICS AND CREDIBILITY TRAPS

A U.S. threat or limited use of force is never the last move in a crisis, nor is it the first. An adversary will view the threat or use of force at any instant in the context of the coercer's past record and, equally important, how it thinks the coercer will respond in the future. As a result, the same action—an air strike, sanctions on trade, and so on—can lead to wildly dissimilar reactions from foes who view it differently: as the first salvo of an overwhelming campaign, the last gasp of a defeated power, or somewhere in between. Establishing and maintaining credibility is an ongoing process rather than a discrete event.

Essential to bolstering credibility is understanding where and how U.S. power will have the most impact. In general, the strategic, political, and diplomatic concerns of adversaries will differ greatly from those of the United States, and these differences often yield adversary advantages that mitigate the U.S. military edge. Most important, adversaries are likely to be fighting for far higher stakes than is the United States. Even if the United States is confronting a WMD-armed adversary in a critical region such as the Persian Gulf, the balance of interests is likely to favor the foe, which may be fighting for regime survival or other core objectives. As such, the adversary's concerns about its own casualties, let alone the civilian casualties of its enemy, are not likely to have a restraining influence on its behavior.

The United States must, in this light, understand what it can and cannot affect: it can determine only the level of pain it inflicts, not the adversary's willingness to accept that pain. Ho Chi Minh's often-quoted statement that the North Vietnamese could endure ten times as many casualties as the United States and nevertheless triumph strikes at the essence of many failed coercive strategies: a misunderstanding of the adversary's willingness to accept punishment. Adversary regimes with little popular input or that capitalize on anti-U.S. nationalism will often endure tremendous suffering. An adversary's willingness to take punishment may fluctuate over time, and designing a strategy that corresponds to these fluctuations will remain an elusive goal for military planners and other strategists. While the U.S. military arsenal may be extremely precise in a technological sense, the ability to finely tune the political effects its use has on an adversary's population, elite, or key regime decision makers remains largely beyond U.S. planners.

This book emphasizes the asymmetry in stakes between the United States and adversaries as a key factor in explaining strategies and outcomes. In doing so, however, we are mindful that today's security environment does not allow for rigorous testing of this variable. With the possible exception of the Persian Gulf War, few standoffs have involved direct and immediate threats to vital U.S. interests. This means that for the time being, public expectations, and hence political constraints, are evolving from no more than a subset of crises and operations along a much larger spectrum of potential conflict. Whether these constraints will hold, loosen, or dissolve during a major conflict involving direct threats to vital U.S. interests remains an open question, as does whether the adversary will take notice.

The low-stakes nature of many of the confrontations facing the United States today could spell problems for future coercive attempts that entail higher stakes. Adversaries also study history, and the lessons they learn in doing so may create misperceptions that ultimately do more harm than good, because the lessons of today's low-stakes contests do not necessarily apply to future, high-stakes confrontations. How many lives, adversary decision makers might ask, would a U.S. president sacrifice to defend Japan from a nuclear attack? reverse the conquest of a NATO ally? stave off a humanitarian crisis in Mexico? If adversary leaders draw lessons from World War II, they may conclude that the United States will sacrifice hundreds of thousands of soldiers. If they draw lessons from Somalia, their answer will be quite different. Reaching the wrong conclusions about U.S. resolve and willingness to sacrifice may lead adversaries to take foolish gambles with tragic consequences.

Saddam Husayn's probable reasoning during the Gulf War should produce caution. Drawing lessons from the U.S. quagmire in Vietnam and the ignominious withdrawal from Lebanon in 1984, Saddam concluded that the United States could not stomach casualties and would eventually back down. He miscalculated the risks the United States would run to defend its substantial interests in the region. Future adversaries may similarly doubt U.S. decisiveness and resolve. Drawing heavily on observations of humanitarian missions or other low-stakes conflicts, they may conclude, for example, that the United States is not likely to escalate beyond air strikes to impose its will.

Compounding the problem of an adversary drawing skewed lessons is pressure on the U.S. side to act even when the circumstances are not auspicious. Air strikes to stop guerrilla forces, sanctions to prompt a regime change, and diplomatic isolation to force a regime to give up a vital domestic goal are only a few examples of an instrument's realistic value being mismatched with its actual use. Yet the United States, as the world's only superpower, often finds itself under tremendous pressure to "do something." This pressure poses a long-term challenge for coercive strategy makers. Because the U.S. public and U.S. allies often see air strikes, sanctions, diplomatic pressure, and other forms of coercion as low-risk, low-commitment measures, policy makers are tempted to use them to demonstrate that they are not ignoring a problem. Yet because these are low-cost tools, they are usually called on when U.S. public or allied commitment is weak—the very situation that makes coercion harder. The prospects of escalation will be difficult in such circumstances, rules of engagement will likely be burdensome, and adversaries will question U.S. credibility. The very strengths of these low-commitment instruments with regard to domestic support and coalition dynamics could become weaknesses if these instruments are used in situations that erode their perceived effectiveness and thus erode U.S. credibility when it employs them in the future.

FINAL WORDS

Failure raises the chances of a destructive spiral. When U.S. instruments fail to coerce, or when the United States concedes to counter-escalation, the damage extends far beyond the immediate crisis. Failure can raise potential adversaries' doubts about the sustainability of U.S. coercive pressure. It can also lead allies or potential allies to cooperate with rather than oppose aggressors. Equally important, the misuse of an instrument can spawn false conclusions, at home and abroad among potential adversaries and allies, about that instrument's true coercive effectiveness.

But the reverse is also true. While U.S. intervention in inauspicious conditions may undermine the credibility of future coercive efforts, successful campaigns can repair some lost credibility. Some features of U.S. coercion are deeply rooted, as are some foreign perceptions of it. There is also room, however, for better projecting resolve and for better deflating of adversaries' confidence that certain counter-coercive strategies will succeed. Successful coercive strategy making requires that sufficient domestic and foreign support be assembled that sudden dips in it do not induce U.S. policy makers to respond with the very restrictions on coercive force that adversaries seek.

Effective coercion in any given crisis depends on cultivating favorable political conditions during the crisis but also far in advance of it. U.S. political strategies should aim at building robust public and international backing for coercive operations through careful and energetic articulation of U.S. interests and alignment of U.S. interests with those of key U.S. partners abroad *before* emergencies arise. On the domestic side, this means not only building the case among both the public and policy elite that certain interests warrant great sacrifices, but also projecting a realistic assessment of risks inherent in defending those interests. On the international side, U.S. diplomacy must aim to shore up partnerships to withstand the strains that naturally arise in any military venture.

Successful coercion, though, is hard. Policy makers face difficult and at times irreconcilable tradeoffs among national interests, the concerns of coalition partners, and the demands of voters at home. Strong leadership can sometimes overcome many limits commonly placed on the use of force, but the constraints will sometimes be too tight. To coerce with credibility—and hence with any chance of success—strong powers must act with restraint. If the United States is to coerce effectively, it must recognize not only the opportunities but also the limitations of available instruments in light of the constraints under which they will be used. Such constraints exist for all forms of military power. When they are understood, the United States will be able to husband its resources and focus its efforts more potently.

Bibliography

Abrahamian, Ervand. *The Iranian Mojahedin.* New Haven, CT: Yale University Press, 1989.

Achen, Christopher H., and Duncan Snidal. "Rational Deterrence Theory and Comparative Case Studies," *World Politics,* Vol. 41, no. 2 (January 1989), pp. 143–169.

Allan, Charles T. "Extended Conventional Deterrence: In from the Cold and Out of the Nuclear Fire?" *The Washington Quarterly,* Vol. 17, No. 3 (Summer 1994), pp. 203–233.

Allison, Graham T. *Essence of Decision.* Glenview, IL: Scott, Foresman and Company, 1971.

Alon, Hanan. *Countering Palestinian Terrorism in Israel: Toward a Policy Analysis of Countermeasures.* Santa Monica, CA: RAND, 1980.

Arkin, William M. "Baghdad: The Urban Sanctuary in Desert Storm?" *Air Power Journal,* Vol. 10, no. 1 (Spring 1997), pp. 4–20.

Arquilla, John. "Bound to Fail: Regional Deterrence After the Cold War," *Comparative Strategy,* Vol. 14, no. 2 (Spring 1995), pp.123–136.

Ascherson, Neal. *Black Sea.* New York: Hill and Wang, 1995.

Atkinson, Rick. "Air Assaults Set Stage for Broader Role," *Washington Post,* November 15, 1995, p. A1.

Atkinson, Rick. *Crusade: The Untold Story of the Persian Gulf War.* Boston, MA: Houghton Mifflin, 1993.

Ayoob, Mohammed. "The Security Problematic in the Third World," *World Politics,* Vol. 43, no. 2 (January 1991), pp. 257–283.

Baker, James E. *The Politics of Diplomacy.* New York: G.P. Putnam's Sons, 1995.

Baldwin, David. *Economic Statecraft.* Princeton, NJ: Princeton University Press, 1985.

Baldwin, David A. "Power Analysis and World Politics: New Trends and Old Tendencies," *World Politics,* Vol. 31, no. 1 (January 1979), pp. 161–194.

Baldwin, David. "The Power of Positive Sanctions," *World Politics,* Vol. 24, no. 1 (October 1971), pp. 19–38.

Baldwin, David A. "The Sanctions Debate and the Logic of Choice," *International Security,* Vol. 24, no. 3 (Winter 1999–2000), pp. 80–107.

Baram, Amatzia. *Building Toward Crisis: Saddam Husayn's Strategy for Survival.* Washington, DC: Washington Institute for Near East Policy, 1998.

Bar-Joseph, Uri. "Variations on a Theme: The Conceptualization of Deterrence in Israeli Strategic Thinking," *Security Studies*, Vol. 7, no. 3 (Spring 1998), pp. 145–181.

Bar-Siman-Tov, Yaacov. *The Israeli-Egyptian War of Attrition, 1969–1970: A Case-Study of Limited Local War.* New York: Columbia University Press, 1980.

Bar-Siman-Tov, Yaacov. "The War of Attrition, 1969–1970." In *Avoiding War: Problems of Crisis Management*, Alexander L. George, ed. Boulder, CO: Westview, 1991, pp. 320–341.

Battles, Jan. "Robinson Hits at Clinical Bombing," *Sunday Times* (London), May 16, 1999, p. 18.

Beale, Michael O. "Bombs over Bosnia: The Role of Airpower in Bosnia-Herzogovina," master's thesis, School of Advanced Airpower Studies, 1997.

Bengio, Ofra. "How Does Saddam Hold On?" *Foreign Affairs,* Vol. 79, no. 4 (July/August 2000), pp. 94–101.

Bennett, Andrew, Joseph Lepgold, and Danny Unger. "Burden-Sharing in the Persian Gulf War," *International Organization,* Vol. 48, no. 1 (Winter 1994), pp. 39–75.

Beres, Louis R. "The Permissibility of State-Sponsored Assassination During Peace and War," *Temple International and Comparative Law Journal*, no. 5 (Fall 1992), pp. 231–249.

Berkowitz, Bruce. "Rules of Engagement for UN Peacekeeping Forces in Bosnia," *Orbis*, Vol. 38, no. 4 (Fall 1994), pp. 635–646.

Bertram, Christoph. "Multilateral Diplomacy and Conflict Resolution," *Survival*, Vol. 37, no. 4 (Winter 1995–1996), pp. 65–82.

Betts, Richard K. "The Delusion of Impartial Intervention," *Foreign Affairs,* Vol. 73, no. 6 (November/December 1994), pp. 20–33.

Betts, Richard K. "The New Threat of Weapons of Mass Destruction," *Foreign Affairs*, Vol. 77, no. 1 (January/February 1998), pp. 26–67.

Betts, Richard K. "What Will It Take to Deter the United States?" *Parameters*, Vol. 25, no. 4 (Winter 1995), pp. 70–79.

Biddle, Stephen. "Victory Misunderstood: What the Gulf War Tells Us About the Future of Conflict," *International Security*, Vol. 21, no. 2 (Fall 1996), pp. 139–179.

Bill, James A. "Morale vs. Technology: The Power of Iran in the Persian Gulf War." In *The Iran-Iraq War: The Politics of Aggression*, Farhang Rajaee, ed. Gainesville, FL: University of Florida Press, 1993, pp. 198–209.

Bird, Chris. "Kosovo Crisis: Yugoslav Media Fear Crackdown amid War Fever," *Guardian*, October 8, 1998, p. 15.

Blackwill, Robert D., ed., *New Nuclear Nations: Consequences for U.S. Policy*. New York: Council on Foreign Relations, 1993.

Blanchard, Jean-Marc F., and Norrin M. Ripsman. "Asking the Right Question: *When* Do Economic Sanctions Work Best?" *Security Studies*, Vol. 9, no. 1–2 (Autumn 1999–2000), pp. 219–253.

Blechman, Barry M., and Tamara Cofman Wittes. "Defining Moment: The Threat and Use of Force in American Foreign Policy," *Political Science Quarterly*, Vol. 114, no. 1 (Spring 1999), pp. 1–30.

Boudreau, Donald G. "The Bombing of the Osirak Reactor: One Decade Later," *Strategic Analysis* (June 1991), pp. 287–301.

Brill, Steven. "War Gets the Monica Treatment," *Brill's Content* (July/August 1999), pp. 103–104.

Bueno de Mesquita, Bruce. *The War Trap*. New Haven, CT: Yale University Press, 1981.

Bundy, McGeorge. *Danger and Survival*. New York: Random House, 1988.

Bush, George, and Brent Scowcroft. *A World Transformed*. New York: Knopf, 1998.

Butcher, Tim, and Patrick Bishop. "NATO Admits Air Campaign Failed," *London Daily Telegraph*, July 22, 1999, p. 1.

Byman, Daniel. "After the Storm: U.S. Policy Toward Iraq Since 1991," *Political Science Quarterly*, Vol. 115, no. 4 (Winter 2000–2001), pp. 493–516.

Byman, Daniel L., Ian Lesser, Bruce Pirnie, Cheryl Benard, and Matthew Waxman. *Strengthening the Partnership: Military Cooperation with Relief Agencies*. Santa Monica, CA: RAND, 2000.

Byman, Daniel L., and Jerrold D. Green. *Political Violence and Stability in the States of the Northern Persian Gulf.* Santa Monica, CA: RAND, 1999.

Byman, Daniel, Kenneth Pollack, and Matthew Waxman. "Coercing Saddam Hussein: Lessons from the Past," *Survival,* Vol. 40, no. 3 (Autumn 1998), pp. 127–152.

Byman, Daniel, and Stephen Van Evera. "Why They Fight: Hypotheses on the Causes of Contemporary Deadly Conflict," *Security Studies,* Vol. 7, no. 3 (Spring 1998), pp. 1–50.

Byman, Daniel, and Matthew C. Waxman. *Confronting Iraq: U.S. Policy and the Use of Force Since the Gulf War.* Santa Monica, CA: RAND, 2000.

Byman, Daniel, and Matthew Waxman. "Defeating U.S. Coercion," *Survival,* Vol. 41, no. 2 (Summer 1999), pp. 107–120.

Byman, Daniel L., and Matthew C. Waxman, "Kosovo and the Great Air Power Debate," *International Security,* Vol. 24, no. 4 (Spring 2000), pp. 1–38.

Byman, Daniel, Matthew Waxman, and Eric Larson. *Air Power as a Coercive Instrument.* Santa Monica, CA: RAND, 1999.

Cambone, Stephen A., and Patrick J. Garrity. "The Future of U.S. Nuclear Policy," *Survival,* Vol. 36, no. 4 (Winter 1994–1995), pp. 73–95.

Camerer, Colin. "Individual Decision-Making." In *The Handbook of Experimental Economics.* Princeton, NJ: Princeton University Press, 1995, pp. 587–703.

Chandler, Robert W. *Tomorrow's War, Today's Decisions.* McLean, VA: AMCODA Press, 1996.

Chernomyrdin, Viktor. "Impossible to Talk Peace with Bombs Falling," *Washington Post,* May 27, 1999, p. A39.

Christensen, Thomas J., and Jack Snyder. "Chain Gangs and Passed Bucks: Predicting Alliance Patterns in Multipolarity," *International Organization* Vol. 44, no. 2 (Spring 1990), pp. 137–168.

Chubin, Shahram, and Charles Tripp. *Iran and Iraq at War.* Boulder, CO: Westview Press, 1988.

Claude, Inis L., Jr. "The United States and Changing Approaches to National Security and World Order," *Naval War College Review,* Vol. XLVIII, no. 3 (Summer 1995), pp. 46–61.

Clinton, William J. "Remarks by the President in Television Address to the Nation," September 14, 1994, http://www.pub.whitehouse.gov/

uri-res /I2R?urn:pdi: //oma. eop.gov.us /1994 /9/15/6.text.1 (accessed on March 14, 2000).

Clinton, William J. "Remarks by the President to Majority 2000," Fairlane Club, Dearborn, MI, April 16, 1999.

Clodfelter, Mark. *The Limits of Air Power: The American Bombing of North Vietnam*. New York: Free Press, 1989.

Cohen, Eliot A. "The Mystique of U.S. Air Power," *Foreign Affairs*, Vol. 73, no. 1 (January/February 1994), pp. 109–124.

Connelly, Marjorie. "Wide U.S. Support for Air Strikes," *New York Times*, December 18, 1998, p. A26.

Cordesman, Anthony H. *The Military Balance in the Gulf, Volume II: Iran and Iraq*. Washington, DC: Center for Strategic and International Studies, January 1998.

Cordesman, Anthony, and Ahmed Hashim. *Iraq: Sanctions and Beyond*. Boulder, CO: Westview Press, 1997.

Cordesman, Anthony H., and Abraham R. Wagner. *The Lessons of Modern War, Vol. II: The Iran-Iraq War*. Boulder, CO: Westview Press, 1990.

Covault, Craig. "NATO Airstrikes Target Serbian Infrastructure," *Aviation Week and Space Technology*, September 11, 1995, p. 27.

Crawford, Leslie. "Unrepentant Peacekeepers Will Fire on Somali Human Shields," *Financial Times*, September 11, 1993, p. 4.

Crossett, Barbara. "Civilians Will Be in Harm's Way If Baghdad Is Hit," *New York Times*, January 28, 1998, p. A6.

Crowther, William. "Moldova After Independence," *Current History*, no. 93 (October 1994), pp. 342–347.

David, Stephen. *Choosing Sides: Alignment and Realignment in the Third World*. Baltimore, MD: Johns Hopkins University Press, 1991.

Davis, Paul K. "Protecting Weak and Medium-Strength States: Issues of Deterrence, Stability, and Decision Making." In *Post Cold-War Conflict Deterrence*. Washington, DC: Naval Studies Board, National Research Council, 1997, pp. 153–181.

Department of Defense Dictionary of Military and Associated Terms. Joint Chief of Staff Publication 1-02. Washington, DC: Department of Defense, 1994.

Des Forges, Alison. *Leave None to Tell the Story: Genocide in Rwanda*. New York: Human Rights Watch, 1999, http://www.hum.org/reports/1991/rwanda.

Douhet, Giulio. *The Command of the Air.* Washington, DC: Office of Air Force History, 1983.

Dowler, Thomas W., and Joseph S. Howard, III. "Countering the Threat of the Well Armed Tyrant: A Modest Proposal for Small Nuclear Weapons," *Strategic Review,* no. 19 (Fall, 1991), pp. 34–40.

Downs, George W., and David M. Rocke. "Conflict, Agency, and Gambling for Resurrection: The Principle-Agent Problem Goes to War," *American Journal of Political Science,* Vol. 38, no. 2 (May 1994), pp. 362–380.

Drezner, Daniel W. "The Trouble with Carrots: Transaction Costs, Conflict Expectations, and Economic Inducements," *Security Studies,* Vol. 9, no. 1–2 (Autumn 1999–Winter 2000), pp. 188–218.

Dunn, Lewis A. "New Nuclear Threats to U.S. Security." In *New Nuclear Nations: Consequences for U.S. Policy*, Robert D. Blackwill and Albert Carnesale, eds. New York: Council on Foreign Relations Press, 1993, pp. 20–52.

Dupuy, T. N. *Elusive Victory: The Arab Israeli Wars, 1947–1974*, 3rd ed. Dubuque, IA: Kendall/Hunt Publishing, 1992.

Dworken, Jonathan. *Improving Marine Coordination with Relief Organizations in Humanitarian Assistance Operations.* Alexandria, VA: Center for Naval Analysis, 1996.

Dworken, Jonathan. "Operation Restore Hope: Coordinating Relief Operations," *Joint Forces Quarterly*, no. 8 (Summer 1995), pp. 14–20.

Eades, Lindsay Michie. *The End of Apartheid in South Africa.* Westport, CT: Greenwood Press, 1999.

Eisenstadt, Michael. *Like a Phoenix from the Ashes? The Future of Iraqi Military Power.* Washington, DC: The Washington Institute for Near East Policy, 1993.

Eisenstadt, Michael. "The Military Dimension." In *Iran Under Khatami*, Patrick Clawson, Michael Eisenstadt, Eliyahu Kanovsky, and David Menashri, eds. Washington, DC: The Washington Institute for Near East Policy, 1998, pp. 71–98.

Eisenstadt, Mike. *The Sword of the Arabs: Iraq's Strategic Weapons.* Washington, DC: The Washington Institute for Near East Policy, 1990.

Erdmann, Andrew P. "The U.S. Presumption of Quick, Costless Wars," *Orbis*, Vol. 43, no. 3 (Summer 1999), pp. 363–382.

Fearon, James D. "Bargaining, Enforcement, and International Cooperation," *International Organization*, Vol. 52, no. 2 (Spring 1998), pp. 269–305.

Feaver, Peter D. "Command and Control in Emerging Nuclear Nations," *International Security*, Vol. 17, no. 3 (Winter 1992–1993), pp. 160–195.

"Fitting Sanctions." *Jane's Defence Weekly*, May 3, 2000 (electronic version).

Flournoy, Michele A. "Implications for U.S. Military Strategy." In *New Nuclear Nations: Consequences for U.S. Policy*, Robert D. Blackwill and Albert Carnesale, eds. New York: Council on Foreign Relations Press, 1993, pp. 135–161.

Foer, Franklin. "Slobodan Milosevic: How a Genocidal Dictator Keeps Getting Away with It," *Slate*, June 20, 1998, http://www.slate.com (accessed on March 11, 1999).

Ford, Franklin L. *Political Murder: From Tyrannicide to Terrorism.* Cambridge, MA: Harvard University Press, 1985.

Franz, (Colonel) David. Testimony before United States Senate Joint Committee on Judiciary and Intelligence, March 4, 1998, http://www.senate.gov~judiciary/franz.htm (accessed on November 17, 1998).

Freedman, Lawrence, ed. *Strategic Coercion.* Oxford: Oxford University Press, 1998.

Freedman, Lawrence, and Efraim Karsh. *The Gulf Conflict, 1990–1991.* Princeton, NJ: Princeton University Press, 1993.

Fursenko, A. A., and Timothy Naftali. *"One Hell of a Gamble": Khrushchev, Castro, and Kennedy, 1958–1964.* New York: Norton, 1998.

Futrell, Robert F. *Ideas, Concepts, Doctrine: Basic Thinking in the United States Air Force.* Maxwell Air Force Base, AL: Air University Press, 1989.

Futrell, Robert F. *The United States Air Force in Korea, 1950–1953.* Washington, DC: Office of Air Force History, 1983.

Gaddis, John Lewis. *We Now Know: Rethinking Cold War History.* New York: Oxford University Press, 1997.

Galtung, Johan. "On the Effects of International Economic Sanctions: With Examples from the Case of Rhodesia," *World Politics,* Vol. 19, no. 3 (April 1967), pp. 378–416.

Gates, Robert M. *From the Shadows*. New York: Simon and Schuster, 1996.

Gause, F. Gregory, III, "Saddam's Unwatched Arsenal," *Foreign Affairs*, Vol. 78, no. 3 (May/June 1999), pp. 54–65.

Gellman, Barton, "Allied Air War Struck More Broadly in Iraq," *Washington Post*, June 23, 1991, p. A1.

George, Alexander. *Forceful Persuasion.* Washington, DC: United States Institute of Peace, 1991.

George Alexander L., and Richard Smoke. *Deterrence in American Foreign Policy: Theory and Practice.* New York: Columbia University Press, 1974.

George, Alexander, and William E. Simons, eds. *The Limits of Coercive Diplomacy*. Boulder, CO: Westview Press, 1994.

"Georgia: Against the Odds," *The Economist*, August 14, 1993.

"Georgia: Tricked and Abandoned," *The Economist*, October 2, 1993.

Gilligan, Andrew. "Russia, Not Bombs, Brought End to War in Kosovo Says Jackson," *London Sunday Telegraph*, August 1, 1999, p. 1.

Glenny, Misha. *The Fall of Yugoslavia.* New York: Penguin Books, 1993.

Gompert, David C. "Rethinking the Role of Nuclear Weapons," *Strategic Forum*, no. 141 (May 1998), pp. 1–4.

Gompert, David, Richard Kugler, and Martin Libicki. *Mind the Gap: Promoting a Transatlantic Revolution in Military Affairs.* Santa Monica, CA: RAND, 1999.

Gompert, David, Kenneth Watman, and Dean Wilkening. "Nuclear First Use Revisited," *Survival,* Vol. 37, no. 3 (Autumn 1995), pp. 27–44.

Gordon, Michael R., "NATO Air Attacks on Power Plants Pass a Threshold," *New York Times*, May 4, 1999, p. A1.

Gordon, Michael R. "NATO Plans Weeks of Bombing to Break Grip of Serb Leader," *New York Times*, April 1, 1999, p. A1.

Gordon, Michael R. "NATO Says Serbs, Fearing Land War, Dig in on Border," *New York Times*, May 19, 1999, p. A1.

Gordon, Michael R., and Eric Schmitt. "Thwarted, NATO Agrees to Bomb Belgrade Sites," *New York Times*, March 31, 1999, p. A1.

Gordon, Michael, and Bernard Trainor. *The Generals' War: The Inside Story of the Gulf War.* Boston, MA: Little, Brown, 1994.

Gourevitch, Philip. *We Wish to Inform You That Tomorrow We Will Be Killed with Our Families: Stories from Rwanda.* New York: Farrar, Straus, and Giroux, 1998.

Gow, James. *Triumph of the Lack of Will: International Diplomacy and the Yugoslav War.* New York: Columbia University Press, 1997.

Graham-Browne, Sarah. *Sanctioning Saddam: The Politics of Intervention in Iraq.* London: I.B. Tauris, 1999.

Gurr, Ted Robert. "Ethnic Warfare on the Wane," *Foreign Affairs*, Vol. 79, no. 3 (May/June 2000), pp. 52–64.

Haass, Richard N. "It's Dangerous to Disarm," *New York Times*, December 11, 1996, p. A21.

Hagan, Joe, and Jerel Rosati, eds. *Foreign Policy Restructuring: How Governments Respond to Global Change.* Columbia, SC: University of South Carolina Press, 1994.

Halperin, Morton. *Limited War in the Nuclear Age.* New York: John Wiley and Sons, 1963.

Harden, Elaine, and John M. Broder. "Clinton's War Aims: Win the War, Keep the U.S. Voters Content," *New York Times*, May 22, 1999, p. A1.

Harris, Arthur. *Bomber Offensive.* London: Greenhill Books, 1990.

Hashim, Ahmed. "The State, Society, and the Evolution of Warfare in the Middle East: The Rise of Strategic Deterrence," *Washington Quarterly,* Vol. 18, no. 4 (Autumn 1995), pp. 53–76.

Havens, Murray Clark, Carl Leiden, and Karl M. Schmitt. *The Politics of Assassination.* Englewood Cliffs, NJ: Prentice-Hall, Inc., 1970.

Hedges, Chris. "Kosovo's Next Masters?" *Foreign Affairs*, Vol. 79, no. 3 (May/June 1999), pp. 24–42.

Heidenrich, John G. "The Gulf War: How Many Iraqis Died?" *Foreign Policy*, no. 90 (Spring 1993), pp. 108–125.

Henkin, Louis. *How Nations Behave: Law and Foreign Policy.* New York: Praeger, 1968.

Hiro, Dilip. *Lebanon: Fire and Embers.* New York: St. Martin's Press, 1992.

Hoffman, David, and Ann Devroy. "Too Many Strings Attached, U.S. Finds," *Washington Post*, February 22, 1991, p. A1.

Holbrooke, Richard. *To End a War.* New York: Random House, 1998.

Hopf, Ted. *Peripheral Visions: Deterrence Theory and American Foreign Policy in the Third World, 1965–1990.* Ann Arbor: University of Michigan Press, 1994.

Hosmer, Stephen T. *Constraints on U.S. Strategy in Third World Conflicts.* New York: Crane Russak and Co., 1987.

Hosmer, Stephen T. *Operations to Remove Enemy Leaders.* Santa Monica, CA: RAND, forthcoming.

Hosmer, Stephen T. *Psychological Effects of U.S. Air Operations in Four Wars, 1941–1991: Lessons for U.S. Commanders.* Santa Monica, CA: RAND, 1995.

Hufbauer, Gary Clyde, et al. *Economic Sanctions Reconsidered.* 2nd ed. Washington, DC: Institute for International Economics, 1990.

Human Rights Watch. "Civilian Deaths in the NATO Air Campaign," Vol. 12, no. 1 (February 2000), http://www.hrw.org/reports/2000/nato/index.htm.

Hunt, Peter. "Coalition Warfare: Considerations for the Air Component Commander," master's thesis, School of Advanced Airpower Studies, Air University Press, June 1996.

Huth, Paul K. *Extended Deterrence and the Prevention of War.* New Haven, CT: Yale University Press, 1988.

Huth, Paul K. "Reputations and Deterrence," *Security Studies,* Vol. 7, no. 1 (Fall 1997), pp. 72–99.

Huth, Paul K., and Bruce Russett. "Testing Deterrence Theory: Rigor Makes a Difference," *World Politics,* Vol. 42, no. 4 (July 1990), pp. 466–501.

The International Institute for Strategic Studies, *The Military Balance 1996–1997.* London: The International Institute for Strategic Studies, 1996.

"Interview: General Wesley Clark," *Jane's Defence Weekly*, July 7, 1999.

Iraqi News Agency Broadcasts, January 9–13, 1991. In FBIS NES-91-009, January 14, 1991.

Janis, Irving L. *Air War and Emotional Stress: Psychological Studies of Bombing and Civilian Defense.* Santa Monica, CA: RAND, 1951.

Janis, Irving L. *Groupthink.* Boston: Houghton Mifflin Company, 1982.

Jehl, Douglas. "In NATO Talks, Bosnia Sets Off a Sharp Debate," *New York Times,* January 11, 1994, p. A1.

Jehl, Douglas. "Only One Arab Nation Endorses U.S. Threat of Attack on Iraq," *New York Times*, February 9, 1998, p. A6.

Jenkins, Simon. "NATO's Moral Morass," *The Times* (London), April 28, 1999.

Jentleson, Bruce W. "The Pretty Prudent Public: Post-Cold War American Public Opinion on the Use of Military Force," *International Studies Quarterly,* no. 36 (1992), pp. 49–74.

Jentleson, Bruce W., and Rebecca Britton. "Still Pretty Prudent: Post-Cold War American Public Opinion on the Use of Military Force," *Journal of Conflict Resolution*, Vol. 42, no. 4 (August 1998), pp. 395–417.

Joseph, Robert G. "Deterring Regional Proliferators," *Washington Quarterly*, Vol. 20, no. 3 (Summer 1997), pp. 167–175.

Kahn, Herman. *On Escalation: Metaphors and Scenarios*. Washington, DC: Praeger, 1965.

Kahn, Herman. *On Thermonuclear War*. Princeton, NJ: Princeton University Press, 1960.

Kahneman, Daniel, and Amos Tversky. "Prospect Theory: An Analysis of Decision Under Risk," *Econometrica,* no. 47 (1979), pp. 263–291.

Kaplan, David E., and Andrew Marshell. *Cult at the End of the World: The Terrifying Story of the Aum Doomsday Cult*. New York: Crown Publishers, Inc., 1996.

Kaplan, Fred M. *The Wizards of Armageddon*. Stanford, CA: Stanford University Press, 1991.

Karnow, Stanley. *Vietnam: A History*. New York: Penguin, 1997.

Kay, David. "Iraq's Weapons of Mass Destruction: A Continuing Challenge." Testimony before the Committee on International Relations, House of Representatives, March 28, 1996. Washington, DC: U.S. Government Printing Office, 1996.

Keaney, Thomas A., and Eliot A. Cohen. *Gulf War Air Power Survey (GWAPS): Summary Volume*. Washington, DC: Government Printing Office, 1993.

Kennedy, Kevin M. "The Relationship Between the Military and Humanitarian Organizations in Operation Restore Hope." In *Lessons from Somalia*, Walter Clarke and Jeffrey Herbst, eds. Boulder, CO: Westview Press, 1997, pp. 99–117.

Keohane, Robert O., and Joseph S. Nye. *Power and Interdependence*. Boston: Little, Brown, 1977.

Khalilzad, Zalmay, and Ian O. Lesser, eds. *Sources of Conflict in the 21st Century, Regional Futures and U.S. Strategy*. Santa Monica, CA: RAND, 1998.

Kirshner, Jonathan. *Currency and Coercion: The Political Economy of International Monetary Power*. Princeton, NJ: Princeton University Press, 1995.

Kirshner, Jonathan. "The Microfoundations of Economic Sanctions," *Security Studies,* Vol. 6, no. 3 (Spring 1997), pp. 32–64.

Kissinger, Henry. *The Necessity for Choice.* New York: Harper & Row, 1961.

Kohut, Andrew, and Robert C. Toth. "Arms and the People," *Foreign Affairs,* Vol. 73, no. 6 (November/December 1994), pp. 47–61.

Kupchan, Charles A. "NATO and the Persian Gulf: Examining Intra-Alliance Behavior," *International Organization*, Vol. 42, no. 2 (Spring 1988), pp. 317–346.

Kuperman, Alan. "Rwanda in Retrospect," *Foreign Affairs*, Vol. 79, no. 1 (January/February 2000), pp. 94–118.

Kuperman, Alan. "The Other Lesson of Rwanda: Mediators Sometimes Do More Damage Than Good," *SAIS Review,* Vol. 16, no. 1 (Winter/Spring 1996), pp. 221–240.

Lambeth, Benjamin S. "Russia's Air War in Chechnya," *Studies in Conflict & Terrorism*, Vol. 19, no. 4 (Winter 1996), pp. 365–388.

Lancaster, John. "Egypt Urges Diplomacy, Not Force, in U.S.-Iraq Dispute," *Washington Post*, November 14, 1997, p. A35.

Lapidus, Gail W. "Contested Sovereignty: The Tragedy of Chechnya," *International Security*, Vol. 23, no. 1 (Summer 1998), pp. 5–49.

Laqueur, Walter. *The New Terrorism: Fanaticism and the Arms of Mass Destruction.* New York: Oxford University Press, 1999.

Larson, Eric V. *Casualties and Consensus.* Santa Monica, CA: RAND, 1996.

Lawson, Mark. "Flattening a Few Broadcasters," *Guardian* (London), April 24, 1999, p. 18.

Lebow, Richard Ned. "Conclusions." In *Psychology and Deterrence: Perspectives on Security,* Robert Jervis, Richard Ned Lebow, and Janice Gross Stein, eds. Baltimore, MD: Johns Hopkins University Press, 1985, pp. 203–232.

Lebow, Richard Ned, and Janice Gross Stein. "Rational Deterrence Theory: I Think, Therefore I Deter," *World Politics*, Vol. 41, no. 2 (January 1989), pp. 208–224.

Lederer, Edith M. "Tuzla Off Limits to Off-Duty Troops," *Detroit News*, February 20, 1997, p. A12.

Lenway, Stephanie. "Between War and Commerce: Economic Sanctions as a Tool of Statecraft," *International Organization,* Vol. 42, no. 2 (Spring 1988), pp. 397–426.

Lepgold, Joseph. "Hypotheses on Vulnerability: Are Terrorists and Drug Traffickers Coerceable?" In *Strategic Coercion,* Lawrence Freedman, ed. Oxford: Oxford University Press, 1998, pp. 131–150.

Lesser, Ian O., and Ashley J. Tellis. *Strategic Exposure: Proliferation Around the Mediterranean.* Santa Monica, CA: RAND, 1996.

Leurdijk, Dick A. *The United Nations and NATO in Former Yugoslavia.* The Hague, Netherlands: Netherlands Atlantic Commission, 1994.

Levite, Ariel, Bruce Jentleson, and Larry Berman. *Protracted Military Interventions: From Commitments to Disengagement.* New York: Columbia University Press, 1992.

Levy, Jack. "Alliance Formation and War Behavior," *Journal of Conflict Resolution,* Vol. 25, no. 3 (September 1981), pp. 581–613.

Levy, Jack. "Loss Aversion, Framing, and Bargaining: The Implications of Prospect Theory for International Conflict," *International Political Science Review,* Vol. 17, no. 2 (1996), pp. 179–195.

Levy, Jack. "Prospect Theory, Rational Choice, and International Relations," *International Studies Quarterly,* no. 41 (1997), pp. 87–112.

Lewy, Guenter. *America in Vietnam.* New York: Oxford University Press, 1978.

Lorch, Donatella. "Disunity Hampering UN Somalia Effort," *New York Times*, July 12, 1993, p. A8.

Lorenz, F. M. "Law and Anarchy in Somalia," *Parameters,* Vol. 23, no. 4 (Winter 1993–1994), pp. 27–41.

Lustick, Ian. "Stability in Deeply Divided Societies: Consociationalism Versus Control," *World Politics,* Vol. 31, no. 3. (April 1979), pp. 325–344.

The Manchester Guardian Weekly, January 20, 1991, p. 21.

Mandelbaum, Michael. "Foreign Policy as Social Work," *Foreign Affairs,* Vol. 75, no. 1 (January/February 1996), pp. 16–32.

Mann, Paul. "Strategists Question U.S. Steadfastness," *Aviation Week and Space Technology*, August 31, 1998, p. 32.

Marr, Phebe. *A Modern History of Iraq*. Boulder, CO: Westview Press, 1985.

Martin, Lisa. "Credibility, Costs, and Institutions: Cooperation on Economic Sanctions," *World Politics,* Vol. 45, no. 3 (April 1993), pp. 406–432.

Mason, Tony. *Air Power: A Centennial Appraisal.* London: Brasseys, 1994.

Matlak, Regis W. "Inside Saddam's Grip," *National Security Studies Quarterly* (Spring 1999) (electronic version).

McNaugher, Thomas L. "Ballistic Missiles and Chemical Weapons: The Legacy of the Iran-Iraq War," *International Security*, Vol. 15, no. 2 (Fall 1990), pp. 5–34.

Mead, Walter Russell. "The Jacksonian Tradition," *The National Interest,* no. 58 (Winter 1999), pp. 5–30.

Meilinger, Phillip S. *Ten Propositions Regarding Air Power.* Washington, DC: Air Force History and Museums Program, 1995.

Meilinger, Phillip S. "The Historiography of Airpower: Theory and Doctrine," *The Journal of Military History,* no. 64 (April 2000), pp. 467–502.

Meilinger, Phillip. "Trenchard, Slessor, and Royal Air Force Doctrine Before World War II." In *The Paths of Heaven: The Evolution of Airpower Theory*, Phillip Meilinger, ed. Maxwell Air Force Base, AL: Air University Press, 1997, pp. 41–78.

Meilinger, Phillip S., ed. *The Paths to Heaven: The Evolution of Airpower Theory.* Maxwell Air Force Base, AL: Air University Press, 1997.

Melman, Yossi. *The Master Terrorist: The True Story Behind Abu Nidal.* New York: Adama Books, 1986.

Melvin, Sheila, "Why Chinese Can Believe Worst About U.S. Bombing," *USA Today*, May 12, 1999, p. 15A.

Menkhaus, Ken. "Complex Emergencies, Humanitarianism, and National Security," *National Security Studies Quarterly,* Vol. IV, no. 4 (Autumn 1998), pp. 53–61.

Mercer, Jonathan. *Reputation and International Politics.* Ithaca, NY: Cornell University Press, 1996.

Meselson, M., Jeanne Guillemin, Martin Hugh-Jones, Alexander Langmuir, Ilona Popova, Alexis Shelokov, and Olga Yampolskaya. "The Sverdlovsk Anthrax Outbreak of 1979," *Science*, no. 266 (November 18, 1994), pp. 1202–1208.

Middle East Watch, *Needless Deaths in the Gulf War: Civilian Casualties During the Air Campaign and Violations of the Laws of War*. New York: Middle East Watch, 1991.

Missiou-Ladi, Anna. "Coercive Diplomacy in Greek Interstate Relations," *The Classical Quarterly*, Vol. 37, no. 2 (1987), pp. 336–345.

Monterey Institute, "Chemical and Biological Weapons Resource Page," http://cns.miis.edu/research/dbw/possess/htm.

Morgan, Patrick M. *Deterrence: A Conceptual Analysis*. Beverly Hills, CA: Sage Library of Social Science, 1977.

Morgan, Patrick M. "Saving Face for the Sake of Deterrence." In *Psychology and Deterrence*, Richard Ned Lebow, Robert Jervis, and Janice Gross Stein, eds. Baltimore: Johns Hopkins University Press, 1985, pp. 125–152.

Morgan, T. Clifton, and Valer L. Schwebach. "Fools Suffer Gladly: The Use of Economic Sanctions in International Crises," *International Studies Quarterly*, Vol. 41, no.1 (March 1997), pp. 27–50.

Morin, Richard. "Poll Shows Most Americans Want Negotiated Settlement," *Washington Post*, May 18, 1999, p. A18.

Morris, Benny. *Israel's Border Wars, 1949–1956*. Oxford: Clarendon Press, 1997.

Mueller, John. *Policy and Opinion in the Gulf War*. Chicago: University of Chicago Press, 1994.

Mueller, John. *Quiet Cataclysm: Reflections on the Recent Transformation of World Politics*. New York: HarperCollins, 1995.

Mueller, John, and Karl Mueller. "Sanctions of Mass Destruction," *Foreign Affairs*, Vol. 78, no. 3 (May/June 1999), pp. 43–53.

Mueller, Karl. "Denial, Punishment, and the Future of Air Power," *Security Studies*, Vol. 7, no. 3 (Spring 1998), pp. 182–228.

Mueller, Karl. "Strategy, Asymmetric Deterrence, and Accommodation." Ph.D. dissertation, Princeton University, Princeton, NJ, 1991.

Natsios, Andrew S. "Humanitarian Relief Intervention in Somalia: The Economics of Chaos." In *Lessons from Somalia*, Walter Clarke and Jeffrey Herbst, eds. Boulder, CO: Westview Press, 1997, pp. 77–98.

Natsios, Andrew S. "The International Humanitarian Response System." *Parameters*, Vol. XXV, no. 1 (Spring 1995), pp. 68–81.

Neff, Donald. *Warriors at Suez*. New York: Simon & Schuster, 1981.

Odell, John S. "International Threats and Internal Politics: Brazil, the European Community, and the United States, 1985–1987." In

Double-Edged Diplomacy: International Bargaining and Domestic Politics, Peter B. Evans, Harold K. Jacobson, and Robert D. Putnam, eds. Berkeley: University of California Press, 1993.

Olson, Mancur, Jr., and Richard Zeckhauser. "An Economic Theory of Alliances," *Review of Economics and Statistics,* Vol. 48, no. 3 (August 1966), pp. 266–279.

O'Toole, Fintan. "NATO's Actions, Not Just Its Cause, Must Be Moral," *Irish Times*, April 24, 1999, p. 11.

Overy, R. J. *The Air War, 1939–1945*. New York: Stein and Day, 1980.

Overy, Richard J. *Why the Allies Won*. New York: W.W. Norton, 1996.

Pape, Robert A. *Bombing to Win*. Ithaca, NY: Cornell University Press, 1996.

Pape, Robert A. "The Air Force Strikes Back: A Reply to Barry Watts and John Warden," *Security Studies*, Vol. 7, No. 2 (Winter 1997–1998), pp. 200–214.

Pape, Robert A. "The Limits of Precision-Guided Air Power," *Security Studies*, Vol. 7, no. 2 (Winter 1997–1998), pp. 91–132.

Pape, Robert A. "Why Economic Sanctions Do Not Work," *International Security*, Vol. 22, no. 2 (Fall 1997), pp. 90–136.

Pape, Robert A. "Why Economic Sanctions *Still* Do Not Work," *International Security*, Vol. 23, no. 1 (Summer 1998), pp. 66–77.

Parks, W. Hays. "Air War and the Law of War," *Air Force Law Review*, no. 32 (1990), pp. 1–226.

Parks, W. Hays. "Rolling Thunder and the Law of War," *Air University Review*, Vol. 33, no. 2 (January/February 1982), pp. 2–23.

Peach, Stuart, ed. *Perspectives on Air Power*. London: The Stationary Office, 1998.

The Pentagon Papers: The Defense Department's History of U.S. Decisionmaking in Vietnam. Gravel edition, Vol. IV. Boston: Beacon Press, 1971.

Perlez, Jane. "Serbia Shuts 2 More Papers, Saying They Created Panic," *New York Times*, October 15, 1998, p. A6.

Perlez, Jane. "U.S. Role Is Not to Disarm, Aide to Top Somali Insists," *New York Times,* December 6, 1992, p. A14.

Peterson, Walter J. "Deterrence and Compellence: A Critical Assessment of Conventional Wisdom," *International Studies Quarterly*, Vol. 30, no. 3 (September 1986), pp. 269–294.

Pillar, Paul R. "Ending Limited War: The Psychological Dimensions of the Termination Process." In *Psychological Dimensions of War*, Betty Glad, ed. Newbury Park, CA: Sage Publications, 1990, pp. 252–263.

Plous, Scott. *The Psychology of Judgment and Decision-Making*. New York: McGraw-Hill, 1993.

Posen, Barry. *Sources of Military Doctrine: France, Britain, and Germany Between the World Wars*. Ithaca, NY: Cornell University Press, 1984.

Posen, Barry R. "The War for Kosovo: Serbia's Political-Military Strategy," *International Security*, Vol. 24, no. 4 (Spring 2000), pp. 39–84.

Posen, Barry R. "U.S. Security Policy in a Nuclear-Armed World (Or: What if Iraq Had Had Nuclear Weapons?)," *Security Studies*, Vol. 6, no. 3 (Spring 1997), pp. 1–31.

Posen, Barry R., and Andrew L. Ross. "Competing Visions for U.S. Grand Strategy," *International Security*, Vol. 21, no. 3 (Winter 1996–1997), pp. 5–53.

Priest, Dana, and Bradley Graham. "Airstrikes Take a Toll on Saddam, U.S. Says," *Washington Post*, January 9, 1999, p. A14.

Putnam, Robert D. "Diplomacy and Domestic Politics: The Logic of Two-Level Games," *International Organization*, Vol. 42, no. 3 (Summer 1988), pp. 427–460.

Quester, George H. "The Continuing Debate on Minimal Deterrence." In *The Absolute Weapon Revisited*, T.V. Paul, Richard J. Harknett, and James J. Wirtz, eds. Ann Arbor, MI: The University of Michigan Press, 1998, pp. 167–188.

Quester, George H. "The Psychological Effects of Bombing on Civilian Populations: Wars of the Past." In *Psychological Dimensions of War*, Betty Glad, ed. Newbury Park, CA: Sage Publications, 1990, pp. 201–214.

Quinlivan, James T. "Coup-Proofing: Its Practice and Consequences in the Middle East," *International Security*, Vol. 24, no. 2 (Fall 1999), pp. 131–165.

Ranstorp, Magnus. *Hizb'Allah in Lebanon: The Politics of the Western Hostage Crisis*. New York: St. Martin's Press, 1997.

Reed, Ronald M. "Chariots of Fire: Rules of Engagement in Operation Deliberate Force." In *Deliberate Force: A Case Study in Effective*

Campaign Planning, Robert C. Owen, ed. Maxwell Air Force Base, AL: Air University Press, 2000, pp. 381–430.

Reisman, W. Michael, and Chris T. Antoniou. *The Laws of War*. New York: Vintage Books, 1994.

Richburg, Keith B. "Aideed 'No Longer Part of the Process': UN Officials in Mogadishu Play Down Failure to Arrest Warlord," *Washington Post*, June 19, 1993, p. A14.

Ricks, Thomas E., David Rogers, and Carla Anne Robbins. "NATO to Reconsider the Issue of Ground Troops in Kosovo." *Wall Street Journal*, April 21, 1999 (electronic version).

Riscassi, Robert W. "Principles for Coalition Warfare," *Joint Force Quarterly*, no. 1 (Summer 1993), pp. 58–71.

Roach, J. Ashley (JAGC, U.S. Navy), "Rules of Engagement," *Naval War College Review*, Vol. 36, no. 1 (January/February 1983), pp. 46–55.

Robins, Carla Anne, and Thomas E. Ricks. "NATO Weighs Plan for Bigger Kosovo Force," *Wall Street Journal*, May 19, 1999 (electronic version).

Roche, James G., and Barry D. Watts. "Choosing Analytic Measures," *Journal of Strategic Studies*, Vol. 14, no. 2 (June 1991), pp. 165–209.

Rodman, Peter W. *More Precious than Peace*. New York: Charles Scribner's Sons, 1994.

Rogers, Elizabeth S. "Using Economic Sanctions to Control Regional Conflicts," *Security Studies,* Vol. 5, no. 4 (Summer 1996), pp. 43–72.

Rose, John P. *The Evolution of U.S. Army Nuclear Doctrine, 1945–1980.* Boulder, CO: Westview Press, 1980.

Rosenthal, Elisabeth, "Public Anger Against U.S. Still Simmers in Beijing," *New York Times*, May 17, 1999, p. A1.

Rowe, David M. "Economic Sanctions Do Work: Economic Statecraft and the Oil Embargo of Rhodesia," *Security Studies,* Vol. 9, no. 1–2 (Autumn 1999–Winter 2000), pp. 254–287.

Sagan, Scott. "The Commitment Trap: Why the United States Should Not Use Nuclear Threats to Deter Biological and Chemical Weapons Attacks," *International Security,* Vol. 24, no. 4 (Spring 2000), pp. 85–115.

Sagan, Scott. *The Limits of Safety: Organizations, Accidents, and Nuclear Weapons.* Princeton, NJ: Princeton University Press, 1993.

Sagan, Scott D. "Rules of Engagement," *Security Studies*, Vol. 1, no. 1 (Autumn 1991), pp. 78–108.

Sagan, Scott D. "Why Do States Build Nuclear Weapons?" *International Security*, Vol. 21, No. 3 (Winter 1996–1997), pp. 54–86.

Sands, David R. "U.S. and Russia Patch Up Relations," *Washington Times*, June 25, 1999, p. A1.

Scarborough, Rowan. "Apaches Were Sent to Scare Serbs," *Washington Times*, May 21, 1999, p. 1.

Schelling, Thomas C. *Arms and Influence*. New Haven, CT: Yale University Press, 1966.

Schelling, Thomas C. *The Strategy of Conflict*. Cambridge, MA: Harvard University Press, 1960.

Schmitt, Michael N. "State-Sponsored Assassination in International and Domestic Law," *Yale Journal of International Law*, no. 17 (Summer 1992), pp. 609–685.

Schow, Kenneth C. "Falcons Against the Jihad: Israeli Airpower and Coercive Diplomacy in Southern Lebanon," master's thesis, School of Advanced Airpower Studies, 1997.

Schulzinger, Robert D. *A Time for War: The United States and Vietnam, 1941–1975*. New York: Oxford University Press, 1997.

Selden, Zachary A. *Economic Sanctions as Instruments of American Foreign Policy*. Westport, CT: Praeger, 1999.

Seybolt, Taylor. *Coordination in Rwanda: The Humanitarian Response to Genocide and Civil War*. Cambridge, MA: Conflict Management Group, 1997.

Seybolt, Taylor B. "The Myth of Neutrality," *Peace Review*, Vol. 8, no. 4 (1996), pp. 521–527.

Shafer, D. Michael. *Deadly Paradigms: The Failure of U.S. Counterinsurgency Policy*. Princeton, NJ: Princeton University Press, 1988.

Shapiro, Jeremy, and Matthew Waxman. "Domestic Constraints on the Use of Air Power." In *Strategic Appraisal: Aerospace Power in the 21st Century*, Zalmay Khalilzad and Jeremy Shapiro, eds. Santa Monica, CA: RAND, 2001.

Shemirani, S. Taheri. "The War of the Cities." In *The Iran-Iraq War: The Politics of Aggression*, Farhang Rajaee, ed. Gainesville, FL: University of Florida Press, 1993, pp. 32–40.

Shimshoni, Jonathan. *Israel and Conventional Deterrence: Border Warfare from 1953 to 1970*. Ithaca, NY: Ithaca University Press, 1988.

Shlaim, Avi. *The Iron Wall: Israel and the Arab World*. New York: W.W. Norton, 1999.

Shogren, Elizabeth. "Rwandans Told World Shares Guilt for Genocide," *Los Angeles Times,* March 26, 1998.

Shultz, George. *Turmoil and Triumph.* New York: Scribner's, 1993.

Simmons, P. J. "Leaning to Live with NGOs," *Foreign Policy,* no. 112 (Fall 1998), pp. 82–96.

Skidmore, David, and Valerie Hudson, eds. *The Limits of State Autonomy: Societal Groups and Foreign Policy Formulation.* Boulder, CO: Westview Press, 1993.

Smith, Jeffrey R. "Tracking Aideed Hampered by Intelligence Failures," *Washington Post*, October 8, 1993, p. 119.

Smoke, Richard. *War: Controlling Escalation.* Cambridge, MA: Harvard University Press, 1977.

Snyder, Glenn H. *Alliance Politics.* Ithaca, NY: Cornell University Press, 1997.

Solonar, V. "Hatred and Fear on Both Banks of the Dniester," *New Times International,* no. 14 (April 1992), pp. 8–9.

Stein, Janice Gross. "Deterrence and Compellence in the Gulf, 1990–91," *International Security*, Vol. 17, no. 2 (Fall 1992), pp. 147–179.

Stein, Janice Gross. "The Arab-Israeli War of 1967: Inadvertent War Through Miscalculated Escalation." In *Avoiding War: Problems of Crisis Management,* Alexander L. George, ed. Boulder, CO: Westview, 1991, pp. 126–159.

Steinberg, Gerald. "U.S. Responses to the Proliferation of Weapons of Mass Destruction in the Middle East," *Middle East Review of International Affairs,* Vol. 2, no. 3 (September 1998) (electronic version).

Stewart, Robert A. *Broken Lives: A Personal View of the Bosnian Conflict.* New York: HarperCollins, 1993.

Stockholm International Peace Research Institute. "Iraq: The UNSCOM Experience." SIPRI Fact Sheet. Stockholm: Stockholm Institute of Peace Research, October 1998, pp. 3–4.

Tanner, Marcus. "Aid Flights Halt on Eve of No-Fly Patrol," *Independent* (London), April 12, 1993, p. 8.

Thomas, Ward. "Norms and Security: The Case of International Assassination," *International Security,* Vol. 25, no. 1 (Summer 2000), pp. 105–133.

Tomes, Robert. "Operation Allied Force and the Legal Basis for Humanitarian Interventions," *Parameters*, Vol. XXX, no. 1 (Spring 2000), pp. 38–50.

Tubbs, James O. "Beyond Gunboat Diplomacy: Forceful Application of Air Power in Peace Enforcement Operations," master's thesis, School of Advanced Airpower Studies, 1997.

United Nations. *The Blue Helmets, A Review of United Nations Peace-Keeping.* New York: United Nations Department of Public Information, 1996.

United Nations High Commissioner for Refugees. *The State of the World's Refugees.* New York: Oxford University Press, 1997.

United Press International. Text of interview with Slobodan Milosevic, April 30, 1999.

United States Strategic Bombing Survey (USSBS). *The Effects of Strategic Bombing on German Morale.* Washington, DC: Government Printing Office, May 1947.

United States Strategic Bombing Survey (USSBS). *The Effects of Strategic Bombing on Japanese Morale.* Washington, DC: Government Printing Office, June 1947.

U.S. Department of Defense. *Conduct of the Persian Gulf War.* Final report to Congress. Washington, DC: Government Printing Office, 1992.

U.S. Department of State, Policy Planning Staff. *Foreign Relations of the United States 1952–1954.* Political annex prepared June 4, 1953, Vol. XV, Part 1. Washington, DC: Government Printing Office, 1984.

Vick, Alan. *Catalyst for Rebellion? Air Campaigns and Civil Unrest in Three Wars.*" Unpublished manuscript, 1998.

Vick, Alan, David T. Orletsky, John Bordeaux, and David A. Shlapak. *Enhancing Air Power's Contribution Against Light Infantry Targets.* Santa Monica, CA: RAND, 1996.

Wallensteen, Peter. "Armed Conflict and Regional Conflict Complexes, 1989–97." *Journal of Peace Research,* Vol. 35, no. 5 (1998), pp. 621–634.

Walt, Stephen M. *The Origins of Alliances.* Ithaca: Cornell University Press, 1987.

Walt, Stephen M. "Why Alliances Endure or Collapse," *Survival,* Vol. 39, no. 1 (Spring 1997), pp. 156–179.

Waltz, Kenneth M. *The Spread of Nuclear Weapons: More May Be Better.* Adelphi paper no. 171. London: International Institute for Strategic Studies, 1981.

Warden, John A., III. "Employing Air Power in the Twenty-First Century." In *The Future of Air Power in the Aftermath of the Gulf War*, Richard H. Shultz, Jr., and Robert L. Pfaltzgraff, Jr., eds. Maxwell Air Force Base, AL: Air University Press, 1992, pp. 57–82.

Warden, John A., III. "The Enemy as a System," *Airpower Journal,* no. 9 (Spring 1995), pp. 40–55.

Watman, Kenneth, and Dean Wilkening. *U.S. Regional Deterrence Strategies.* Santa Monica, CA: RAND, 1995.

Watts, Barry M. "Theory and Evidence in Security Studies," *Security Studies*, Vol. 7, no. 2 (Winter 1997–1998), pp. 13–169.

Waxman, Matthew C. "Emerging Intelligence Challenges," *International Journal of Intelligence and Counterintelligence,* Vol. 10, no. 3 (Fall 1997), pp. 317–331.

Waxman, Matthew C. *International Law and the Politics of Urban Air Operations*. Santa Monica, CA: RAND 2000.

Waxman, Matthew C. "Siegecraft and Surrender: The Law and Strategy of Cities as Targets," *Virginia Journal of International Law*, Vol. 39, 1999.

Webster, Charles, and Noble Frankland. *The Strategic Air Offensive Against Germany,* Vol. 1. London: H.M. Stationary Office, 1961.

Weigley, Russell F. *The American Way of War: A History of United States Military Strategy and Policy*. New York: Macmillan, 1973.

Wendt, Alexander. "The Agent-Structure Problem in International Relations Theory," *International Organization,* Vol. 41, no. 3 (Summer 1987), pp. 335–370.

White House, *The Clinton Administration's Policy on Managing Complex Contingency Operations,* Presidential Decision Directive-56, May 1997.

Wilkening, Dean, and Kenneth Watman. *Nuclear Deterrence in a Regional Context.* Santa Monica, CA: RAND, 1995.

Willett, T., and M. Jalaighajar. "U.S. Trade Policy and National Security," *Cato Journal,* Vol. 3, no. 3 (1983), pp. 717–728.

Wohlstetter, Albert. "The Delicate Balance of Terror," *Foreign Affairs,* Vol. 37, no. 2 (January 1959), pp. 213–236.

Wolf, Franklin R. "Of Carrots and Sticks, or Air Power as a Nonproliferation Tool," master's thesis, School of Advanced Airpower Studies, 1994.

Woodward, Susan L. *Balkans Tragedy: Chaos and Dissolution After the Cold War*. Washington, DC: Brookings Institution, 1995.

Wu Dunn, Sheryl, Judith Miller, and William J. Broad. "How Japan Terror Alerted World," *New York Times*, May 26, 1998, p. 10

Yu, Bin, "What China Learned from Its 'Forgotten War' in Korea," *Strategic Review* (Summer 1998), pp. 4–16.

Zengel, Patricia. "Assassination and the Law of Armed Conflict," *Military Law Review*, no. 134 (Fall 1991), pp. 123–156.

Zimmerman, Tim, "Coercive Diplomacy and Libya." In *The Limits of Coercive Diplomacy,* Alexander George and William E. Simons, eds. Boulder, CO: Westview Press, 1994, pp. 201–228.

Index

Abu Nidal, 74
active defenses, 221
adversaries. *see also* authoritarian regimes
  counter-coercion by, 42–43, 142–48, 194–99, 171, 219
  decision making by, 3, 31–32, 46–47
  in humanitarian interventions, 176
  interests of, 237
  international legal norms and, 148–49
  optimism of, 143
  pressure points of, 30, 44–46
  values of, 44
  vulnerabilities of, 3, 19
Afghanistan
  air strikes against, 88, 135–36, 232
  insurgents in, 118, 119
  terrorists in, 88, 119, 135–36, 232
agreements, predecisional, 165
aid workers, 177, 181–82, 182n9, 187–88. *see also* humanitarian interventions
Aideed, Mohamed Farah. *see also* Somalia
  air strikes against, 171
  assassination attempts on, 153
  humanitarian interventions and, 182–83
  intelligence about, 186
  media coverage of, 195
  military resources of, 191, 191n23
  on public opinion, 144
  United Nations and, 191
Air Corps Tactical School (ACTS), 92, 92n7
air strikes, 88–99
  in Afghanistan, 88, 135–36, 232
  for assassination, 94–95
  in the Balkan conflict, 1, 88, 89, 122, 136, 167
  in Bosnia, 90, 121
  capabilities of, 90–92
  casualties from, 89–90. *see also* casualties
  against Chechen forces, 91, 95
  against civilians, 90, 96–99, 186
  collateral damage from, 138, 139
  on convoys, 142n33
  denial and, 16, 90–92
  effectiveness of, 31, 234
  in Egypt, 97
  against electric power grids, 98
  against elites, 92–93
  escalation and, 88–89
  in the Gulf War, 34, 88, 91, 93–94, 95, 97–98
  indigenous ground troops and, 121, 121n89
  against industrial sites, 92, 96
  in the Iran-Iraq War, 97, 98
  in Iraq, 34, 88, 91, 93, 94–95, 97–98
  by Israel, 4, 89, 97
  in Japan, 69–71, 92
  in the Korean War, 122, 139–40
  in Kosovo, 28, 40, 89, 136
  against leaders, 94–95
  in Libya, 89, 93–94, 94n11
  limited use of, 16
  morale and, 69–71, 70–71n38
  Pape on, 31, 50n1
  precision, 89, 95, 122, 232–33, 232n2
  public opinion on, 138n18
  resistance to, 70, 93
  role of, 20, 50, 88–89, 124
  rules of engagement for, 167
  social effects of, 96, 97–98
  strategic, 10, 16, 122, 122n93
  strengths and weaknesses of, 230, 234
  terrorists and, 88, 91, 135–36, 232
  unrest and, 69–71, 96, 97–98
  Vietnam War, 41, 58, 80, 80n62, 91, 139–40
  World War II, 95, 97

World War II (Germany), 31, 44, 58, 70–71, 86, 92
World War II (Japan), 31, 44, 69–71, 70n33, 92
Al Firdos bunker, 147, 147n45
Algeria, 52, 205
alliances. *see* coalitions; international cooperation
Allied Force operation. *see* Operation Allied Force
Allison, Graham, 13
analysts, vs. policy makers, 234–36
anthrax, 210
antiwar movement, 137n16
Arab-Israeli wars
Suez War (1956), 42, 52, 53, 69, 77
Yom Kippur War (1973), 80–81
War of Attrition (1969–70), 35–36, 66–67, 67n23
Arab states. *see also* specific states
Gulf War and, 168, 171
on no-fly zones, 160–61
on Saddam Husayn, 169
weapons of mass destruction and, 206
Aristide, Jean-Bertrand, 183
Arms and Influence (Schelling), 15
assassination, 72–76. *see also* decapitation
acknowledgment of, 73
air strikes for, 94–95
of nonstate actors, 190
Palestinian terrorists and, 73–74
as self-defense, 75n52
attitudes, public. *see* public opinion
audience costs, 36–37, 36n12
Aum Shinrikyo, 209n17
authoritarian regimes
characteristics of, 130
civilian causalities and, 222
commitment to, 74–75
media coverage and, 149–50
power base of, 59–60
pressure points of, 45
public opinion in, 148
urest in, 62–63
weakening mechanisms and, 77
weapons of mass destruction and, 214–15, 224

backfire potential, 35–36, 224–25
background threats, 32–33
Baker, James, 73
Baldwin, David
on coercive instruments, 123
on deterrence, 7
on economic pressure, 35
on military force, 19
on power, 16, 18
on sanctions, 235
Balkan conflict. *see also* Bosnia; Kosovo; Milosevic, Slobodan; Serbia
air strikes in, 1, 88–90, 121, 122, 136, 167
casualties in, 89, 90, 144–45
coalitions in, 159–60, 166–67, 172
coercive mechanisms used in, 54, 57
collateral damage and, 142
command procedures in, 163–65
Dayton peace accords, 135, 183
electric power grids and, 98
escalation of, 169
field commanders in, 193, 193n27
France and, 161, 172
Germany and, 172
Great Britain and, 161
ground forces in, 32, 100n30, 101–2, 160, 166–67
hostages and, 145
human-shield tactics in, 197–98
Italy and, 172
leaders in, 193–94. *see also* Milosevic, Slobodan
media coverage of, 71, 149
military resources in, 192–94
NATO and, 1, 5, 116, 119–21, 169–70, 172, 193
NATO casualties in, 28
NATO summit on, 162
Operation Allied Force. *see* Operation Allied Force
Operation Deliberate Force, 40, 90, 121, 141, 191–92
political isolation in, 116
public opinion on, 138n18
public will and, 144–45
rules of engagement for, 141, 166–67, 189, 190, 198
Russia and, 116, 172
threat credibility in, 169–79
United Nations and, 160, 193
UNPROFOR mission, 160, 161, 163, 166–67, 189, 189n22
Bar-Siman-Tov, Yaacov, 66
Baram, Amatzia, 61
Belgrade, Yugoslavia, 142
benefits, 10, 11, 78. *see also* cost-benefit analysis
bin Laden, Osama, 94
binary metrics, of success, 33–34, 33–34n5, 35
biological weapons. *see also* weapons of mass destruction
access to, 210
costs of, 218
cults and, 209n17

escalation and, 218
Gulf War and, 208
Iraq and, 210
in the post–Cold War era, 203
regional powers with, 205
Soviet Union and, 208n16
threat of, 210
utility of, 211
vaccine-resistant, 221
blackmail, 6n5, 10
Bosnia. *see also* Balkan conflict
air strikes in, 90, 121
coalitions and, 159, 166–67
command procedures in, 163–65
hostages in, 145
human-shield tactics in, 197–98
humanitarian interventions in, 180, 181, 183, 188, 197–98
military resources of, 192–94
militias, 191–92
NATO and, 120–21, 183
nonstate actors in, 191–92
Operation Deliberate Force, 40, 90, 121, 141, 191–92
refugees in, 183
rules of engagement in, 141, 189, 190, 198
UNPROFOR mission and, 163, 166–67, 189, 189n22
botulinum, 210
Britain. *see* Great Britain
brute force, 3, 4–6, 100, 124
vs. denial, 78, 80
examples of, 52, 54, 55, 56, 57, 58
Bush, George H.W., 217
Bush, George W., 204

Cambodia, 183
Camp David Accords, 9
case studies, 5, 15, 51–59
Castro, Fidel, 109
casualties. *see also* civilian casualties
from air strikes, 89–90
in the Balkan conflict, 89, 90, 144–45
from ground forces, 100
in the Gulf War, 89, 89n3, 135, 143–44
in humanitarian interventions, 184–85
in Kosovo, 89
lack of concern for, 222
minimizing, 232
public opinion and, 136–37, 136n15, 143–44
public will and, 142
from sanctions, 111, 111n64, 111n66, 112
sensitivity to, 134–42, 143–44, 173, 184–85, 214
U.S. military, 130
in the Vietnam War, 143
weapons of mass destruction and, 213–14
Chechen forces
air strikes against, 91, 95
coercive mechanisms used against, 54
Dudayev's assassination and, 74
hostages and, 198
military resources of, 194
unrest and, 68
chemical weapons. *see also* weapons of mass destruction
access to, 210
Egypt and, 211
escalation and, 217
Gulf War and, 208, 217
in the Iran-Iraq War, 210–11
Iraq and, 39, 68, 104–5, 210, 211, 217
Japan and, 209n17
Libya and, 220
nuclear threats and, 39
in the post–Cold War era, 203
regional powers with, 205
threat of, 21
UN destruction of, 210
utility of, 211
Chernomyrdin, Viktor, 116
Chile, 62
China, 2, 56
Chirac, Jacques, 198
Christmas bombings (Vietnam War), 33
civil unrest. *see* unrest
civil war, 133–34
civilian casualties
in the Balkan conflict, 90
enemy, 223–24
in the Gulf War, 137, 140, 147, 147n45
in Kosovo, 89
lack of concern for, 222
policy maker sensitivity to, 98, 136–42, 184–85, 214, 223–24
from sanctions, 111, 111n64, 111n66, 112
in Somalia, 137, 146
civilians
air strikes against, 90, 96–99
disaffection of. *see* unrest
in the Gulf War, 97–98, 137, 140, 147, 147n45
national interests and, 140
punishment of, 66
Saddam Husayn and, 137, 148
sanctions and, 139, 148, 223–24
suffering of, 45, 65, 97–98, 130, 137–42, 146, 196

targeting restrictions and, 139–42, 146, 147, 186–87, 196, 233
in the Vietnam War, 137, 141–42, 147
well-being of, 65, 76, 77
Clark, Wesley, 101n31
Clinton, William J.
on Haiti, 133
on Iraqi weapons inspections, 131
on Kosovo, 156–57n8
on Rwanda, 192
on Somalia, 153
on weapons of mass destruction, 204
Clodfelter, Mark, 80n62
coalitions, 152–74
ad hoc, 154
agenda of, 159–63
in the Balkan conflict, 159–60, 166–67, 172
breaking, 152, 156, 171–72, 194
building, 128, 172–73
coercive instruments for, 156
collateral damage and, 173
consensus in, 162
control of, 158, 163–67
counter-coercion and, 171–72
credibility of, 169–71
decision making in, 165–66
definition of, 154
domestic, 157
domestic politics and, 156, 171
economic sanctions and, 156
escalation and, 19, 158, 166–69, 171
escalation dominance and, 167–69
goals of, 158, 159–60
in the Gulf War, 155–56, 160–61, 162–63, 168
for humanitarian interventions, 175–76, 185–86
Iraq and, 34, 159, 160–61, 162–63, 169
in the Korean War, 155, 168
limitations of, 158–71
military forces and, 155, 173
national interests and, 159–60, 165
negative objectives and, 161
political isolation and, 156
predecisional agreements for, 165
public opinion of, 157
regional interests in, 173
role of, 154–58, 156n5
rules of engagement and, 158, 165, 166
in Somalia, 152–53, 159, 168–69, 171
threats by, 162
unity of, 170–71
in the Vietnam War, 155
weapons of mass destruction and, 203, 215–16
in World War II, 154–55, 155n3
coercion
backfire potential of, 35–36
vs. brute force, 4–6, 100
categories of, 6–9
context of, 127–29
definition of, 1, 3–9, 6n5, 30
vs. deterrence, 7–9
dynamics of, 37–46, 236–39
effectiveness of, 239–40
future of, 229–40
measuring, 31
models of, 10–14
studies of, 14–17
successful, 33–37, 39n17, 85
theory of, 15, 23, 30–47
third-party, 82–85, 86
in today's world, 14–21
coercive contests, 218–24, 233–34
coercive instruments, 87–124. *see also* specific instruments
assessment of, 123–24
combinations of, 31–33, 120–23
context of, 31
costs of, 235–36, 238–39
credibility and, 240
definition of, 28
effectiveness of, 234–35
low-risk, 238–39
mechanisms and, 50
misuse of, 239
nonmilitary, 230–31
in strategy, 27–28
strengths and weaknesses of, 230–31
success of, 33–37
value of, 32–33, 238
coercive mechanisms, 48–86. *see also* specific mechanisms
in the Balkan conflict, 54, 57
commonly used, 50–82
decision making and, 59
effectiveness of, 85–86, 234–35
examples of, 52–58
multiple, 50–51
third-party, 82–85
coercive strategy, 27–29
challenges to, 229–34
coalitions and, 173
domestic politics in, 239–40
goals of, 34–35
mechanisms in, 48
politics and, 229, 236
success of, 239–40
weakening mechanisms in, 229
coercive threats. *see* threats
Cohen, Eliot, 88–89, 135
Cohen, William, 136

Cold War era
coercion, 14–15
decapitation threats, 72
deterrence and, 205
escalation dominance and, 40
insurgency during, 117
insurgents, 117, 118
nuclear threats during, 14, 87, 103, 208n16, 222
vs. the post–Cold War era, 1, 16–18, 127
sanctions, 109
weakening mechanisms in, 76n54
collateral damage
from air strikes, 138, 139
in the Balkan conflict, 142
coalitions and, 173
exploitation of, 151
in the Gulf War, 140
political constraints on, 138
risk aversion and, 147–48, 148n45
in the Vietnam War, 231–32
weapons of mass destruction and, 223–24
Combined Bomber Offensive, 5
command and control
in coalitions, 158, 163–67
national, 165
command procedures, 163–65, 167
compellence, 6–9, 6n5
complex contingency operations, 175n1
concessions, 9–10, 37, 64–65
Congo, 118
contras, 118–19
cost-benefit analysis, 10–14, 38
costs
audience, 36–37, 36n12
of biological weapons use, 218
of coercive instruments, 235–36, 238–39
of concessions, 37, 64–65
of defiance, 9
definition of, 11
of escalation dominance, 38
of ground forces, 100–101
of inducements, 10n13
of insurgency support, 118–19, 123, 234–35
of nuclear weapons, 103
perceived, 85
of resistance, 15
of sanctions, 107–8, 111–12
sunk, 12
threatened, 42
of weapons of mass destruction, 103, 201, 203, 212–13, 222, 224
counter-coercion, 42–43, 142–48. *see also* adversaries
coalitions and, 171–72
by nonstate actors, 194–99
weapons of mass destruction for, 219–21
counterescalation, 42–43, 239
counterforce, 219–21
counterthreats, 43, 143, 214
coups, 60–61, 62
credibility, 18, 237
of coalitions, 169–71
coercive instruments and, 240
technology and, 231–32
of threats, 169–71, 221
traps, 236–39
crises, 15, 29, 143
high-stake, 223, 238
low-stake, 131
Croatia, 121, 160
cruise missiles, 232, 232n2
Cuba, 109, 205
Cuban missile crisis, 10, 13, 54, 104
culture, 11–12, 150

damage. *see* costs
Dayan, Moshe, 83
Dayton peace accords, 135, 183
deaths. *see* casualties
decapitation, 72–76
acknowledgment of, 73
air strikes for, 94–95
definition of, 50, 50n1
examples of, 53, 54, 55, 56, 57
legal issues and, 75–76
by nonstate actors, 73–74
of nonstate actors, 190
as self-defense, 75n52
success of, 74–75, 74n50
decision making
by adversaries, 3, 31–32, 46–47
in coalitions, 165–66
coercive mechanisms and, 59
collective, 13, 14
cost-benefit analysis in, 11
in the Cuban missile crisis, 13
culture in, 11–12
elites in, 13
goals in, 12–13
in humanitarian interventions, 177–80
by leaders, 12–14
by policy makers, 42
rational, 11, 12
by regimes, 13–14
threats and, 32, 49, 51
values in, 12–13
defeat, 2, 62, 80–81
defenses, for weapons of mass destruction, 221–22, 224
defiance, 9, 64, 64n18, 65, 69
Deliberate Force, 40, 90, 121, 141, 191–92

democracy, 59, 133, 214
denial, 78–82
  air strikes and, 16, 90–92
  vs. brute force, 78, 80
  definition of, 50, 50n1
  examples of, 52, 53, 54, 55, 56, 57
  flexible response as, 76n54
  ground forces and, 100
  nonstate actors and, 194–95
  success of, 79
Deny Flight, 160, 167–68
Desert Fox, 93, 131, 223
Desert Storm, 34, 100, 168. *see also* Gulf War
  air strikes and, 91
  casualties, 135
  lessons of, 5, 206–7
deterrence, 6–9
  vs. coercion, 7–9
  Cold War era and, 205
  definition of, 6, 6n5
  general vs. immediate, 6–7
  nuclear weapons and, 7n9
  of provocations, 230
  weapons of mass destruction and, 204–6, 207, 219–24, 219n32
developing countries
  power base of, 60–61
  weapons of mass destruction and, 204, 207
dictatorial regimes. *see* authoritarian regimes
diplomacy, 6n5, 15, 82, 240
displaced persons, 182–83. *see also* refugees
domestic politics, 130–51
  coalitions and, 156, 171
  in coercive strategy, 239–40
  constraints on, 20
  in escalation dominance, 43–44
  in the post–Cold War era, 127–29
  of regional powers, 207–8
Dominican Republic, 54, 62
Douhet, Giulio, 17, 69, 96
drug trafficking, 200
Dudayev, Dzhokhar, 74, 95, 194

economic assets. *see also* infrastructure attacks
  destruction of, 79–80, 79n61, 139
economic sanctions, 35, 62, 77, 106–10, 111, 156. *see also* sanctions
Egypt
  air strikes against, 97
  chemical weapons and, 211
  Israeli-Egyptian War of Attrition and, 35–36, 66–67, 67n23
  Suez Canal crises and, 42, 52, 53, 69, 77
  weapons of mass destruction and, 205
  Yom Kippur War and, 80–81
Eisenhower, Dwight, 103
El Dorado Canyon operation, 93–94, 95
elections, 183
electric power grids, 48–49, 98
elites
  air strikes against, 92–93
  casualty sensitivity and, 136, 137
  in coercive strategy, 44–45
  consensus of, 131–32n3
  in decision making, 13
  in Iraq, 46
  Milosevic and, 63
  as the power base, 60, 62–63
  public opinion and, 51, 131–32n3
  public policy and, 44–45
endowment effect, 41, 41n22
Eritrea, 100, 179
escalation. *see also* escalation dominance
  air strikes and, 88–89
  of the Balkan conflict, 169
  biological weapons and, 218
  chemical weapons and, 217
  coalitions and, 19, 158, 166–69, 171
  counterthreats and, 43
  domestic politics and, 20
  in humanitarian interventions, 176, 199
  impartiality and, 189
  inadvertent, 35–36
  nonstate actors and, 197–98
  nuclear weapons and, 7n9, 105, 217–18
  overcoercion and, 36–37
  public opinion and, 37n13
  of sanctions, 108
  sudden, 41–42
  threats and, 35–36
escalation dominance, 30, 38–44
  coalitions and, 167–69
  in the Cold War era, 40
  components of, 39n17
  costs of, 38
  definition of, 40n20
  in humanitarian interventions, 176, 199
  nuclear threats and, 39–40, 221
  politics in, 43–44
  weapons of mass destruction and, 202, 212–16, 217, 223
Ethiopia, 100, 179, 205
ethnic cleansing, 133

false alarms, 208n16
feedback cycles, 151, 171
field commanders, 193, 193n27
flexible response, 76n54

force
brute. *see* brute force
limited. *see* limited force
military. *see* military force
foreign policy, 1–2, 19–20, 150
Former Yugoslavia. *see* Balkan conflict; Serbia
France
Algerian insurgents and, 52
Balkan conflict and, 161, 172
Iraq and, 159
Rwanda and, 179–80
Suez Canal crises and, 42, 52
funding, for insurgents, 119

Gause, F. Gregory, 111, 112
genocide, 133, 180
geopolitics, 17
George, Alexander, 15, 39n17, 42, 159, 213
Germany. *see also* Nazi Germany; World War II
air strikes against, 31, 44, 58, 70–71, 86, 92
Balkan conflict and, 172
inducements by, 9
occupation by Russia, 85–86
goals
of coalitions, 34, 158, 159–60
of coercive strategy, 34–35
in decision making, 12–13
of leaders, 12–13
of sanctions, 114
Gorazde, 170
governments. *see* regimes
grand strategy, 27n1
Great Britain
Balkan conflict and, 161
gunboat diplomacy, 87
Malayan guerillas and, 52
Suez Canal crises and, 42, 52, 77
UN inspections and, 61
Greece, 172
ground forces, 99–102. *see also* military force
air strikes and, 121, 121n89
in the Balkan conflict, 32, 100n30, 101–2, 160, 166–67
casualties from, 100
coalitions and, 155
costs of, 100–101
denial and, 100
in the Gulf War, 34, 100, 102
in humanitarian interventions, 185–86
in the Korean War, 122
in Kosovo, 32, 100n30, 101–2
NATO, 101–2, 101n31
rules of engagement for, 166–67
strengths and weaknesses of, 234–35
guerrilla forces, 79, 91. *see also* insurgents; nonstate actors
Gulf War. *see also* Husayn, Saddam; Iraq
air strikes in, 34, 88, 91, 93–94, 95, 97–98
biological weapons and, 208
casualties of, 89, 89n3, 135
casualty sensitivity and, 143–44
chemical weapons and, 208, 217
civilian causalities in, 98, 137, 140, 147, 147n45
civilians and, 140
coalitions in, 155–56, 160–61, 162–63, 168
collateral damage in, 140
decapitation threats in, 73, 73n46, 93, 94, 95
domestic politics and, 142
ground forces in, 34, 100, 102
justification of, 157
lessons of, 5, 206–7
nuclear threats during, 39, 217
public opinion on, 132–33, 142
purpose of, 34, 132–33
rules of engagement for, 140
Soviet Union and, 162–63
gunboat diplomacy, 87

Haiti, 4, 55, 133, 157, 183
Hamas, 75
Hezbollah, 2, 53, 64–65, 74, 89
history, 3, 78
lessons of, 5, 206–7, 234, 238
value of, 18, 22, 23
Hitler, Adolf, 4n3
Ho Chi Minh, 143, 237
Holbrooke, Richard, 197–98
hostages, 145, 197–98
human rights, 157, 178–79
human-shield tactics, 146, 196–97
in Bosnia, 197–98
in Somalia, 196–97
humanitarian interventions, 20, 175–200
aid workers and, 177, 181–82, 182n9, 187–88
in Bosnia, 180, 181, 183, 188, 197–98
casualties in, 184–85
coalitions for, 175–76, 185–86
coercion in, 175, 176–77
constraints on, 183–90
decision making in, 177–80
during the 1990s, 128
escalation in, 176, 199
ground forces and, 185–86
in Haiti, 183

impartiality and, 187–88, 189
intelligence gathering and, 186–87
in Kosovo, 178, 179, 183, 184
media coverage of, 179, 185
military force for, 175–76, 177, 181–90, 195–98, 199
motivation for, 128
national interests and, 184
nongovernmental organizations in, 157–58, 182n9
nonstate actors and, 128, 176, 182–83, 188–89, 190–94
in the post–Cold War era, 127–29
public opinion on, 132
refugees and, 179, 180, 182–83, 185, 185n13
rules of engagement for, 189–90, 195–97
in Rwanda, 185, 185n13
sanctions and, 111–12
in Somalia, 152–53, 181, 181n7, 182–84, 182n9, 189
in the Sudan, 178, 179
supplies for, 181–82, 181n7
target discrimination in, 186–87, 196
humanitarian organizations. *see* nongovernmental organizations
Husayn, Saddam. *see also* Gulf War; Iraq
air strikes against, 93, 94, 95
Arab states on, 169
on casualty sensitivity, 143–44
coalition rifts and, 156
decapitation threats and, 73, 73n46, 93, 94, 95
denial mechanisms and, 81–82
nuclear threat and, 39, 104–5, 104–5n40, 217
on the oil-for-food program, 148
policies of, 137, 137n17
political isolation of, 62
power base of, 45–46, 61–62, 231
public opinion of, 132–33
reasoning of, 11, 238
rivals to, 45–46
sanctions and, 110, 112, 113–14
Scud missile attacks by, 168, 171, 215
weaknesses of, 231
Hutus, 179–80

impartiality
escalation and, 189
in humanitarian interventions, 187–88, 188n17, 189
inaction, 240
India, 205, 214
indirect pressure, 82–85
Indonesia, 205
inducements, 9–10, 10n13
industrial sites
air strikes against, 92, 96
sanctions and, 106
UN inspections of, 61–62, 61–62n11, 81–82
as weakening mechanisms, 76
for weapons of mass destruction production, 220, 220n3
information gathering. *see* intelligence gathering
information infrastructure, 233
infrastructure attacks, 76, 139, 191, 233
inspections, for weapons of mass destruction, 55, 61–62, 81–82, 93, 113–14, 155–56, 169
instruments. *see* coercive instruments
insurgents
Afghan, 118, 119
Algerian, 52
Cold War era, 118
funding for, 119
impact of, 120
in Iraq, 118
Kurdish, 41, 79, 160, 179
Nicaraguan, 118–19
support for, 117–20, 117n82, 123, 234–35
intelligence gathering, 186–87, 232
intercontinental ballistic missiles, 212, 215
interdependence, 46n33
interdiction, 87
interests
of adversaries, 237
national. *see* national interests
regional, 173
internally displaced persons, 182–83. *see also* refugees
international cooperation. *see also* coalitions
breaking, 194
building, 151
geopolitics and, 17
for humanitarian interventions, 184
in Kosovo, 156–57, 156–57n8
media portrayals and, 150
in Operation Allied Force, 156–57
for sanctions, 106
weapons of mass destruction and, 215–16
international criminal court, 157–58
international isolation. *see* political isolation
international legal norms
adversarial compliance with, 148–49
on decapitation, 75–76
exploitation of, 145
military force and, 133, 138

invasions, 8, 99–102
investment sanctions, 108
Iran. *see also* Iran-Iraq War
  chemical weapons and, 211
  Kurdish insurgents and, 41, 79
  mujahedin and, 118, 119
  political isolation of, 115
  sanctions against, 55, 108
  weapons of mass destruction and, 205–6, 208
Iran-Iraq War
  air strikes in, 97
  chemical weapons use in, 210–11
  civilian suffering in, 97–98
  coercive mechanisms in, 52
  unrest and, 67–68
Iraq. *see also* Gulf War; Husayn, Saddam; Iran-Iraq War
  air strikes against, 34, 88, 91, 93, 94–95, 97–98
  air strikes by, 97, 168, 171, 215
  biological weapons and, 210
  casualty sensitivity and, 222
  chemical weapons and, 39, 68, 104–5, 104–5, 210, 211, 217
  civilian causalities in, 98, 137, 140, 147, 147n45
  civilian suffering in, 97–98, 148
  coalitions and, 34, 159, 160–61, 162–63, 169
  coercive mechanisms used against, 55
  electric power system, 98
  elites of, 46
  France and, 159
  ground forces against, 34, 100, 102
  infant mortality in, 111n64
  insurgents in, 118
  Kurds and, 41, 79, 183
  military resources of, 112–13, 229
  nuclear reactors in, 4, 220
  nuclear threats and, 39, 104–5, 104–5n40, 217
  oil-for-food program and, 111, 111n63, 112, 148
  public opinion on, 131, 132–33, 134n9
  Saddam Husayn's policies and, 46, 137, 137n17
  sanctions against, 55, 62, 110–14, 111n63
  Scud missiles, 168, 171
  support for Iranian insurgents, 119
  UN inspections of, 55, 61–62, 81–82, 113–14, 155–56, 169, 210
  weapons of mass destruction program, 110, 112–14, 133, 161, 205–6, 208, 220n33
  withdrawal from Kuwait, 11, 34, 35, 100
Ireland, 153
Islamic Revolutionary Guard Corps, 208
isolation. *see* political isolation
Israel
  air strikes by, 4, 89, 97
  assassination by, 74, 75
  Iraqi Scud missiles and, 168, 171, 215
  Lebanese Hezbollah and, 2, 53, 64–65, 89
  nuclear threats by, 205, 206
  Osiraq nuclear reactor strike, 4, 219n32, 220
  Palestinian terrorists and, 41, 53–54, 64–65, 73–74, 83–85, 198
  Suez Canal crises and, 42, 52, 53
  Syria and, 7, 7n7
  third-party coercion by, 83–84
  weapons of mass destruction and, 205, 214
  Yom Kippur War and, 81
Israeli-Egyptian War of Attrition (1969–1970), 35–36, 42–43, 66–67, 67n23, 97
Italy, 108, 153, 172

Jackson, Michael, 116
Japan, 7, 44, 209n17
  air strikes against, 31, 44, 69–71, 70n33, 92
Jervis, Robert, 16
Jordan
  Palestinian terrorists in, 41, 53, 83–84
  Syrian invasion of, 7, 7n7
  unrest in, 84
justification of military force, 132–34

Kahn, Herman, 15, 40, 40n20, 221
Karadzic, Radovan, 193
Kashmir, 118
Kennedy, John F., 104
Keohane, Robert O., 46n33
Kirschner, Jonathan, 107, 109
Korean War, 2, 5, 43
  air strikes in, 122, 139–40
  coalitions in, 155, 168
  ground forces in, 122
  nuclear threats during, 39, 103, 122, 168, 168n25
  rules of engagement for, 139–40
Kosovo, 101–2. *see also* Balkan conflict; Milosevic, Slobodan; Serbia
  air strikes in, 28, 40, 89, 136
  ground forces and, 32, 100n30, 101–2
  humanitarian interventions in, 178, 179, 183, 184

international cooperation in, 156–57, 156–57n8
NATO and, 116, 119–20, 157n9
rules of engagement in, 190
Kosovo Liberation Army (KLA), 119–20, 183
Kurds, 41, 79, 160, 179, 183
Kuwait. *see also* Gulf War
Iraqi withdrawal from, 11, 34, 35, 100

land grabs, 99–102
Laos, 56, 79, 205
Laqueur, Walter, 209n17
Larson, Eric V., 136n15
leaders. *see also* decapitation
air strikes against, 94–95
authoritarian regimes, 12
in the Balkan conflict, 193–94
decision making by, 12–14
defiance of, 64, 65, 69
foreign pressure and, 36–37
goals of, 12–13
motivation of, 60n5
power base of, 59–65
removal of, 72–76
weaknesses of, 231
League of Nations, 108
Lebanon, 54, 84–85, 146
Hezbollah, 2, 35, 53, 64–65, 74
Lebow, Richard Ned, 16
legal norms. *see* international legal norms
Lepgold, Joseph, 200
Levy, Jack, 12, 12n17, 41, 41n22
Lewy, Guenter, 137n16
Liberia, 188
Libya
air strikes against, 89, 93–94, 94n11
chemical weapons and, 220
coercive mechanisms used against, 56
rules of engagement for, 140–41
weapons of mass destruction capabilities, 205
limited force, 3, 5–6, 16
The Limits of Coercive Diplomacy (George and Simons), 15
Linebacker operations, 41, 57, 80, 80n62, 91
loss aversion, 12, 12n17
low-stake crises, 131
lowest common denominator effect, 162

major powers, 17, 18–19, 106, 107, 238
Malayan guerillas, 52
manufacturing facilities. *see* industrial sites
market economies, 107–8
Mason, Tony, 164
massive retaliation, 76n54
Mead, Walter Russell, 142–43
means-end-chain, 27, 48
mechanisms. *see* coercive mechanisms
media coverage
authoritarian regimes and, 149–50
of the Balkan conflict, 71, 149
of humanitarian interventions, 179, 185
of nonstate actors, 195, 197–98
public opinion and, 150
real-time, 150
of sanctions, 112
of Somalia, 195
of the Vietnam War, 149–50, 198–99
military defeat, 2, 62, 80–81
military force. *see also* air strikes; ground forces
coalitions and, 155, 173
constraints on, 20, 134–50, 236, 240
conventional, 235
for election security, 183
foreign policy and, 2
high-technology, 135, 136, 145, 146, 231–32
for humanitarian interventions, 175–76, 177, 181–90, 195–98, 199
international legal norms and, 133, 138
justification of, 132–34
as the last resort, 134
limited use of, 3, 5–6, 16
political isolation and, 116
public opinion on, 130–31, 132–34
role of, 3–4, 132–33
strengths and weaknesses of, 230–31
utility of, 19
weapons of mass destruction and, 206–7, 219
military victory, 78–82
militias, 177, 191. *see also* nonstate actors
Milosevic, Slobodan. *see also* Balkan conflict; Serbia
air strikes against, 1, 94
coalitions and, 172
elites and, 63
ground forces and, 101–2
media coverage of, 71, 149
political isolation of, 116
on public will, 144–45
Radovan Karadzic and, 193
unrest and, 71
missile defense systems, 221
missiles
cruise, 232, 232n2
intercontinental ballistic, 212, 215
Scud, 168, 171, 215
for weapons of mass destruction delivery, 211–12, 215
Mladic, Ratko, 193–94

Mogadishu, 135, 146, 168–69, 229
morale
  air strikes and, 69–71, 70–71n38
  hostages and, 198
morality, 133
Morgan, Patrick, 6
motivation
  asymmetric, 200
  for humanitarian interventions, 128
  of leaders, 60n5
  of nonstate actors, 200
  of regional powers, 204–8
  weapons of mass destruction and, 213
Mount Igman, 169
Mueller, John, 111, 111n66, 139
Mueller, Karl, 111, 111n66, 139
mujahedin, 118, 119
Mujahedin-e Khalq (MEK), 119
multilateralism, 134
multinational coalitions. *see* coalitions
Muslims, 121
My Lai massacre, 137

Nassar, Gamal Abdel, 66, 67n23, 69
national control, 165
national interests, 29, 230, 237, 240
  civilian casualties and, 140
  coalitions and, 159–60, 165
  humanitarian interventions and, 184
  morality and, 133
  weapons of mass destruction and, 215–16, 223–24
nationalism, 71, 237
NATO
  air strikes, 88, 90, 98
  Balkan conflict and, 1, 116, 119–21, 162–65, 169–70, 172, 193
  in Bosnia, 120–21, 183
  casualties in Serbia, 89
  coercive mechanisms used by, 54, 57
  command procedures, 163–65, 167–68
  ground forces, 101–2, 101n31
  in Kosovo, 116, 119–20, 157n9
  Operation Allied Force. *see* Operation Allied Force
  Operation Deliberate Force, 40, 90, 121, 141, 191–92
  Operation Deny Flight, 160, 167–68
  peacekeepers, 145, 153, 183, 188, 197–98
  in Serbia, 5, 28, 89
  summit on the Balkans, 162
  threat credibility and, 169–70
  unity of, 172
Nazi Germany
  air strikes against, 58, 70–71, 92
  coercive mechanisms used against, 55
  invasion of Russia, 4, 4n3
  loss of Berlin, 5
  public relations efforts by, 44
Neff, Donald, 69
negotiation, 63, 85
neutrality, 188n17
Nicaraguan insurgents, 118–19
no-fly zones, 160–61, 197
noncombatants. *see* civilians
nongovernmental organizations, 112, 153, 157–58, 179, 182n9. *see also* aid workers; humanitarian interventions
nonstate actors. *see also* guerrilla forces; terrorists
  assassination of, 190
  in Bosnia, 191–92
  counter-coercion by, 194–99
  decapitation threats by, 73–74
  denial and, 194–95
  escalation and, 197–98
  humanitarian interventions and, 128, 176, 182–83, 188–89, 190–94
  media coverage of, 195, 197–98
  motivation of, 200
  public opinion and, 195
  rules of engagement and, 197, 198
  in Somalia, 188, 191
Normandy invasion, 44, 155n3
North Atlantic Treaty Organization. *see* NATO
North Korea. *see also* Korean War
  casualty sensitivity and, 222
  nuclear weapons program, 34–35, 56, 58, 80
  weapons of mass destruction capabilities, 205, 206
nuclear reactors, 4, 219n32, 220
nuclear threats. *see also* nuclear weapons
  chemical weapons and, 39
  during the Cold War era, 14, 87, 103, 208n16, 222
  escalation dominance and, 39–40, 221
  during the Gulf War, 39, 217
  by Israel, 205, 206
  during the Korean War, 39, 103, 122, 168, 168n25
  Saddam Husayn and, 39, 104–5, 104–5n40, 217
  as weakening mechanisms, 76–77
nuclear weapons, 9, 15, 104. *see also* nuclear threats; weapons of mass destruction
  access to, 209
  costs of, 103
  escalation and, 7n9, 105, 217–18
  false alarms and, 208n16
  North Korea and, 34–35, 56, 58, 80

in the post–Cold War era, 202–3
regional powers with, 202–3, 205, 209–10
strengths and weaknesses of, 234–35
threatened use of, 21, 102–5
utility of, 211
weapons of mass destruction and, 207, 218
Nye, Joseph S., 46n33

Oakley, Robert, 144
occupation, 85–86
oil embargoes, 114n76
oil-for-food program, 111, 111n63, 112, 148
Operation Allied Force
casualties in, 89
goal of, 28
ground forces and, 100n30, 101–2
international cooperation in, 156–57
media coverage of, 71
public support for, 137n17
rules of engagement for, 141
success of, 40
Operation Barbarossa, 4
Operation Deliberate Force, 40, 90, 121, 141, 191–92
Operation Deny Flight, 160, 167–68
Operation Desert Fox, 93, 131, 223
Operation Desert Storm. *see* Desert Storm
Operation El Dorado Canyon, 93–94, 95
Operation Provide Comfort, 179
Operation Restore Hope, 196
Operation Support Hope, 180
Operation Turquoise, 180
optimism, 143
Organization of African Unity, 153
Organization of American States (OAS), 62
organizations, nongovernmental. *see* nongovernmental organizations
Osiraq nuclear reactor strike, 4, 219n32, 220
outcomes, 28, 48
overcoercion, 36–37
overconfidence, 11–12
Overy, Richard, 31, 155n3

pain. *see* suffering
Pakistan, 118, 153, 205
Palestinian Liberation Organization (PLO), 64–65, 64n18, 84–85, 198
Palestinian terrorists
assassination of, 74
assassination threats by, 73–74
in Jordan, 41, 53, 83–84
in Lebanon, 53, 54, 64–65, 84–85
Syria and, 35
Panama, 110
Pape, Robert
on air strikes, 31, 50n1
on coercion, 6n5, 28n2
on denial, 78, 79
on German occupation, 85–86
on Korea, 122
on sanctions, 109
on strategic bombing, 10, 16
on the War of Attrition, 67n23
passive defenses, 221
peace operations, 175n1. *see also* humanitarian interventions
peacekeepers, 183, 188
in the Balkans, 145, 197–98
in Somalia, 153, 168
Persian Gulf War. *see* Gulf War
policy makers
on air strikes, 88–89
vs. analysts, 234–36
decision making by, 42
elites and, 44–45
military force and, 20
reality and, 28–29
threats and, 12
weapons of mass destruction and, 217
political isolation, 105–6, 114–17, 123
in the Balkan conflict, 116
coalitions and, 156
of Iran, 115
military force and, 116
of Saddam Husayn, 62
of South Africa, 115
political victory, 80–81
politics. *see also* domestic politics
coercive strategy and, 229, 236
collateral damage and, 138
counter-coercion and, 142–48
in escalation dominance, 43–44
geopolitics, 17
goals of, 12–13
technology and, 233
popular disaffection. *see* unrest
popular support. *see* public opinion
population. *see* civilians
Posen, Barry, 27n1, 224
post–Cold War era
vs. the Cold War era, 1, 16–18, 127
domestic politics in, 127–29
humanitarian interventions in, 127–29
nuclear weapons in the, 202–3
weapons of mass destruction and, 201–2, 203
power base
of developing countries, 60–61
elites as, 60, 62–63
negotiation and, 63

of regimes, 59–60, 92–94
of Saddam Husayn, 45–46, 231
sanctions and, 106
susceptibility of, 61
power base erosion, 50, 59–65
examples of, 52, 53, 54, 55, 56
power, unrealized, 18, 51
predecisional agreements, 165
Presidential Decision Directive-56, 175n1
pressure points, 30, 44–46, 59
constant, 32–33
weakening mechanisms as, 77–78
propaganda, 149–50, 195
prospect theory, 12
Provide Comfort operation, 179
provocations, 230
public opinion
on air strikes, 138n18
in authoritarian regimes, 148
on the Balkan conflict, 138n18
casualties and, 136–37, 136n15, 143–44
of coalitions, 157
of defiance, 65
elites and, 51, 131–32n3
escalation and, 37n13
on the Gulf War, 132–33, 142
on humanitarian interventions, 132
on Iraq, 131, 132–33, 134n9
media portrayals and, 150
on military force, 130–31, 132–34
of Milosevic, 63
nonstate actors and, 195
regimes and, 51, 148
role of, 19, 240
of Saddam Husayn, 132–33
of threats, 68–69
unrealized power and, 51
on weapons of mass destruction, 214, 217
public policy. *see* policy makers
public relations, 43–44
public will. *see* will
punishment, 50n1, 66, 237. *see also* suffering

Qaddafi, Mohammar, 93–94

Rambouillet accords, 28, 54
Red River Valley Dikes, 147, 149–50
refugees, 179, 180, 182–83, 185, 185n13
regimes. *see* authoritarian regimes
audience costs to, 36–37
decision making by, 13–14
media coverage of, 149–50
political isolation of, 115–17
power base of, 59–65, 92–94
pressure points of, 44–45
public opinion and, 51, 148
rogue, 17
sanctions and, 106, 109–10, 113–14
weaknesses of, 231
weapons of mass destruction and, 206
regional interests, 173
regional powers, 208–12
domestic politics of, 207–8
motivations and characteristics of, 204–8
nuclear weapons and, 202–3, 205, 209–10
weapons of mass destruction and, 201, 204–12, 215–16
relief operations. *see* humanitarian interventions
Republican Guard (Iraq), 93
resolve. *see* will
Restore Hope operation, 196
risk, 50n1, 207, 233
risk aversion, 147–48, 148n45, 225
Rolling Thunder campaign, 56, 79–80, 79n61, 149–50
rules of engagement, 139–42
for air strikes, 167
for the Balkan conflict, 141, 166–67
in Bosnia, 141, 189, 190, 198
coalitions and, 158, 165, 166
definition of, 139n21
for ground forces, 166–67
for the Gulf War, 140
for humanitarian interventions, 189–90, 195–97
for the Korean War, 139–40
in Kosovo, 190
for Libya, 140–41
nonstate actors and, 197, 198
restrictions on, 147
in Somalia, 168–69, 189, 189n21
for the Vietnam War, 139–40, 141–42
Russia, 2, 4, 108
air strikes by, 91, 95
on the Balkan conflict, 116, 172
Chechens and, 54, 68, 74, 91, 95, 194, 198
German fears of, 85–86
support for insurgents by, 117, 117n83
Rwanda
humanitarian interventions in, 179–80, 185, 185n13
intelligence gathering in, 186
military force in, 192
support for insurgents by, 117–18
Zaire refugee camps and, 182
Rwandese Patriotic Front (RPF), 180

Sadat, Anwar, 81
safe areas, 170

Sagan, Scott, 104–5n40
salmonella bacteria, 209n17
sanctions, 105–10
  casualties from, 111, 111n64, 111n66, 112
  children and, 111, 112
  civilian suffering and, 139, 223–24
  Cold War era, 109
  costs of, 107–8, 111–12
  against Cuba, 109
  against the Dominican Republic, 62
  economic, 106–10, 111
  effectiveness of, 109–10, 112–14, 234
  escalation of, 108
  goals of, 114
  humanitarian issues and, 111–12
  vs. inducements, 9
  international cooperation for, 106
  investment, 108
  against Iran, 55, 108
  against Iraq, 55, 62, 110–14, 111n63
  by major powers, 106, 107
  media coverage of, 112
  against Panama, 110
  political damage from, 111–12
  regimes and, 106, 109–10, 113–14
  against Russia, 108
  strengths and weaknesses of, 234
  studies of, 16–17
  on technology, 108
  trade, 106, 106n43, 108, 109
  types of, 108
  United Nations, 107
Sandinistas, 118–19
Sarajevo, 169, 170
Schelling, Thomas, 3, 6n5, 14, 15, 85
Scud missiles, 168, 171, 215
security forces, 60–61, 71
self-defense, assassination as, 75n52
Serbia. *see also* Balkan conflict; Kosovo; Milosevic, Slobodan; Operation Allied Force
  air strikes against, 1, 88, 89, 122, 136
  air strikes by, 160
  casualties in, 144–45
  electric power grids and, 98
  ground forces and, 32, 100n30, 101–2
  media coverage and, 71, 149
  military resources in, 192–94
  NATO and, 28, 116
  political isolation of, 116
  public opinion of, 138n18
  public will and, 144–45
  rules of engagement for, 141
  UNPROFOR and, 160, 161
shared control, 158, 163–67
siege warfare, 66
Simons, William E.
  on coalitions, 159
  on coercion, 6n5
  on escalation, 16, 42
  on motivation, 213
  on success, 39n17
Sinai peninsula, 81
Smoke, Richard, 40
smuggling, 109
social effects of air strikes, 96, 97–98
Somali National Alliance, 191
Somalia. *see also* Aideed, Mohamed Farah
  civilian casualties in, 137, 146
  coalitions in, 152–53, 159, 168–69, 171
  coercive mechanisms used in, 57
  human-shield tactics in, 196–97
  humanitarian interventions in, 152–53, 181, 181n7, 182–84, 182n9, 189
  media coverage of, 195
  military resources of, 191, 191n23, 229
  nonstate actors in, 188, 191
  Operation Restore Hope, 196
  rules of engagement in, 168–69, 189, 189n21
  target discrimination in, 187
  United Nations in, 152–53, 191, 195, 196–97
South Africa, 115
South Korea, 205, 206. *see also* Korean War
Soviet Union. *see also* Cold War era; Russia
  biological weapons use by, 208n16
  Cuban missile crisis and, 10, 54, 104
  demise of, 1, 14
  Gulf War and, 162–63
  Israeli-Egyptian War of Attrition and, 43
  on Nicaragua, 118–19
  nuclear threats and, 87, 222
Srebrenica, 170
Stalin, Joseph, 4n3
Stein, Janice Gross, 16, 34
strategic bombing, 10, 16, 122, 122n93
strategy
  coercive. *see* coercive strategy
  grand, 27n1
success, 33–37, 39n17
  binary metrics of, 33–34, 33–34n5, 35
Sudan, 149, 178, 179, 205
Suez Canal crises, 42, 52, 53, 69, 77
suffering
  acceptance of, 237
  vs. benefits, 10
  of civilians, 45, 65, 97–98, 130, 137–42, 146, 196
  exploitation of, 45
  in the Iran-Iraq War, 97–98

as a weakening mechanism, 76
weapons of mass destruction and, 214–125
suitcase bombs, 221
sunk costs, 12
superpowers, 17, 238
Support Hope operation, 180
support, public. *see* public opinion
susceptibility, 46, 46n33, 61
Syria
casualty sensitivity and, 222
Jordan and, 7, 7n7
Palestinian terrorists and, 35
weapons of mass destruction capabilities, 205

Taiwan, 2, 205, 214
target discrimination
future challenges in, 233
in humanitarian interventions, 186–87, 196
targeting restrictions, 139–42, 146, 147
technology
conflicts and, 17
credibility and, 231–32
expectations of, 232–33
information, 233
limitations of, 233
military, 135, 136, 145, 146, 231–32
politics and, 233
sanctions on, 108
strengths and weaknesses of, 231–34
terrorists. *see also* nonstate actors; Palestinian terrorists
in Afghanistan, 88, 119, 135–36, 232
air strikes against, 88, 91, 135–36, 232
as nonstate actors, 199–200
weapons of mass destruction and, 209n17
Tet Offensive, 198–99
Thailand, 205
third-party coercian, 82–85, 86
threats, 3, 4–5, 33, 42. *see also* counterthreats; nuclear threats
analyzing, 37
back up for, 61n10
background, 32–33
by coalitions, 162
credibility of, 169–71, 221
decision making and, 32, 49, 51
escalation and, 35–36
policy makers and, 12
predicting results of, 72
public opinion of, 68–69
weapons of mass destruction as, 21, 102–5, 128–29, 231
trade sanctions, 106, 106n43, 108, 109
Trujillo regime, 62
Turkey, 160, 179
Turquoise operation, 180
Tutsis, 180

UNAMIR, 179–80
United Nations
Balkan conflict and, 160, 193
command procedures, 163–65
destruction of chemical weapons, 210
impartiality of, 187
on Iraq, 110
mandates, 157, 157n9, 167
peacekeepers, 145, 153
sanctions, 107
Security Council Resolution 687, 110, 110n60
Security Council Resolution 794, 152
Security Council Resolution 816, 160
in Somalia, 152–53, 191, 195, 196–97
UNOSOM II mission, 152–53, 195
UNPROFOR mission, 160, 161, 163, 166–67, 189, 189n22
weapons of mass destruction inspections, 61–62, 81–82, 93, 113–14, 155–56, 169
United Nations Assistance Mission for Rwanda, 179–80
United Nations Special Commission, 81–82, 112
United Task Force, 152
UNOSOM II, 152–53, 195
UNPROFOR, 160, 161, 163, 166–67, 189, 189n22
unrealized power, 18, 51
unrest, 65–72
air strikes and, 69–71, 96, 97–98
in authoritarian regimes, 62–63
definition of, 50
examples of, 52, 53, 54, 55, 56, 57
Iran-Iraq War and, 67–68
nonstate actors and, 194–95
value of, 72
USSR. *see* Soviet Union

vaccine-resistant biological weapons, 221
values
of adversaries, 44
in decision making, 12–13
in foreign policy, 150
the Vatican, 87, 153
victory
denial of, 78–82
political, 80–81
Vietnam syndrome, 135

Vietnam War
  air strikes, 41, 58, 80, 80n62, 91, 139–40
  antiwar movement and, 137n16
  casualty sensitivity and, 143
  Christmas bombings, 33
  civilians in, 137, 141–42, 147
  coalitions in, 155
  coercive mechanisms used in, 56, 57, 58
  collateral damage in, 231–32
  limitations of, 2
  Linebacker operations, 41, 57, 80, 80n62, 91
  media coverage of, 149–50, 198–99
  Red River Valley Dikes, 147, 149–50
  Rolling Thunder campaign, 56, 79–80, 79n61, 149–50
  rules of engagement for, 139–40, 141–42
  Tet Offensive, 198–99
Vietnam, weapons of mass destruction capabilities, 205
vulnerability
  of adversaries, 3
  of power base support, 61
  vs. susceptibility, 46, 46n33
  weapons of mass destruction and, 216, 220, 223

Walt, Stephen M., 156n5
War of Attrition. *see* Israeli-Egyptian War of Attrition (1969–1970)
Warden, John, 16
warlords. *see* nonstate actors
weakening mechanisms, 76–78, 229
  in the Cold War era, 76n54
  examples of, 54, 55, 56, 57
  nuclear threats and, 76–77
  weapons of mass destruction and, 220–21
  world powers and, 18–19
weapons of mass destruction, 112, 201–25. *see also* biological weapons; chemical weapons; nuclear weapons
  access to, 209, 209n17
  authoritarian regimes and, 214–15, 224
  backfire potential and, 224–25
  casualties and, 213–14
  coalitions and, 203, 215–16
  coercion and, 216–18
  coercive contests and, 218–24
  collateral damage and, 223–24
  constraints on, 213–15
  vs. conventional superiority, 206–7, 219
  costs of, 103, 201, 203, 212–13, 222, 224
  for counter-coercion, 219–21
  dangers of, 20, 203–12
  decapitation threats and, 73
  defenses for, 221–22, 224
  deterrence and, 204–6, 207, 219–24, 219n32
  developing countries and, 204, 207
  escalation dominance and, 202, 212–16, 217, 223
  hidden facilities for, 220, 220n33
  Iran and, 205–6, 208
  Iraq program for, 110, 112–14, 133, 205–6, 208, 220n33
  Israel and, 205, 214
  missiles for, 211–12, 215
  motivation and, 213
  national interests and, 215–16, 223–24
  nuclear weapons and, 104
  in the post–Cold War era, 128–29, 201–2
  predelegated authority for, 208
  public opinion on, 214, 217
  regional powers and, 201, 204–12, 215–16
  risk aversion and, 225
  sanctions and, 110, 112–14
  as status symbols, 206
  suffering and, 214–125
  terrorists and, 209n17
  threatened use of, 21, 102–5, 128–29, 231
  types of, 208–12
  UN inspections of, 55, 61–62, 81–82, 93, 113–14, 131, 155–56, 169
  utility of, 211
  vulnerability and, 216, 220, 223
  weakening mechanisms and, 220–21
  will and, 214
Weigley, Russell, 231
well-being, 65, 76, 77
will
  casualties and, 142
  high-technology and, 146
  history and, 238
  Milosevic on, 144–45
  nonstate actors and, 194
  projecting, 151
  role of, 18
  vs. strength, 19
  weapons of mass destruction and, 214
withdrawal, 8, 9
WMD. *see* weapons of mass destruction
Wohlstetter, Albert, 15
World Vision, 182n9
World War II, 2, 4–5, 85–86
  air strikes, 95, 97
  air strikes in Germany, 31, 44, 58, 70–71, 86, 92

air strikes in Japan, 31, 44, 69–71, 70n33, 92
coalitions in, 154–55, 155n3
coercive mechanisms used in, 55, 58
Doolittle raid, 44
Normandy invasion, 44, 155n3
Operation Barbarossa, 4
public relations in, 43–44

Yom Kippur War, 80–81
Yugoslavia. *see* Balkan conflict; Serbia

Zaire, 182